D0896851

With Joyful Acceptance, Maybe

With Joyful Acceptance, Maybe

Developing a Contemporary Theology of Suffering in Conversation with Five Christian Thinkers: Gregory the Great, Julian of Norwich, Jeremy Taylor, C. S. Lewis, and Ivone Gebara

MOLLY FIELD JAMES

WIPF & STOCK · Eugene, Oregon

WITH JOYFUL ACCEPTANCE, MAYBE
Developing a Contemporary Theology of Suffering in Conversation with Five
Christian Thinkers: Gregory the Great, Julian of Norwich, Jeremy Taylor,
C. S. Lewis, and Ivone Gebara

Wipf & Stock
An Imprint of Wipf and Stock Publishers
199 W. 8th Ave., Suite 3
Eugene, OR 97401
www.wipfandstock.com

ISBN 13: 978-1-62032-280-2
Manufactured in the U.S.A.

To my grandparents
Walker and Nancy Field
Everett and Catherine Fisher
for inspiring and supporting
a love of learning
and for showing me how
to live with joyful acceptance.

Contents

Foreword

To SUFFER IS PART of the human lot in life. Modern medicine and technology have not eliminated suffering from our lives, although they have been involved in morphing the forms of suffering we experience from those caused by accidents and workplace injury into those associated with chronic diseases and neurological problems. We are increasingly aware of the suffering of the poor and powerless, struck by the randomness of the socio-political lottery that drops one soul into luxury and another into hell on earth.

Molly James joins a long line of serious Christian thinkers who have tried to come to terms with the fact they confess the Messiah has come, but a world without suffering has not appeared. She's worked up a provocative and imaginative typology of ways of coming to terms, or "explaining," suffering in a redeemed world. James makes a fine contribution to our discussion of what is arguably the most important issue in Christian thought and ethics today. She's taught me a lot.

David H. Smith
Senior Lecturer, Yale University
Poynter Senior Fellow, Indiana University

Preface

WRITING ABOUT GRIEF IS not an entirely cerebral or academic exercise. One does not usually choose to write about grief only out of intellectual curiosity. I am no different. To grapple with questions of loss, grief, suffering, and pain is an intellectual task for me, but it is also a spiritual one. My desire to examine past and current approaches to grief in the hopes of drawing on them for contemporary Christians arises out of my own experiences, both personal and professional.

In the spring of 1993, when I was thirteen, I was diagnosed with bone cancer. I underwent a year of treatment that included chemotherapy and surgery to remove my left collarbone. I missed weeks of school, lost my hair, spent countless days on the couch feeling as though I had the flu. Those were just the physical effects. Far more challenging to deal with as a teenager were the spiritual wounds of cancer. Facing the realities of a life-threatening illness and facing my own mortality meant I lost my childhood innocence. It meant the future no longer seemed a sure thing. It meant my vision was narrowed to the here and now. It meant I was afraid tomorrow would not come.

Blessedly, I am cured and here to write these words. I did not have to face the immediacy, only the possibility of my own death. Nonetheless, I grieved. I grieved over my loss of innocence and the reality of my own mortality.

As an Episcopal priest, I have also seen this process of grief in the face of illness and suffering in my professional work. As a hospital chaplain and a parish priest, I have witnessed suffering and death. I have come to realize that the grieving process is not limited to the times when someone dies—it is a normal part of the human response to suffering.

Acknowledgments

In preparation for my doctorate I was privileged to work closely with Kelton Cobb, Mike Higton, and Ian Markham. Along with them I have been tremendously blessed with gifted teachers, mentors, friends, and family who have inspired and challenged me in the course of my academic work, my ministry, and my writing. I am deeply grateful for all of them.

Introduction

Christian Theologies of Suffering Across the Centuries

THE PAGES THAT FOLLOW examine the work of five theologians who have particular insight into issues of grief: Gregory the Great, Julian of Norwich, Jeremy Taylor, C. S. Lewis and Ivone Gebara. Their writings offer ways of thinking about and living with suffering that, in turn, can help offer a way for contemporary Christians to accept the reality of suffering that is endemic to the human experience, while also raising questions about when suffering ought not to be accepted and, in fact, ought to be fought against.

DEFINING SUFFERING AND GRIEF

First, it is important to establish what is meant by suffering and grief, even though (as shall be seen) each thinker has a distinct take on what constitutes suffering and grief. It is perhaps best to start with suffering, as that is the phenomenon that prompts grief. Whereas, grief is the psychological and spiritual response to the experience of suffering. In order to really engage with suffering, it is important to dig into the meaning of "to suffer." The etymology of the word is "sub" (under) and "ferre" (to bear).[1] Etymologically, then, suffering is to bear under something. This sense of being under gets at an important aspect of suffering—the sense of something being imposed. One definition in the *Oxford English Dictionary* is, "to go or pass through, be subjected to, undergo, experience (now usually something evil or painful)," and in

1. "Suffer," *Oxford English Dictionary Online,* 2nd ed. Oxford: Oxford University Press, 1989. http://dictionary.oed.com/entrance.dtl.

its transitive sense, to suffer also means, "to have (something painful, distressing, or injurious) inflicted or imposed upon one; to submit to with pain, distress, or grief."[2] To suffer, then, is to be the subject of some difficult or painful experience.[3]

As noted above, grief can be seen as the emotional, physical, and spiritual response to an experience of loss. Indeed, the *OED* defines grief as "mental pain, distress, or sorrow" and even "deep or violent sorrow."[4] Grief is the noun used to describe the act of grieving; therefore, it is also important to examine the definition and etymology of "grieve." Etymologically, "grieve" has its roots in "gravis" (heavy) and "grave."[5] The root of "gravis" connects with the understanding of suffering discussed above, the sense of being under something, and adds the dimension of weight to that burden. Having "grave" at its root, of course, gives grief connotations of death and mortality.

The descriptive language of Nicholas Wolterstorff, a theologian who reflects on suffering after the tragic death of his son, also provides an understanding of suffering and grief from the perspective of the one who suffers. He defines suffering as: "When something prized or loved is ripped away or never granted—work, someone loved, recognition of one's dignity, life without physical pain—that is suffering."[6] Wolterstorff's powerful language is that of loss and absence, something taken away or never given, which means that grief, then, is not limited only to the "grave"; it is experienced any time there is "significant loss."[7]

While it is possible to simply define grief as our response to suffering, it is not as easy to define suffering as a burden that is imposed. As will be seen in subsequent discussion, the reality of suffering is more complicated. In the *Westminster Dictionary of Christian Ethics* John Macquarrie defines suffering first and foremost as "the opposite of action." The entry goes on to explain that the experience of suffering is about undergoing "a series of events initiated from the outside and

2. Ibid.

3. This understanding is echoed in the *Dictionary of Psychology*, which defines suffering as "the experience of pain or acute distress, either psychological or physical." See "suffering" in *APA Dictionary of Psychology*.

4. "Grief," *Oxford English Dictionary Online*, 2nd ed. Oxford: Oxford University Press, 1989. http://dictionary.oed.com/entrance.dtl.

5. Ibid.

6. Wolterstorff, *Lament for a Son*, 89.

7. See "grief" in *APA Dictionary of Psychology*.

leading to a state of affairs which is not desired."[8] This goes along with an understanding of suffering as something imposed from without, but Macquarrie does not leave it there. In defining suffering, Macquarrie also touches on the important Christian theme—which has its roots in the sufferings of Christ—of suffering as good or redemptive in nature. The question of whether, how, or when suffering can be redemptive (and even seen as a good) will be explored in greater detail later, but it is an important question to note in establishing an understanding of suffering. Macquarrie's position is that "[b]ecause so much suffering has this apparently senseless character, it is generally regarded as a duty to relieve suffering whenever possible." Yet his view of suffering's redemptive value is not entirely negative. He also understands that there is an intimate connection between suffering, love, and sympathy. It is the experience of suffering that allows us to feel love and sympathy more deeply. Even in this connection between suffering and sympathy, we see how suffering cannot be seen only as a negative imposed from without.[9]

CONTEXT

Understanding the definitions and etymologies of the terms "suffering" and "grief" provides a helpful foundation. They are, however, still two very broad terms that can encompass a wide range of the human experience, and their roots and etymologies do not necessarily dictate how writers use them. Suffering and grief also connect to a variety of other important theological issues that are beyond the scope of this book. Chiefly, perhaps, would be the issue of evil. Evil is an issue that has engaged theologians and philosophers through the centuries, particularly the question of theodicy: whether or not we can affirm the existence or benevolence of God in the midst of evil or suffering. The focus of this book, however, is on the place suffering has in the relationship between human life and God rather than on questions of theodicy and the existence or benevolence of God.

The notion of evil does have relevance to the experience of suffering, and it is worth acknowledging that suffering can be described as the result of encountering evil in its different forms. A distinction

---

8. Macquarrie, "Suffering," *Westminster Dictionary*, 608.
9. Ibid.

between three kinds of evil: metaphysical, physical, and moral, is generally attributed to seventeenth-century thinker Gottfried Leibniz in his work *Theodicy*. According to Leibniz, metaphysical evil describes the world as being in a state of imperfection; it refers to the reality of existential evil in the world, the kind of evil that happens and does not seem to have a direct or discernible cause. The second kind of evil is physical evil, which Leibniz understands to be the experience of suffering. Physical evil is what is experienced by humanity as a result of living in an imperfect world. The third type of evil is moral evil, which is sin.[10] It is the evil experienced as a result of harmful actions by humanity itself. John Macquarrie shares this distinction of evils, and particularly the understanding of physical or natural evil. For Macquarrie, natural evil is the "inevitable accompaniment" to life in this world. Yet Macquarrie draws the important distinction that natural evil is to be seen as "an instrument of God's justice, whereby he punishes the wicked." For Macquarrie, natural evil is to be understood (as it is for Gregory) as "an instrument of God's education for the human race."[11] These distinctions among types of evil are important, for they help to illuminate the nature and origins of suffering. The thinkers I'll discuss, in varying degrees, share in these distinctions, and distinguishing the types of evil is an important aspect in understanding how we respond to the experience of evil.

Through conversation with the five theologians we seek to gain greater insight into how they understood suffering to be redemptive. To affirm the redemptive nature of suffering is not a new idea. It is a Christian belief founded in the Old Testament prophets (e.g., Isaiah 53) and is at the heart of the theology of the cross and the Eucharist. The church in its first generation promoted the message that Christ gave himself up, suffered, to redeem all of humanity.

We will also explore how and when suffering is not redemptive and not to be accepted, but rather refused and fought against. It is important to highlight this question of how and when suffering is to be accepted as well as ask other questions, such as: What are the fruits of suffering? What are the blessings and the gifts to be found in the midst of the pain and darkness? These areas of exploration encounter foundational truths of the Christian faith. The major touchstones of the

10. Leibniz, *Theodicy*, 139.

11. Macquarrie, *Principles of Christian Theology*, 258.

Christian faith that will be discussed, as they relate to suffering, are: the human condition (the nature of human experience); God's providence (the role of God's power); Christ (how his suffering helps us understand our own); salvation (the redemptive quality of suffering); and eternal life (how a belief in an afterlife impacts our perspective on suffering). Overall, there is a tension in Christianity. On the one hand, sin (that which is opposed to God's will), evil, and suffering are realities present in the world and in individual lives. Simultaneously, though, Christians must never let go of their conviction that God wills human flourishing. This is a conviction that finds eloquent expression in the Gospel of John, where it is written, "For God so loved the world that he gave his only Son, so that everyone who believes in him may not perish but may have eternal life."[12] At the heart of the Christian faith is the belief that God loves the world and desires all people have life and have it abundantly (John 10:10).

The remainder of this Introduction is divided into three parts. First, a presentation of the typological method that is used in the book; second, a survey of significant, relevant literature in the areas of grief and suffering; and third, an introduction to the five thinkers and the subsequent chapters.

TYPOLOGY

There are many possible ways to approach the issue of suffering. Given the complexity of the issue and the breadth of experiences commonly subsumed under the concept of grief as the human response to suffering, it is challenging to try to categorize or construct a typology. The reality is that human experience is messy. It does not easily fit into boxes or categories. A typology, however, offers a framework, a way of accessing and understanding the theologians and their work.

The value and imperfections of a typology can be understood by examining the work of the thinkers Max Weber and H. Richard Niebuhr. In his book, *Christ and Culture,* twentieth century Protestant theologian Niebuhr uses a typology to examine the issue of how Christians relate to their culture from a variety of perspectives. In his first chapter, he acknowledges both the value and the drawbacks of this

12. John 3:16.

method. He offers the reminder that constructing a typology is to leave the complicated realm of human experience and move to the orderly realm of intellectual categories. Of course, in the dialectic between experience and category, we are reminded that inevitably "no person or group ever conforms completely to a type."[13] Despite the fact that constructing a typology is an inherently imperfect endeavor, it does have value. Niebuhr notes that while at the micro, individual, and specific level typologies do not always seem accurate, they do have value in painting a picture of broader trends. In making his own apology for his typology of Christ and culture, Niebuhr argues that his particular typology "though historically inadequate, has the advantage of calling to attention the continuity and significance of the great *motifs* that appear and reappear in the long wrestling of Christians with their enduring problem."[14] Niebuhr attempts to show how a typology can be a useful tool for looking at a broad swath of history and identifying points of connection and continuity across the centuries.

Like Niebuhr, Max Weber sees value in typologies for their ability to provide a scholarly framework. Max Weber's work on "ideal types" was predominately in the area of economics and history, but on a methodological level his work is nonetheless applicable. Weber offers the reminder that in order to talk about anything, words and constructs are necessary. They are used, and scholarship is improved by an awareness of that use. "If the historian (in the widest sense of the word) rejects an attempt to construct such ideal types as a 'theoretical construction' . . . the inevitable consequence is either that he consciously or unconsciously uses other similar concepts without formulating them verbally and elaborating them logically or that he remains stuck in the realm of the vaguely 'felt.'"[15] Constructs are necessary to give structure, meaning, and force to ideas. Constructs make ideas more comprehensible and help ease the translation of ideas from one discipline to another.

Weber engages in this practice of translation across disciplines by himself using examples from the history of Christianity. Weber offers "Christianity in the Middle Ages" as an example of a construct, acknowledging that it is, in and of itself, a nebulous concept, but when it is used as a "stable concept," it can provide valuable information to

13. Niebuhr, *Christ and Culture*, 43–44.

14. Ibid., 44.

15. Weber, "Objectivity in Social Science," 21–22.

scholars. He acknowledges that ideal types have problematic validity if they are seen as representing facts, but "[o]n the other hand, such presentations are of great value for research and of high systemic value for expository purposes when they are used as conceptual instruments for *comparison* and the *measurement* of reality. They are indispensable for this purpose."[16]

The goal here is to present the writings of the five theologians as offering five types of responses to suffering. It endeavors to compare them with one another in order to better understand their theologies and the implications of those theologies. The five theologians represent different types of acceptance of suffering. Gregory, Julian, and Jeremy Taylor are quick to accept the reality of suffering. For them, the question "Why do we suffer?" is the wrong question. The right question is "How do we respond *when* we suffer?" For them, the occurrence of suffering is seen in a very positive light. They do not engage in meek acquiescence or mere forbearance; suffering provides a fruitful opportunity. For Gregory, suffering is to be accepted because it offers an opportunity to be cleansed from sin. For Julian, suffering is to be accepted because it is through suffering we are brought to the great reward of union with God. For Taylor, suffering is to be accepted because it offers a new way to live a more holy life. For Lewis and Gebara, on the other hand, an acceptance of suffering does not come so easily. Lewis struggles mightily in the wake of his wife's death to accept the reality of his own suffering. He offers a model of how to fully grieve the pain we feel and how grappling with that pain can lead to a place of acceptance. For Gebara, acceptance comes only once we have established that the suffering we experience or witness is endemic to the human experience and not the result of persecution and injustice. If it is the former, then it is to be accepted. If it is the latter, then it is not to be accepted; it is to be combated.

Of course, none of these five thinkers fit perfectly into a particular type of acceptance. They are not always distinct in their understandings of acceptance. They do have much in common. All of the theologies have nuances and richness that are lost when they are categorized. The use of a typology, therefore, endeavors to elucidate the dominant themes found in each and to compare and contrast them in light of those themes.

16. Ibid., 23 and 25.

In the spirit of Weber's work, I offer models of thinking theologically about the issue of suffering, all the while acknowledging they are not the only possible models we could draw from within the Christian tradition. As one discovers in constructing an essence of Christianity, Weber reminds us that ideal types are always ideal in the mind of the author, and may not fit with others' understanding of the same topic.[17] Authors must acknowledge their own imprint on the ideal types that emerge—because they have constructed them—while simultaneously acknowledging the lenses through which the material is viewed. As Weber notes, "[t]hey are all attempts, on the basis of the present state of our knowledge and the available conceptual patterns, to bring order into the chaos of those facts which we have drawn into the field circumscribed by our *interest*."[18] As noted in the preface, I come to this endeavor as one who has grieved and will grieve. I come seeking solace and a theological framework with which to understand the reality of suffering and loss. I bring a willingness to sit with the questions and live in those gray areas where there are no easy answers. I come with a belief that to gain a greater understanding of suffering is to gain a deeper understanding of the nature of the Trinitarian God. Those are my interests that no doubt circumscribe the nature of this work. I also come with the humble acknowledgment that this work cannot possibly fully explore the nature of grief and suffering. No matter how we may search, we are ultimately confronted with the reality of the divine mystery and an awareness of the truth that much is beyond full comprehension. Yet, in the face of this reality, may the acknowledgment of the mystery never hold us back from the desire for better self-understanding or the desire to better understand God. To construct a typology of suffering is then, as Weber notes, to endeavor to create order out of chaos. It is an inherently imperfect exercise, but that does not mean it is not a worthwhile endeavor.

RELEVANT PERSPECTIVES

The field of literature dealing with issues of suffering and grief is an immense one, and it is beyond the scope of this work to offer a complete

17. Ibid.
18. Ibid., 32.

survey. This section will endeavor, however, to highlight and discuss some major works in the field that come closest to this book. First, it is perhaps helpful to see books on suffering and grief as existing in two categories. The first category—including Søren Kierkegaard, Dorothy Soelle, and Stanley Hauerwas—consists of those reflections that deal with suffering and grief from a theological frame of reference. The second category—including Elisabeth Kübler-Ross, St. Augustine, and Nicholas Wolterstorff—consists of writings that have a greater emphasis on personal experience. As the five theologians in this study—Gregory the Great, Julian of Norwich, Jeremy Taylor, C. S. Lewis and Ivone Gebara— are ones who write theologically and from their own experience with suffering, both categories are important.

Elisabeth Kübler-Ross

In a discussion of suffering and grief it is important to touch upon an author whose work also focuses on the question of acceptance of suffering: Elisabeth Kübler-Ross, author of *On Death and Dying*. The work of Kübler-Ross was revolutionary in its time, and it is valuable because it brings in the perspective of the dying person. Kübler-Ross is best known for the account of the five stages of grieving that developed out of her work: denial, anger, depression, bargaining and acceptance.[19] These stages can provide a valuable framework and be helpful in understanding the dying and grieving process. While her work has had significant impact on how suffering, grief, and death are viewed in American society, it is being discussed first to note how it differs from the work of this book. I will not focus on acceptance as a stage in her progression, nor seek to provide a Christian path with her stage as the end goal. It can become difficult for anyone who has studied her stages, however, to avoid seeing them as milestones to be reached rather than signposts. Kübler-Ross herself cautions her readers not to view the stages too narrowly. She writes, "We have discussed so far the different stages that people go through when they are faced with tragic news—defense mechanisms in psychiatric terms, coping mechanisms to deal with extremely difficult situations. These means [stages] will last for different periods of time and will replace each other or exist at times

19. Kübler-Ross, *On Death and Dying*, 265.

side by side."[20] Having this caution is helpful, because stages are often thought of in linear terms. Kübler-Ross actually provides a chart of the process in her book that shows one moving in a linear fashion through the stages from diagnosis to death.[21]

Like a typology, Kübler-Ross's stages provide a simplified framework for understanding and talking about death and loss. Her stages may have become absorbed into the psyche of American culture, but they must not be seen as the only way to understand the dying process. A number of scholars have stood up to critique her work, and their voices are worth heeding. In *Death: Confronting the Reality,* William Phipps writes, "It should be pointed out that the stages of dying may be more in Kübler-Ross' mind than in the clinical data she presents. Other clinical psychologists who have worked with dying patients do not find evidence of a standard progressive pattern."[22] Phipps goes on to cite from two thanatologists who strongly disagree with her work. They do not share her belief that people move through stages and believe people have many more varied responses than the five she identified.[23] Perhaps the largest problem in the work of Kübler-Ross work is it has moved from a description *of* the dying process to a prescription *for* the dying process. "Indeed, Kübler-Ross has done a disservice in going beyond describing how people die to recommending how they ought to die."[24]

Other scholars share these critiques of Kübler-Ross's stages. James Carpenter writes, "Kübler-Ross's preoccupation with acceptance represents a selective blindness to other and different approaches which might be no less commendable."[25] Carpenter is especially critical of the way the stages seem to be set up as moving toward the goal of acceptance. "Acceptance alone has a positive ring, because it places the dying patient beyond the struggles and defiance with which Kübler-Ross associates the first four stages. Acceptance is a victory and a transition to a life after death. This emphasis is troublesome, for it rests upon a simplistic and arguable progression through stages."[26]

20. Ibid., 147–48.

21. Ibid., 265.

22. Phipps, *Death*, 51.

23. Ibid., 52.

24. Ibid.

25. Carpenter, "Accepting Death," 42.

26. Ibid.

Others criticize her goal-oriented portrayal of the stages because what it implies about death seems to run counter to the Christian tradition. In his critique of Kübler-Ross, George Kuykendall says, "significantly for Christians, Kübler-Ross' world-view conflicts strongly with biblical testimonies. . . . Death is primarily, according to the biblical accounts, neither 'a part of life' nor the 'last stage of growth,' but a terrible disruption of the life God's people live with God and, as such, a subject of fear, loathing, and pain."[27] Kuykendall also believes a Christian approach to caring for the dying that does not see death as a problem to be solved, as Kübler-Ross does, but rather as a reality to be faced with care and faith in God's abiding love, is far better.[28]

The criticisms of Kübler-Ross's work show that while she endeavored to provide a universal account of the grieving process, it is still one bound to a specific ideology that believes grief can be defined by its stages, and it is one that does not fit well with central tenets of Christian theology. We should, therefore, see the work of Kübler-Ross for what it is: an influential work that offers insight into issues around death and dying. It offers an intriguing framework. It is, though, only one approach. It need not be seen as the "right way" to die or grieve. Her work is notable because of its influence in society, but as it was written by a medical professional it does not get to the heart of the issue of developing a *theology* of suffering.

St. Augustine

The writings of St. Augustine are noteworthy because they provide one of the earliest descriptions of how the experience of suffering and grief is transformed by Christian faith. In *Confessions,* he writes of his grief over the loss of his friend; yet despite his moments of utter misery, he does not lose his faith. He writes: "Yet if our tearful entreaties did not reach your ears, no remnant of hope would remain for us. How does it come about that out of the bitterness of life sweet fruit is picked by groaning and weeping and sighing and mourning? Does the sweetness lie in the hope that you hear us?"[29] The Christian faith affirms not only

---

27. Kuykendall, "Care for the Dying," 45.

28. Ibid., 48.

29. Augustine, *Confessions,* 58–60.

that God hears a person's cry, not only that one is not alone in grief, but also that those lost are never truly lost. As Augustine wrote of the death of his friend, "[t]hough left alone, he loses none dear to him; for all are dear in the one who cannot be lost. Who is that but our God, the God who made heaven and earth and filled them?"[30] Christian confidence is in the reality of eternal life and the hope of resurrection. This hope for resurrection is not only a belief in a reunion with those who have been loved and lost, but also in a God who is constantly bringing out new life in the midst of death. The value of remembering God as Creator and Sustainer is evident in Augustine's writing on his grief at the death of his mother. He writes:

> Finally, I fell asleep and on waking found that in large part my suffering had been relieved. Alone upon my bed I remembered the very true verses of your Ambrose. For you are 'Creator of all things./ You rule the heavens./ You clothe the day with light/ And the night with the grace of sleep./ So rest restores exhausted limbs/ to the usefulness of work./ It lightens weary minds/ And dissolves the causes of grief.' From then on, little by little, I was brought back to my old feelings about your handmaid, recalling her devout attitude to you and her holy gentle and considerate treatment of us, of which I had suddenly been deprived. I was glad to weep before you about her and for her, about myself and for myself. Now I let flow the tears which I had held back so that they ran as freely as they wished. My heart rested upon them, and reclined upon them because it was your ears that were there, not those of some human critic who would put a proud interpretation on my weeping.[31]

Like the preachers in *This Incomplete One* (discussed below), Augustine is able to feel gratitude for the gift of his mother's life. His recollection of Ambrose's words help him broaden his perspective, to be reminded not only of God's greatness, but also of God's nearness.

Søren Kierkegaard

Over a millennium after Augustine wrote, Søren Kierkegaard continues the thread on how the Christian faith can transform the experience of

30. Ibid., 61.
31. Ibid., 176.

suffering. His theology of suffering is well expressed in his *Christian Discourses: Joyful Notes in the Strife of Suffering.* These writings focus on the theme of joy in the midst of suffering. Although Kierkegaard's writing is not always known for its joyful tenor, joy is evident throughout this work. It is not the joy of a "Pollyanna;" it is a joy that arises alongside an awareness of the existence of sin in the world. He affirms again and again, "sin only is man's ruin."[32] Like Dorothee Soelle (who will be discussed below) and Julian of Norwich, Kierkegaard advocates seeing things from a broader perspective. Kierkegaard wants his readers to remember, "We suffer only *once*, but we triumph eternally."[33] We are to see our suffering as a small instance in light of eternity. In the midst of pain and suffering we are to keep in mind a vision of eternity drawn from Revelation 20 where there is only joy—no death, no tears. Kierkegaard believes if suffering is seen in light of eternity, then it will be seen for what it really is: an illusion. He does not deny the reality of the experience of physical pain and emotional anguish, but he wants to assert ultimately suffering does not have real substance. Unlike God and all that is good, suffering does not last.[34] This is also true of losses. Even if we lose a friend or possessions, we have only lost something temporal. That which is eternal cannot be truly lost; it may be transfigured, but it is not lost. "Thou loses thus an earthly friend—thou gainest a transfigured friend." For Kierkegaard there is great joy in knowing what is gained in the end is eternal, and, therefore, greater than whatever was lost. No matter what we may lose—friends, possessions, even life itself—we have ultimately lost nothing, because in God we have gained all.[35] This belief that in losing we gain is a central tenet of the Christian faith, most profoundly expressed in baptism. We read in the *Book of Common Prayer,* that in the waters of baptism, "we are buried with Christ in his death. By it we share in his resurrection. Through it we are reborn by the Holy Spirit."[36] We need not despair in the midst of suffering because we have life and joy in Christ that are eternal and cannot be taken away.

---

32. Kierkegaard, *Christian Discourses*, 128, 138, 148, 153, 163.

33. Ibid., 103.

34. Ibid., 107.

35. Ibid., 142–46 and 151.

36. *Book of Common Prayer*, 306.

As for Gregory the Great, for Kierkegaard suffering is also an opportunity to be cleansed and purified: "For as gold is purified in the fire, so is the soul in suffering."[37] As with Gregory, Julian, and Taylor, Kierkegaard seems to accept the reality of suffering. His question is not "Why do we suffer?" but rather "What joys, what blessings may be gained from suffering?" He wishes to help his readers see how suffering need not be viewed as evil or horrible, but rather as a challenge with the potential to bear some beautiful fruit.

Kierkegaard recognizes how situations of suffering and affliction offer the potential for great hope. As countless writings attest, from St. Paul and St. Augustine to the five theologians examined here, hope is not absent in suffering. In fact, it can certainly be argued, as Kierkegaard does, hope is *most* present in the midst of suffering. Kierkegaard believes the presence of hope is due to the fact that suffering recruits hope. He believes the potential for hope is in all people as a gift from God, and it is in suffering that hope is brought forth. He invites his readers to see affliction not as a "pressure that depresses," but one which uplifts. Like a geyser of water, suffering can be a pressure that lifts up rather than beats down.[38] This provides an interesting nuance to the etymology of suffering that evokes images of bearing a burden. This is a view that would be affirmed by many, particularly Gregory, Julian and Taylor.

Along this same line, Kierkegaard goes on to affirm that suffering not only uplifts us, it can also make us stronger. In the midst of suffering it is important to focus on faith and the strength that comes from God. "If the sufferer, despondent and low-spirited, perhaps in despair, would stare fixedly upon how weak he has become—no, there would be nothing joyful in that. But if he would look away from that, to perceive what signified that he has become weak, who is it that becomes strong, that this is God—then that is indeed joyful." The strength that arises in suffering is not our own; it is God at work within us. God is strength and to be without him is utter weakness. In allowing weakness, we let go of the illusion that success is possible on our own, and instead turn ourselves over to God. In weakness we find true strength, and that is where joy is to be found.[39]

37. Kierkegaard, *Christian Discourses*, 108.

38. Ibid., 115–17.

39. Ibid., 131, 134, and 137.

Suffering is often seen as misfortune, but Kierkegaard goes to great lengths to proclaim that suffering is, in fact, good fortune because it brings us closer to the goal of eternity. In the midst of suffering we may grieve and perceive ourselves to be a victim of tragedy, feeling powerless to overcome the tribulations, but that is because our focus is in the wrong place. Giving in to weakness allows our focus to be on eternity and brings one closer to God. Turned over in this way, one's misfortune is transformed. Kierkegaard writes, "When in misfortune it seems impossible to budge from the spot, when in the impotence of suffering it is as if one could not move a foot—then eternity makes of misfortune good fortune." Like the five theologians examined below, Kierkegaard sees faith as a tool for transforming grief into joy.[40]

Another glimpse into Kierkegaard's views on suffering and grief can be found in his essay, "The Work of Love in Remembering One Dead." Like Taylor, Kierkegaard believes the reality of death helps one see life more clearly. "Yes, once again we go out to the dead in order *there* to get a look at life: this is the way the sharp shooter operates—he seeks out a place where the enemy cannot attack him but from which he can attack the enemy and where he can have perfect quiet for observation." The grief experienced at the death of a loved one is an opportunity to look at life, and it presents an opportunity to love. Kierkegaard believes there is a duty to those who have died and the way they are remembered reveals a lot about oneself and how one loves. In fact, death is a test of how unselfish love really is. "If one wants to make sure that love is completely unselfish, he eliminates every possibility of repayment." To love one who is dead is a free act of unselfish, faithful love. Kierkegaard believes this act of loving those who are dead offers a profound life lesson: humanity is called to love. "Remember one who is dead, and in addition to the blessing which is inseparable from this work of love, you will also have the best guidance to rightly understand life: that it is one's duty to love the men we do not see, but also those we do see."[41] It is in loving those dead we truly learn to live as Jesus taught, "You shall love your neighbor as yourself."[42] The experience of loss, like any other cause of grief, has the possibility, according to Kierkegaard, to teach and

40. Ibid., 155–56 and 163.

41. Kierkegaard, *Works of Love*, 317, 319–20, 325, 329.

42. Mark 12:31.

to deepen faith. If we engage in the "works of love," our own lives and the world will be enriched. That is the promise of faith, the gift of grief.

Kierkegaard is notable because his writings share many of the themes found in the writings of Gregory, Julian, and Taylor, including the focus on the joy that can be found in suffering, the belief in suffering as cleansing, and the focus on the afterlife. It is not surprising he shares these themes, for we could argue that Gregory, Julian, and Taylor had a role in shaping the Christian tradition that Kierkegaard inherited. Kierkegaard is a significant figure on the Christian landscape of theology of suffering, and could, therefore, merit a much larger role in the conversation presented here. Yet it is because Gregory, Julian, and Taylor had a role in shaping the tradition Kierkegaard inherited, and because less attention has been paid to their theologies of suffering and grief, that they are given places in the central conversation that follows.

Dorothy Soelle

Soelle is a contemporary theologian continuing to write on the theme of how Christian faith can transform grief, but she is critical of much of the attitude toward suffering she sees present in Western society. Her book *Suffering* was written in the midst of the Vietnam War and only a generation away from the Holocaust. It seeks to discover what meaning may be found in the midst of profound suffering. It is a work that engages deeply with the issues and desires to find light in the midst of the darkness. I am also strongly critical of the apathy Soelle sees dominating so much of Western society.

In her critique of apathy, Soelle does a disservice to her readers by the strong emotion evident in the book. She acknowledges in her introduction it is a book written "out of the bitterness" of those who protest against the war in Vietnam. There is nothing inherently wrong with bitterness being the motivation for a book. The difficulty is, at times, that her bitterness comes across as accusation. It is in her section on apathy and Vietnam that her anger is most evident. She paints a rosy picture of Vietnam and sees Americans as predominately apathetic, overcome by anti-communist feelings and unwilling to hear about the suffering of the Vietnamese. Soelle is right to be angry about the atrocities and the horrors of war. Yet she paints a too black-and-white picture of the conflict. Her critique of apathy would be more effective if it were nuanced and less accusatory.

After arguing strenuously against apathy, Soelle moves on to affirm the importance of making meaning out of suffering. It is this section of her book that is most relevant. She asserts that trying to uphold meaninglessness is absurd. Grief grounded in faith can be fruitful. She writes, "The grief that God works conforms us more closely to Christ and makes us more alive, more capable both of pain and of love."[43] Yet she does not seem to have a very high opinion of organized religion. She believes traditional practices of prayer are "as good as dead and buried," and believes religious belief does not add depth, only the vocabulary and ritual through which we can express our experience of suffering. Soelle does come to the conclusion that suffering can be understood as redemptive and meaningful when it is seen in a larger, communal context. She believes we cannot ask why an individual person has suffered. Hope is found in the belief that there is an ultimate good end for all of humanity. No longer is one to view "existence in terms of individual lives;" we must have a vision of hope that encompasses all of humanity. In responding to the story of the death of a young boy, she acknowledges an inability to offer direct hope about him as an individual. There is no way to bring him back, but she says, "[w]e can live in such a way that our life portrays a hope that other children will suffer no longer."[44]

The importance of community seems to be at the heart of Soelle's writings. She emphasizes community in her vision of the future. As with the above statement about children, she, like Gebara, believes one way to deal with suffering is to work together to fight against it. She believes there is much suffering that can be alleviated through social action. "We can change the social conditions under which people experience suffering. We can change ourselves and learn in suffering instead of becoming worse. We can gradually beat back and abolish suffering that still today is produced for the profit of a few." Soelle also acknowledges that no matter how hard we might work, there will also be suffering that cannot be alleviated. In the face of that unavoidable suffering, she counsels empathy. She exhorts her readers to join with those who are

43. Soelle, *Suffering*, 134.
44. Ibid., 76–78, 157, 173.

suffering by sharing the pain and "not leaving them alone and making their cry louder."[45]

There is no disputing the value of Soelle's cry to fight against unjust suffering, nor the call to stand with those who suffer. They are calls shared particularly by liberation theologians, including Gebara, and by many others across the world today and in centuries gone by. The commandment to "love thy neighbor" certainly affirms that an ethic of caring and preventing harm is at the heart of the Christian faith. Her overwhelming emphasis on community, however, does not seem sufficient for pastoral care or Christian theology. In the face of a personal loss, of one's own child for example, is it truly comforting to be given only the hope that someday other children will not suffer? Christianity certainly affirms the value of community, and of an eschatological vision of ultimate redemption and transformation, but does it not also equally affirm the precious value of each individual life? The parables of Jesus, which are so constitutive for the Christian faith, depict God as intimately, even extravagantly, concerned with the importance of individual lives. "Which one of you, having a hundred sheep and losing one of them, does not leave the ninety-nine in the wilderness and go after the one that is lost until he finds it?"[46] Are Christians, therefore, called to a theology of suffering that is not only communal in nature, but which also offers a personal and individual element that can comfort in the face of personal grief? Theology must not only call Christians to action in support of each other; it must also comfort those who suffer. Comforting theology is found in a vision of God that affirms God's love of humanity as God's own, special, individual children. Such a vision of God is present in Julian of Norwich's parable of the lord and the servant; she sees a God who guides the faithful through the darkness of their lives. Such a vision promotes an intimacy with God that seems lost if the focus is only on community. Soelle does not want God to remain "an alien superior power" and prefers to understand God as "that which occurs between people."[47] Yet if God is only "that which occurs between people," then God is no longer God. God has been reduced to an emotion or an intangible connection that ignites a relationship. Christians would not deny that connection; it is a part of the work of the Holy

45. Ibid., 178.
46. Luke 15:4.
47. Soelle, 173.

Spirit. Yet to focus solely on the Holy Spirit's actions between people is to neglect the fullness of the Trinitarian God. While acknowledging that God is at work in human relationships, Christians simultaneously maintain God is manifest both in the sustaining actions of the Holy Spirit, and as Creator and Redeemer. For Christians, God is a superior power, just not an alien power. Through the presentation of the five theologians, I offer it is possible to develop a theology of suffering that maintains God as a benevolent, superior power without relinquishing the intimacy of the divine-human relationship.

Stanley Hauerwas

Contemporary Christian ethicist Stanley Hauerwas continues to uphold the tradition that Christian faith can transform grief. His work *God, Medicine and Suffering* is written as response to works, like that of Rabbi Harold Kushner, that focus on explaining, "why God allows us to experience pain and suffering." Hauerwas believes framing the question this way is a theological mistake. Hauerwas is more interested in dealing with the question behind the question—more interested in understanding *why* people often ask the questions of why and how God allows suffering. He acknowledges the human desire for an understanding and an explanation, but believes "we cannot afford to give ourselves explanations for evil when what is required is a community capable of absorbing our grief." What Hauerwas is advocating is an approach to suffering that is focused on living with it, and on the Christian community's response to suffering. He is not interested in, and is even angered at, attempts to explain away suffering. In his book he relates the stories of children suffering (and in some cases dying) from life-threatening illnesses. The illness of a child is, perhaps, the most poignant example of suffering that cannot be explained. The child is too young to have sinned, and therefore, to have brought this on herself. A child who is ill and dying is a paramount example of innocent and inexplicable suffering.[48]

Like Soelle, Hauerwas is focused on the importance of community, but unlike Soelle, he is focused on the importance of upholding the beliefs and traditions of organized religion. Hauerwas's goal is

---

48. Hauerwas, *God, Medicine, and Suffering*, ix–xi.

to remind Christians and Christian communities of their role in the midst of inexplicable suffering. It is to hold strong to the truths of the Christian faith and to "call on the best wisdom we have developed as a Christ-formed people." Drawing on this wisdom allows Christians "to show the patience that does not try to discern any 'purpose' behind the suffering" and to allow that patience to inspire great care for those who are suffering. There are those who would take a case of innocent suffering as a reason to assume that either God does not exist or God is not good and merciful. For Hauerwas, a response to suffering that denies God's existence or tries to narrowly define God is wrong because it cuts us off from the gifts of the Christian tradition that can help us live with suffering.[49]

This focus on how to live with suffering is one Hauerwas shares particularly with Jeremy Taylor, whose work *Holy Living and Dying* is a manual devoted to helping people live more faithfully in the midst of suffering and the challenges of life. Hauerwas offers an important reminder of where our focus should be in response to suffering, but he does not follow Taylor in offering a wealth of instruction on how to live with suffering. Hauerwas's work is focused on convincing his reader why the focus must be shifted, not on how we are to live once we have found the new focus. Hauerwas's argument is important, but his work does not provide as practical a resource as Taylor's.

Nicholas Wolterstorff

Hauerwas's focus on how to live with grief, and how the Christian faith can be transformational in the midst of grief, is a theme prevalent in much of the literature written by theologians reflecting on personal experiences of grief. One example of this literature is the collection of sermons entitled *This Incomplete One: Words Occasioned by the Death of a Young Person*. Sermons certainly are an opportunity for theological reflection on grief and loss, and since they are so paramount in the Christian tradition, they are also an opportunity to affirm hope. In his forward to the book, Nicholas Wolterstorff notes the common elements of these sermons: "Amidst the grief over the brevity of this child's life, there is gratitude for his or her presence in our midst. This child was

---

49. Ibid., 68 and 89.

a gift. The grief does not smother the gratitude. And death, they all affirm, is not the end. We grieve, but not as those who have no hope. Yet none says that since death is not the end, we should not grieve. Though grief does not smother hope, neither does hope smother grief."[50] It is important to affirm that this hope is authentic, it is not meant to gloss over the depths of the pain that is felt. As Wolterstorff notes, the sermons "[a]ll affirm the great worth of our love of our children. . . . None says that it's not really so bad – that we should get over it, put it behind us, get on with things."[51] None of these preachers is advocating that loss is something one can get over. Like Kuykendall they do not see death as a problem to be solved, but as a reality with which we must live.

Wolterstorff is, of course, very qualified to reflect theologically on the loss of a child. He is a well-known theologian, and his own son, Eric, died in a climbing accident at the age of twenty-five. Wolterstorff's own reflections were collected in *Lament for a Son* and published in the hopes of providing comfort to fellow mourners.[52] In his book, Wolterstorff provides valuable theological reflection on the meaning of suffering. As noted above, he offers a basic definition: "When something prized or loved is ripped away or never granted—work, someone loved, recognition of one's dignity, life without physical pain—that is suffering."[53] In his reflections, though, he realizes that that definition does not fully capture the reality of suffering, it only describes its occurrence. "What it *is,* I do not know. . . . I understand nothing of it. Of pain, yes: cut fingers, broken bones. Of sorrow and suffering, nothing at all. Suffering is a mystery as deep as any in our existence. It is not of course a mystery whose reality some doubt. Suffering keeps its face hid from each while making itself known to all."[54] This acknowledgment of the mystery and incomprehensibility of suffering is important. To so acknowledge prevents us from merely railing in anger at the seeming misfortune. To acknowledge the mystery is to affirm the heart of the Christian faith; it is to leave open the possibility of blessing, the possibility of resurrection in the midst of loss and death. Resurrection is a possibility, a truth that Wolterstorff himself eloquently

50. Wolterstorff, *This Incomplete One*, x.

51. Ibid., ix.

52. Wolterstorff, *Lament for a Son*, 7.

53. Ibid., 89.

54. Ibid.

affirms: "Suffering may do us good—may be a blessing, something to be thankful for. This I have learned. . . . Suffering may be among the *sufferer's* blessings. . . . In the valley of suffering, despair and bitterness are brewed. But there also character is made. The valley of suffering is the vale of soul-making." Of course, to affirm the reality of blessing in the midst of suffering is not to see suffering as something to be sought out because it is character building. Wolterstorff recognizes how living with suffering requires holding two seemingly contradictory, simultaneous truths. Like Gregory, Wolterstorff acknowledges the growth that is possible through suffering. For Wolterstorff, however, while we may come to be grateful for the fruits of suffering, that does not stop us from crying out in anguish at the pain of the loss.[55]

Wolterstorff's writing in *Lament for a Son* is much like Lewis's, as it is the reflections of a theologian in the midst of deep personal grief. In his own writings, and through the collection of sermons he edited, Wolterstorff helps develop an understanding of what suffering means and establishes a framework for discussing the human response to suffering. Because, like Lewis, Wolterstorff is a twentieth-century theologian who offers permission for Christians to feel the pain of their grief, he too could have merited a place in the central conversation of this book. Yet Lewis's writings offer opportunities to engage with him at multiple stages in his life journey through fiction and nonfiction. It was, therefore, the variety of Lewis's texts that merited his inclusion.

These works show how developing a theology of suffering out of our own personal experiences of suffering is not a new or strange idea, as it has long established grounds within the Christian tradition. The works of the authors presented above offer great insights, but they do not provide the unique combination of perspectives offered in the five thinkers discussed below.

FIVE THEOLOGIANS ON SUFFERING AND GRIEF

This book brings together the voices of five Christian theologians who, separately and together, offer valuable theological insights and approaches to the issues of suffering and grief. They are five disparate voices from across the centuries. One of the important questions to be

55. Ibid., 96–97.

addressed is whether or not their voices are in fact so disparate as their chronology, locations, and experiences would have them seem to be. Among all the thinkers there is a tendency toward a way of thinking that affirms the element in the Christian tradition that focuses on what is beyond the here and now. The belief is expressed by Paul in his letter to the church in Corinth, in which he wrote: "Now I know only in part; then I will know fully."[56] The five thinkers vary in their emphasis and balance between the then and the now, but their affirmation of both is a unifying theme. The following pages provide an overview of the five thinkers and their individual perspectives.

Gregory the Great

Gregory the Great was pope in the sixth century in the midst of plagues, wars, and famines. The chapter on Gregory's theology of suffering and grief is grounded in his treatise on *Pastoral Care*, most specifically his instructions on how to care for the sick (part 3, chapter 12), and also draws on his sermons and his commentary on Job. Gregory's work is specifically addressed to those who are in a position to minister to and care for the sick. There is much in this section, however, that reveals Gregory's own beliefs about suffering and how we should respond to suffering. Gregory strongly believes suffering is a gift that cleanses us from sin. Suffering is also seen as a discipline from God. In modern society where politeness and care are meant to reign, all this talk of discipline and sin may seem cruel. Yet it is important to note that Gregory saw suffering as a gift and admonished his readers to keep in mind the sufferings of Christ. There is to be hope and consolation because Christ suffered. No one is alone in the midst of suffering, and no suffering can be as great as Christ's. Christians are to follow the example of Christ and be patient in the midst of suffering. As Gregory writes, "And who with healthy reasoning can be ungrateful for his suffering if God himself did not go without punishments, even though he was without sin?" For Gregory, suffering is part of the reality of existence, and in Christ there is the hope of overcoming suffering because there is the promise of everlasting life. In the grand scheme, the sufferings of one individual are small indeed. Suffering pales in comparison with the great salvific

---

56. 1 Corinthians 12:12b.

work accomplished by Christ on the cross. Gregory ultimately offers a theology of suffering that is one of acceptance, and he sees suffering as a matter of ascetic discipline that is both divinely and personally imposed.[57]

Julian of Norwich

The examination of the theology found in the text of fourteenth-century English mystic Julian of Norwich, *Revelations of Divine Love,* will center on her parable of the lord and the servant. This story describes a servant who was rushing to do his lord's bidding and fell into a ditch and injured himself. The servant is blinded by his own suffering and cannot see that his lord is still watching over him. In fact, his lord knows he will recover, and there is a great reward awaiting him. Through this parable and her own reflections on it, Julian, like Gregory, offers a reminder to keep perspective in the midst of suffering. We are to remember God's vision is much greater and broader than humanity's. From the parable, we may also trust that God does not abandon his servants, but rather leads them to a better place.

This does not mean we are to seek out suffering because it is redemptive. Rather, the knowledge that God is leading us to a reward is meant to be a source of consolation and comfort in the midst of suffering. The suffering will come; there is no doubt about that. What is important to remember is God is present, guiding, leading us through the suffering to a place of greater union with him. Julian's acceptance of suffering is grounded in the faith that we are being led to that place of union with God.

Jeremy Taylor

Jeremy Taylor, like Gregory the Great, offers a manual for his readers. Taylor's manual, however, is directed at lay people rather than clergy. The discussion of Taylor, a seventeenth-century Anglican priest in England, will focus on his work, *Holy Living and Holy Dying,* which seeks to put death in the forefront of people's minds so as to inspire them to

---

57. Gregory the Great, *The Book of Pastoral Rule,* 115–18.

live more meaningful and holy lives.[58] Like the other thinkers, Taylor helps to put individual human suffering into a global and even cosmic context. On the surface, Taylor seems to have a negative, pessimistic view of the world: "The prosperity of this world is so infinitely soured with the overflowing of evils." Yet at the heart of Taylor's writing is a faith-filled hope and the significant truth that death, and the grief that results from the evils of the world, are what lend meaning to life. Taylor also admonishes his readers that living with an acceptance of suffering and an awareness of the certainty of death can enable us to lead a more spiritually meaningful life. As Taylor encourages, "This is a place of sorrows and tears, of great evils and constant calamity; let us remove from hence, at least in affections and preparations of mind." Taylor's acceptance of suffering is grounded in a belief in the importance of a virtuous response to suffering – one of patient and hopeful forbearance.[59]

C. S. Lewis

C. S. Lewis is a twentieth-century Anglican who died in 1963. He is an author not typically considered a theologian, but beloved by many. There is, however, much theology in what he writes, and the value of his work is both its depth and approachability. One of the gifts of his work is it is firmly grounded in his own personal experience, particularly the death of his wife. His questions and struggles are not abstract—they are his own—and they articulate some universal human questions and struggles. The discussion of Lewis will focus primarily on *A Grief Observed,* with some consideration of other works, including *The Problem of Pain, The Chronicles of Narnia,* and *Letters to Malcolm,* which also address the issues of suffering and grief. Especially in *A Grief Observed,* Lewis offers an example of living and struggling with questions. He does not jump to quick or easy answers; rather, he brings his reader on his own journey as he lives into the pain and challenges of his grief. Lewis is an example of courage and of faith. He has no hesitation in questioning God and expressing his anger. "Lord, are these your real terms? Can I meet H. again only if I learn to love you so much that I

---

58. Although originally published as two works: *Holy Living* and *Holy Dying,* they quickly became bound together and have since been published usually as a single work with the title *Holy Living and Dying.*

59. Taylor, *Holy Living and Dying,* 326 and 330.

don't care whether I meet her or not?"[60] Lewis serves as an example of the value of asking difficult questions and the reward of learning to live with them. It is through his grappling with his own pain and questions that Lewis comes to develop his own understanding of acceptance, and he therefore shows acceptance need not be devoid of grieving. For Lewis, acceptance can be seen as a place of rest that we come to after struggling through the depths of grief.

Ivone Gebara

Ivone Gebara is a contemporary Brazilian liberation theologian who works and writes from a feminist perspective. Her book *Out of the Depths: Women's Experience of Evil and Salvation* is grounded in her own work, as well as the writings of other Latin American women. She questions much of the established theology on suffering. She raises questions as to whether traditional views of understanding suffering and grief are appropriate for women and others on the margins. She reminds us how issues of gender, power, culture, and class play a role in how we experience suffering. Gebara notes "the message of Jesus on the cross leads us to believe that suffering that comes from injustice will lead us to redemption, to victory over our enemies. . . . Through experience we can say how much, in practice, this theology accentuates the victimization of women and encourages them in domestic and familial martyrdom."[61] Gebara helps us think critically about how theology is formulated and how suffering is understood. Her writings offer insight into when suffering is unjust. Gebara advocates an approach to theology grounded in the specificity of individual experience. The discussion of Gebara will, therefore, also draw on her engagement with author Isabel Allende and her memoir, *Paula*. The memoir tells Allende's story of suffering as her daughter dies, and of her suffering under the dictatorship in Chile. Gebara's perspective raises critical questions that must be asked on the road to formulating a theology of suffering, as she offers the reminder that not all suffering is to be accepted. Along with her criticisms, Gebara does promote acceptance of suffering which has been identified as endemic, rather than unjust.

60. Lewis, *A Grief Observed*, 79–80.
61. Gebara, *Out of the Depths*, 107.

CONCLUSION

The final chapter serves as a forum to bring these five thinkers into conversation with each other and to construct a nuanced theology of suffering that draws on their varying perspectives. The five thinkers do share a belief that suffering can offer meaning and growth; suffering can lead to a place of greater spiritual knowledge and toward union with God. Gregory, Julian, and Jeremy Taylor remind us this is the gift of suffering. Lewis and Gebara remind us of the value of asking questions and even expressing anger along the way.

This contemporary theology seeks to nuance a belief in the redemptive nature of suffering, affirming suffering is a reality that has value and meaning in the context of the Christian tradition, but not seeking to promote suffering as something that should be sought out. In fact, not all suffering is even to be accepted, as Christians are called to stand in opposition to suffering that is a result of moral evil and injustice. Other suffering, however, is a result of natural evil; it is an existential fact, a reality of the human experience. When faced with the reality of existential suffering, these five thinkers explain the possibility of living with and moving through the anguish created by that suffering. The Christian story reminds us that salvation is possible, not only in a cosmic sense, but on a tangible level in the daily lives of individual people. Whether it is because we have come to accept the reality of existential suffering or because we have joined the fight with those who are victims of injustice, in the end we hope it will be possible to join Julian and say, "all shall be well."[62]

62. Julian of Norwich, *The Showings*, 72. Throughout this book, the quotes from Julian's *Shewings* have been updated to more modern English in consultation with the translation of Colledge and Walsh as noted.

1

Gregory on Grief: "The Great Teacher"[1]

LATE SIXTH-CENTURY ROME WAS in a state of decline. The seat of the empire had moved to Constantinople, so Rome was no longer the center of the empire. Central Italy had been invaded by the Lombards who "terrorized the population." "[W]orn down by decades of intermittent, vindictive warfare"and a half century of plague, Rome saw its population drop to a quarter of what it had been a hundred years before, making the city "a ghost of its former self." This reality was evident in that the glorious Circus Maximus was deserted and many of the edifices of Rome's glory days were crumbling.Gregory offers a unique window into the realities of suffering in his age, as well as a theological approach to the experience of grief. Gregory is also widely known for his writings, which are foundational to much of Western Christian theology.[2] This chapter aims to focus predominately on his handbook entitled *Pastoral Care* or *Rule* (*Liber Regulae Pastoralis*), which provides a guide for bishops and ministers in their work, and his commentary on the book of Job. Both of these works provide great insight into the mind of Gregory regarding the issues of suffering and grief.

Gregory is a logical starting point for this typology because in many ways his work is foundational for Christian theology regarding suffering and grief. He begins with Scripture and the life, death, and resurrection of Jesus Christ. Scripture is foundational in Gregory's

1. Gregory the Great. *The Books of the Morals, Vol. I, .v.xxviii.*

2. Although it is interesting to note that "many now see Gregory's pastoral, ascetic, and soteriological positions to be more aligned with the Eastern Fathers of his era than with St. Augustine." Gregory the Great, *The Book of Pastoral Rule*, 10.

work, and it is for him the supreme authority. There are additional resources that ground Gregory's work, including the Councils of the Church, the writings of other Church Fathers (particularly Augustine), and greek philosophers. As Gillian Evans notes, Gregory "draws on whatever has been said by earlier Christian authors as he needs it, but so often without acknowledgment that the question of his knowledge of many individual authors remains uncertain."[3]

CONTEXT

In order to best understand Gregory's beliefs and writings about suffering and grief, it is important to gain a sense of the forces at work in the context in which he lived and upon him as a person. The broader context of life in Europe in the Middle Ages, like that of Rome itself, was a precarious one. Julia Smith describes it thus: "men and women in early medieval Europe lived intimately with deprivation and death. In the face of intermittent climatic disasters, periodic epidemics, and harsh everyday living conditions, the population of Europe laboured to produce a living from the land and to raise children to carry on their efforts. Most lived at or near subsistence level; others reflected on the meaning of human existence and its moral qualities amid the fearfulness of unexpected death and the likelihood of death."[4] The constancy of warfare was also an issue in Gregory's lifetime. As Markus notes, "From the 530s until well after Gregory's death Italy was never again at peace for more than short spells."[5]

Gregory was born into this chaos, likely around 540, the son of a prominent Roman family. Gregory's professional life began in the secular world. Gregory thought that, like Boethius, he could live a devout life as a layman, and, in line with his aristocratic status, he became the Prefect of Rome in 573. Yet this political career was short lived. Dudden believes that in his time as Prefect, Gregory's "anxieties must have been great. Swarms of Lombards beset the city, and all communications with Constantinople were cut off." It may have been a particular set of events, or perhaps it was a growing realization, but it became clear to Gregory

3. Evans, *The Thought of Gregory the Great*, 8.

4. Smith, *Europe after Rome*, 51.

5. Markus, *Gregory the Great and His World*, 3.

not long after he became Prefect that he "lacked the moral strength" to combine secular employment with his religious devotion, and so Gregory became a monk.[6] Even the lure of wealth could not entice him to maintain a secular life; rather, Gregory saw wealth as something to be given away. Gregory's inheritance allowed him to found six monasteries in Sicily and one in Rome (in his father's palace), and it left him with enough money to give to the poor.[7]

Gregory did not become the abbot of the monastery he endowed; instead, he lived as a monk at the one he founded in Rome, and that simple life brought him great joy.[8] In the view of Peter Brown, "This was the life for which he considered himself best suited—not the life of a pious lay person 'in the world,' but a secluded life, undertaken for his own good, lived without 'worldly' cares, as a monk devoted to the contemplation of God." It seems that whatever Gregory chose to do, he chose to do it well and to the highest standard. Gregory's monastery (founded in his father's palace) was "a center of fierce asceticism and, above all, heavy learning."[9]

Gregory was first called out of monastic life to be a papal emissary to the Imperial Court in Constantinople, but that did not stop his asceticism. In fact, because Italy was not particularly important to the court at the time, Gregory was allowed ample time to maintain the routine of his monastic life while in Constantinople.[10] In 590 the plague again struck Rome, and Gregory was called again to service in the church, this time as pontiff.[11] To be elected supreme leader of the church was, of course, a high honor. It spoke highly of Gregory's faith and character, but it was a post he did not want. "Congratulations poured in on him from every side, but his answers were only a perpetual wail of lamentation. He declared on his conscience that he 'undertook the burden of the dignity with a sick heart;' he was 'so stricken with sorrow that he could scarcely speak;' 'the eyes of his soul were darkened with grief.'" Indeed, Gregory wrote in a letter after his election, "Under the pretence of being made a bishop, I am brought back to the world; for I am now

6. Dudden, *Gregory the Great*, 3, 11, 16, and 103–4; Brown, 200–1.

7. Evans, *The Thought of Gregory the Great*, 4–5.

8. Ibid., 5.

9. Brown, *The Rise of Western Christendom*, 201.

10. Ibid.

11. Evans, *The Thought of Gregory the Great,* 5.

more in bondage to earthly cares than I ever was as a layman. I have lost the deep joy of my quiet, and while I seem outwardly to have risen, I am inwardly falling down."[12] These lines evidence Gregory's regret and grief at his own election. Despite his feelings of lament, Gregory did not deny the call to lead or ultimately refuse the position. It is a bit ironic that one who would eventually be given the title "The Great," was to enter into his pontificate so reluctantly. On the other hand, perhaps it was the qualities of his life as a monk, his simplicity, humility, and strong faith that helped make him a great pope. Despite ill health that ultimately left him "[r]acked with pain and unable to walk," Gregory served as pope for fourteen years, until his death in March of 604.[13]

Before moving on to examine his pontificate in greater detail, it is worth noting that living in the times he did, Gregory shared with the early church the sense of immediacy regarding the end of the world, a view emphasized in many of his sermons.[14] As Richards notes, "[t]he imminent end of the world dominated Gregory's thinking, and his writings are informed by the urgent necessity to prepare for this."[15] This dominant theme in Gregory's thinking can make his writing seem uncomfortably gloomy, but that label should not apply to all of Gregory's work.[16] He may be a man strongly influenced by the devastation, destruction, and personal suffering he witnessed, but that does not make him a man without hope. There is much judgment and admonition in his work, but there is also evidence of a deep faith and abiding hope. He does not discount the reality of great suffering around him and in his own body, but he also does not discount the ever-present possibility of redemption. Gregory holds his emphasis on the end of the world in tension with a need to figure out how to live with suffering. If Gregory truly thought the end of the world was imminent, why would he spend the beginning of his pontificate writing a handbook for bishops and priests on how to minister to the people? Although there is certainly evidence of Gregory's belief in the immediacy of the end of the world, his prolific writings and the manner in which he cared for his flock

12. Dudden, *Gregory the Great*, 226. Also Gregory the Great, *Pastoral Care*, 3–4.

13. Richards. *Consul of God*, 259.

14. Moorhead. *Gregory the Great*, 6. On his belief regarding the end of the world, see particularly Homilies 3, 17, 20, and 35 in Gregory, *Forty Gospel Homilies*.

15. Richards, *Consul of God*, 53.

16. Moorhead, *Gregory the Great*, 44.

would seem to indicate otherwise.[17] It is, however, possible he believed in the importance of caring the best he could for his flock in whatever time they had or that his belief in the end of the world came and went, depending on the level of catastrophes he and his people were experiencing. Since he was not one to be lazy or complacent, it is likely a belief in the imminent end of the world was not going to keep him from the labors to which he believed God had called him.

PONTIFICATE

As noted above, Gregory came to power in a time of great suffering. As Carole Straw notes: "A world of wars, famine, and plague shaped Gregory's spirituality and his activities as pope."[18] Gregory was up to the task and has been praised for his skills as a pastor and as an administrator. His upbringing, self-assurance, strong spirituality, and practical, administrative skills were gifts he brought to the papacy. John Moorhead notes that Gregory "is generally regarded as one of the outstanding figures in the long line of popes, and by the late ninth century had come to be known as 'the Great', a title which is still applied to him."[19] Gregory was not a pope who was caught up in the trappings of the office or intoxicated by power. He continued, as much as possible, to live the life of a monk, even while he held the highest office in the church. Apparently, Gregory did not allow visitors to prostrate themselves in front of him. He did not see himself as a "lord." Even though he lived humbly, Gregory did not shirk from leadership. The voluminous nature of Gregory's correspondence testifies to his hard work, particularly as the chief administrator of the church. Over 800 of Gregory's letters survive, and they likely numbered in the thousands. The majority of these letters were rescripts that involved his "ruling on administrative and ecclesiastical matters."[20]

One does wonder whether Gregory would have been considered "Great" had he not had so many challenges to deal with in the course of his papacy. As pope, he was responsible for feeding the city of Rome from the harvest of the patrimony of St. Peter, which was a collection

17. Ibid.; Markus, *Gregory the Great and His World*, 205; Richards, *Consul*, 53; Demacopoulos, *Five Models*, 143 and 157.

18. Straw and Collins. *Gregory the Great*, 1.

19. Moorhead, *Gregory the Great*, 1 and 3.

20. Brown, *Rise of Western Christendom*, 212. Also see Volz, *The Medieval Church*, 30–31.

of over four hundred estates under the control of the papacy.[21] Many of these estates had previously been "neglected, usurped, ravaged, or lost to predators, the Lombards, or the Eastern emperor," but Gregory reclaimed lands for the papacy and believed their bounty should be used to "alleviate poverty."[22] Additionally, the church's treasury served as the bank for the civil administration of Rome. Since the Emperor in Constantinople frequently needed reminding of Italy's existence and therefore seemed ignorant of the issues facing Romans, Gregory "acted independently to stave off famine by seeing to the needs of the sick and starving, using his own private resources."[23] It would seem, then, that Gregory's "greatness," both as an administrator and as a pastor, were not only a result of his circumstances, but rather a combination of circumstances and character.

In seeing all the challenges of Gregory's pontificate and how he responded to them, we begin to get a sense of Gregory's beliefs about suffering. Gregory had to minister to a people in a constant state of fear. As Richards notes, "The characteristic state of the ordinary man in the Middle Ages, as of his late antique counterpart, was one of fear—fear of the plague, fear of invasion, fear of the tax-collector, fear of witchcraft and magic, fear above all of the unknown."[24] For Gregory, though, the reality of fear in everyday life was not necessarily a negative. He believed that fear can be purgative, a "cleansing fire" that could help conform our lives to God's will.[25] Additionally, Gregory's seeing himself as the *praedicator* (the one called to warn of the end of time), meant that he lived in a state of excitement rather than one of fear or panic.[26]

In his response to the plague, we can see that Gregory exemplified the typical view of his day —suffering was due to sinful behavior—because he used the epidemic to call upon the people to repent. In one of his sermons during the plague, he called on the people to assemble "with contrite hearts and amended lives, with devout minds and with tears . . . so that when the strict Judge sees that we punish our faults ourselves, He may refrain from passing the sentence of condemnation,

---

21. Brown, *Rise of Western Christendom*, 206.

22. Volz. *The Medieval Church*, 29.

23. Brown, *Rise of Western Christendom*, 206; Volz, *The Medieval Church*, 29.

24. Richards, *Consul of God*, 16.

25. Straw and Collins, *Gregory the Great*, 22 and 24.

26. Brown, *Rise of Western Christendom*, 213.

now ready to be pronounced against us."[27] As will be explored in more depth later, Gregory's take on suffering, as exemplified in this response to the plague, was to view it as an opportunity for people to repent and restore themselves to right relationship with God.

ASCETICISM AND PERSONAL SUFFERING

As stated in the preface, writing about suffering is rarely a merely intellectual exercise. It is often one borne out of personal experience. Gregory is no different on this front. He writes on suffering as one who knows first hand what it is to feel pain and grief. In Gregory's efforts to reach out to those in need and his calls for repentance in his sermon during the plague, we can also see that he did not consider himself separate from the sufferings of his people. Perhaps part of the reason he was not callous about the sufferings of others was the fact that he himself suffered physical pain and emotional anguish.

The ascetic practices of Gregory's early days as a monk ruined his health and meant that for the remainder of his life "his energies were sapped by constant illness." As Richards notes, "For Gregory, pain was an inescapable fact of life. Throughout his pontificate he was almost continuously ill, his suffering increasing as his reign wore on. His severe asceticism had completely undermined his constitution, ruining his digestive system and leaving him prey to the summer fevers which infested Rome." Richards goes on to quote from one of Gregory's letters, in which he wrote, "For many a long year has passed since I have been afflicted by frequent pains in the bowels. The powers of my stomach having broken down, I am continually weak; and I gasp under the weight of successive slow fevers." It is of little surprise, then, that Gregory chose to write a commentary on Job, that biblical figure who himself knew such great suffering.[28] Theologically, Gregory can be said to have had a high view of suffering and its redemptive value. In some of his own writings, though, it is evident he did not always live out that view. In 599 Gregory wrote, "I am so tormented with gout and painful anxieties that life itself is to me most grievous suffering. Every day I

---

27. Dudden, *Gregory the Great*, 218.

28. Richards, *Consul of God*, 45. Periodic references to his own illnesses are also evident in his *Homilies*. See Homilies 22 and 34.

sink through pain. Every day I look for the relief of death."[29] That statement is a marked contrast to his theology, which promotes acceptance and forbearance in the midst of suffering and the value of suffering as a scourge that cleanses us of sin. He does not praise his suffering for its character-building value, rather, like anyone who is in the midst of severe pain, he wishes only for relief.

The emphasis on asceticism is not only an aspect of Gregory's personal life and practice; it is a central part of his theology. Gregory believes in the body are both humanity's punishment and humanity's salutary discipline. As Straw notes, "By God's ordinance the universe is so arranged to educate man that he might eventually return to God."[30] The suffering we undergo, then, is a part of our education. It is the corrective discipline through which one finds the way back to God. Yet for Gregory suffering is not merely something that we undergo; as evidenced by his own practices, it is something to be sought out. We are to practice asceticism and self-deprivation because of its great redemptive value. Straw sees in Gregory that "[t]o control one's reaction to suffering and temptation is to be master of all the possible disasters the devil can devise. Even the darkest moments of trial are somehow triumphant with man's defeat of evil." What matters for Christians is the ability to control our bodies and to resist the temptation to sin, for in so doing we triumph and move closer to God. The value in ascetic practices is not only that they help us persevere in resisting temptation, but they also help us define what is good. We more fully understand and appreciate the good in the world when we, like Gregory, knows the misery of suffering.[31] Gregory's emphasis on asceticism is also a significant part of his legacy. Demacopoulos believes "Gregory's most significant contribution, one that had both administrative and theological consequences, was his asceticizing of spiritual direction. By completing the merger between ascetic and clerical strands of the pastoral tradition, Gregory did nothing less than redefine Christian leadership."[32]

Gregory not only suffered from physical ailments (mostly brought on by his ascetic practices) including fevers, gout, and intestinal pain, he also suffered from anxiety and emotional distress. Gregory took his

29. Dudden, *Gregory the Great*, 38.

30. Straw, *Gregory the Great*, 128 and 141.

31. Ibid., 145–46.

32. Demacopoulos, *Five Models of Spiritual Direction,* 129.

life and his role seriously. The act of writing a manual to instruct bishops is clear evidence that he firmly believed it mattered greatly how one lived, especially as a leader of the church. As can be seen by his response to his election, Gregory was anxious and fearful that he might not be able to fulfill the role of chief pastor of the church. If Gregory began his pontificate in a state of anxiety, and given the challenges the church faced during that time, it seems quite likely that worry and anxiety continued to plague him for the remainder of his life.

Gregory's emotional anguish is, perhaps, most evident in his above-noted response to his own election. Yet the seriousness with which Gregory took his job is evident in his careful, dedicated administrative involvement in the affairs of the church and the empire. His role as head of the church in the Western Empire meant responsibility for the well being of thousands of people—many of whom depended on him for their basic survival as well as spiritual guidance. For a man who would have liked nothing better than to live out his days quietly serving God behind the walls of a monastery, it is perhaps of little surprise the language in his letters at the time of his election is that of sorrow, grief and loss. His use of this language is notable and meaningful. To hear a pope and a saint grieve over the loss of the life he hoped and wished for himself is intriguing, not only because it may be a source of comfort to an average Christian, but because it points to a contrast between Gregory's theology and experience. Gregory holds up the idea, particularly in *The Pastoral Rule*, that grieving is a sin, for it is the inappropriate response to suffering or to a challenge given by God. We are to welcome the gift as an opportunity for spiritual growth, but, initially at least, Gregory did not live out this belief. First he grieved, and only after that grief was he able to live into the new reality of his responsibility and to use his new situation for the spiritual betterment of himself and others. Gregory did live out his belief that suffering is an educational opportunity, and the contrast between his personal statements of grief and the theology he espouses in his writings suggest a desire to teach his flock a way to respond to suffering he wished himself capable of living out.

A THEOLOGY OF SUFFERING
FROM GREGORY'S WRITINGS

An understanding of Gregory's views on suffering can be gained from many of his writings. The two most significant and influential are *The Book of the Pastoral Rule (Liber Regulae Pastoralis)* and his *Moralia* (a commentary on the book of Job). *The Book of the Pastoral Rule* is Gregory's manual of instruction for ministers. The sections on how to minister to those who are suffering particularly offer insight into Gregory's views on suffering. The book has proved its worth in that it continues to be a classic, if not *the* classic work on pastoral care. In fact, Thomas Oden describes Gregory as one who "astutely gathered up the pastoral wisdom of the patristic period and energetically set in motion the basic direction of the medieval pastoral tradition."[33] The book is divided into four parts. The first part focuses on the nature of the pastoral office; the second focuses on the life of the pastor. The third part is about how to minister to particular types of people, and the fourth with how a pastor should guard against pride. It is the third part that is most instructive of Gregory's view on suffering and that which has been the most influential. As Henry Davis notes in his introduction, written well over a millennium after Gregory's manual, "He deals with nearly forty different classes of people. . . . It is this part of the work which commends it to succeeding generations, and still serves as a source of knowledge, inspiration, and enlightenment to rulers, pastors in high office or low, preachers, and confessors."[34] Oden also describes it as the "indispensible [sic] guide to pastoral counseling" for more than a thousand years.[35]

The *Moralia* is a long and extensive commentary on the book of Job. Given the sufferings of his own life, it is, as Jeffrey Richards writes, "perhaps small wonder that he chose for his greatest exegetical work to expound the tribulations and patience of Job."[36] Gregory's sufferings were present even in the writing process itself, as completing the *Moralia* (his commentary on Job) "was not done without difficulty, for his health had been in a deplorable state for years, and he shook with slow but continual fevers." Although Job's sufferings likely had personal

33. Oden, *Care of Souls*, 12.
34. Gregory the Great, *Pastoral Care,* 8.
35. Oden, *Care of Souls*, 27.
36. Richards, *Consul of God*, 45.

significance for Gregory, the book of Job is also an important book for the Christian tradition. As Pierre Batiffol expresses this, "The fundamental allegory of the book of Job is based on the idea that Job by his trials is a prototype of the passion of Christ."[37] Job offers an example of innocent suffering. Job does not fit the traditional understanding of suffering as punishment for sin. The writer of the story establishes Job as blameless and yet he suffers greatly. The question of why Job suffers offers insight in Gregory's views on suffering and the human experience.

Humanity, Sin, and Evil

Early in his commentary, Gregory addresses the question of why Job suffers. Since Job did not sin, his suffering is not a form of punishment. In Gregory's view, however, this does not mean his suffering is empty or without cause. Gregory states, "Thus, that we may uphold the truth of God in word, and His equity in deed, the blessed Job is at one and the same time not afflicted without cause, seeing that his merits are increased, and yet he *is* afflicted *without cause*, in that he is not punished for any offence [sic] committed by him." Job's suffering is not without cause because it is inflicted so that his merits might increase. By the "blows the virtue of patience gained increase, and the gloriousness of his reward was augmented by the pains of the scourge."[38] Gregory thus offers an answer to the old question of why does a benevolent and just God allow his children to suffer? Gregory does not hold with Hauerwas that this is the wrong question, for Gregory easily asserts that suffering is a cleansing scourge and it increases virtue. Suffering refines and improves our character. As he writes in the *Pastoral Rule*, "For unless it was his plan to give them an inheritance after correction, he would not concern himself to educate them through affliction."[39]

---

37. Batiffol. *Saint Gregory the Great*, 119 and 122.

38. Gregory the Great, *The Books of the Morals*, Vol. I.iii.

39. Ibid., *The Book of Pastoral Rule*, 115. The quotes from Pastoral Rule in this work are taken from George E. Demacopoulos's translation because it is the most updated translation, and one which works from "a reproduction of the text contained in a manuscript believed to be transcribed by Gregory's secretary," a text which was unavailable to previous English translators. Demacopoulos, therefore, while indebted to earlier translations, is able to better convey Gregory's original meaning than other translations. See 23–25.

Suffering is to be an educational experience, but not one inflicted by our fellow humans. In discussing the sufferings of Job, it is important to note Gregory's harsh condemnation of Job's friends. It is a condemnation that would likely be appreciated by C. S. Lewis and Ivone Gebara, two fellow Christians who speak out (in subsequent chapters) against human behavior that adds further strife to our suffering. As noted above, Gregory sees Job's friends as adding to his suffering. Elsewhere, he goes so far as to refer to them as heretics.[40] Gregory criticizes Eliphaz for being "ignorant of the rules of consoling" and "offering insult to the afflicted man." The friends are to blame for their narrow-mindedness that assumes Job suffers for some sin or wickedness on his part. The friends do not see Job for who he is, "a righteous man, and [one who is] besieged with the strokes of God's hand."[41]

Interestingly, Gregory criticizes Job's friends for narrowly holding to the view that suffering is punishment for sin. It would seem, though, that while Gregory (like Job's friends) may first jump to this conclusion, he does leave open the reality of innocent suffering in the world. One wonders how his sermon in the midst of the plague (quoted earlier) might have been different, if he had seen his role being that of consoler rather than critic. As it is written, he certainly sounds more like Job's friends than the ideal consoler he portrays as their contrast. The contrast between his sermon and his chiding of Job's friends raises intriguing questions about Gregory's view of human nature. Is it simply that he knew no other human could measure up to Job's innocence? Was he too profoundly aware of his own faults and those of his own generation to believe the plague was not some form of divine retribution? Was innocent suffering only the stuff of legends, saints, and Scripture—could it not be found in his own era? If there is no possibility of innocent suffering in Gregory's time, then it would seem appropriate to call Gregory's views gloomy. Yet this Gregory is also the pope who continually gave from the bounty of the church to alleviate the suffering of the poor. So it seems in Gregory's view, not all suffering is punishment. Sometimes the innocent do suffer. The important question for Gregory is not the why of suffering, but rather a question of how we respond in the midst of suffering.

40. Ibid., *The Books of the Morals,* Vol. I, viii.
41. Ibid.,v.

Human Response to Suffering

While Gregory certainly acknowledges the role of human sinfulness in the experience of suffering (as evidenced in his sermon on the plague), on the whole, Gregory advocates an acceptance of the experience of suffering, with an emphasis on how to live with it. This means an acceptance of both God's will (which is the source of suffering) and the effects of suffering. Accepting suffering does not only mean surrendering to the pain we experience; it also means doing the spiritual work of accepting suffering as God's will and as an opportunity for repentance and amendment of life.

Physical affliction is to be welcomed not only because it promises a later reward, but also because it offers the reward of spiritual learning in the here and now. Gregory writes, "The sick should consider how healthy the heart becomes from bodily suffering, which recalls the mind to the knowledge of itself and renews the memory of illness that the healthy person typically disregards. Thus the spirit, which is lead out of itself by pride, recalls through the suffering of the flesh the condition to which it is subject."[42] It may be Gregory is referring to the finite nature of human existence when he mentions the "condition." Suffering is an occasion to recall the frail and fragile nature of human existence, but it also seems Gregory is referring to the reality of our own sinfulness. In connection with the above quotation, Gregory also cites Proverbs 20:30: "Blows that wound cleanse away evil; beatings make clean the innermost parts." In this verse and in Gregory's belief in the cleansing value of physical affliction we can see how he would have the high opinion of whipping. Returning to the idea of the connection between outward and inward suffering, it is worth noting that Gregory believed bodily suffering causes people to revisit their sins, which can, therefore, cause greater suffering. In that reflection, "we bring back before our eyes all of our evil actions; and through our external suffering, we lament internally all the more for what we have done. Therefore, it comes to pass that with the open wounds of the body, the secret lashes of the belly cleanse us all the more, because the hidden wound of lament

42. Ibid., *Pastoral Rule,* 116. The Latin translated as suffering is *molestia,* which refers to trouble or vexation, and in this passage the emphasis is on having a physical problem. See Lewis and Short, *A Latin Dictionary,* 1158. Whenever Latin words are cited from Gregory, this is the text that is used: Westhoff, *S. Gregorii Papae I.*

cleanses our iniquities."[43] Reflecting on our sins need not be a cause for grief, because it can also cleanse us from sin and help prevent future sin. As Gregory writes, "The sick should be advised to consider how beneficial bodily affliction can be, because it both cleanses sins already committed and prevents others from being accomplished. Moreover, by external lashes, bodily affliction inflicts the wounded mind with the wounds of penance."[44] The lashes of which Gregory writes can be seen on both a literal and symbolic level. They affect the body, but can also be a spur to spiritual reflection and repentance. Suffering can be viewed as a divine punishment for our sins, and also as a tool to prevent future sins. While some suffering may be a chastisement from God, all suffering allows for reflection that can promote an amendment of life and prevent further sinful actions. It is through that act of reflection we can come to an understanding of whether our suffering is a punishment for sinful actions or a push from God to grow in our spiritual stature.

Grief as Sin

The realization of this great opportunity in the midst of suffering only happens if we do not commit further sin in the midst of suffering. Gregory goes so far with the idea of acceptance as to advise those who grieve emotionally in the midst of it. He writes, "On the other hand, the patient should be advised that they not pity themselves on the inside for what they appear to tolerate on the outside. Otherwise they will corrupt by internal malice the great virtue of sacrifice that they outwardly offer. Moreover, their sin of self-pity, which humans do not recognize but which is identified as sin by divine examination, will become worse in proportion to the fraudulent show of virtue before others."[45] We are to be patient in the midst of suffering; grieving over the suffering is to add sin to the situation—a sin visible to God if not to others. We are not to grieve, not to have self-pity, because suffering is a gift from God

43. Gregory the Great, *Pastoral Rule,* 117. In the previous paragraph he indicates that by "belly," Gregory actually means "mind." The Latin *nequitas* has not only a sense of bad actions, but of being worthless or having a corrupt nature. See Lewis and Short, 1201–2.

44. Gregory the Great, *Pastoral Rule,* 124.

45. Ibid., 104–5. The Latin *intus malitiae* is referring to one's internal nature, and can mean ill will and spite in addition to malice. See Lewis and Short, 1103.

that leads to reward, and to grieve is to reject God's gift. Grieving over our suffering also takes us away from the primary task of reflection and repentance, and may lead to stagnation in our spiritual life. To grieve is to also engage in the sin of deception, for if we give an outward appearance of noble sacrifice but inwardly grieve, we deceive ourselves and others. Acceptance is being patient in the midst of suffering, not furthering our suffering by engaging in sinful behavior.

It is significant to note the use of the word "patient," which is *patientia* in Gregory's Latin. Not merely about waiting or not making a fuss, as is often understood in modern times, *patientia* is about enduring, bearing, and suffering. It is quite an appropriate word to use to describe how someone should respond to suffering with endurance and a willingness to bear the burden. It is interesting the word itself denotes suffering, and that Gregory considers patience a virtue. The exercise of virtue is not meant to be a simple or easy endeavor; it is one of hard work and sacrifice, and therefore, it includes suffering. The use of *patientia* also seems to be in line with the use of ascetic language that Demacopoulos finds so prevalent in the *Pastoral Rule*. Demacopoulos writes, "the language of virtue/vice conveys ideals that are distinctively ascetic. This language evinces the internal struggle with sin characteristic of renunciation. No other medium provides such an in-depth assessment of one's spiritual condition." Demacopoulos also sees the language of virtue as referencing or drawing on the vows of Benedictine monasticism.[46] Gregory seems to be applying the standards of his own life and ascetic behavior as a guideline for all Christians. The virtue of patience, so greatly exemplified by monks who engage in ascetic behavior, is also to be practiced by the average Christian.

It is also important to note the use of the word "sin" in the passage quoted above is not an editorial choice. Gregory himself uses the word *peccatur*, which should be translated as sinner or transgressor. At its root is *pecco*, which means "to miss or mistake anything; to do so amiss, to transgress, to commit a fault, to offend, sin."[47] As will be discussed below, Gregory exhorts his readers to maintain hope and perspective, and so it seems logical he would refer to grief as sin. To grieve is to

---

46. Gregory the Great, *Pastoral Rule*, 21 and 95. For *patientia,* see Lewis and Short, 1314.

47. Muller. *Dictionary*, 219–20; Lewis and Short, *A Latin Dictionary*, 1320.

fall away from our trust in God, to lose perspective and hope. It is to transgress and to offend God.

It is also important that the use of "pity" is not an editorial choice. In this connection, Gregory uses the verb *doler,* which means both to feel ache and pain in the physical sense and also "to grieve for, deplore, lament, be sorry for, be afflicted at or on account of anything."[48] Given Gregory's own experience of physical suffering, it is not surprising he chose a verb that means suffering in both the physical and emotional senses. Given Gregory's understanding that grief can be sin, the focus on physical pain is also significant because physical suffering is often a consequence of sin. If we deepen our suffering by self-pity in our hearts over the experience, which is a sinful act in Gregory's mind, then we are likely to add to our own physical experience of grief. Grieving our hearts is not merely a metaphor or a spiritual idea; the experience of grief has physical manifestations. If we add to our experience of anxiety and emotional distress, then we will feel physically worse as well. It would seem, therefore, Gregory understands physical suffering as a necessary consequence of sin, particularly given that he believes suffering can be divine punishment for sin.

For Gregory, the sin of grief can manifest itself as a desire for revenge against those who might be to blame for our suffering.[49] He writes that even those who are patient in the midst of suffering may, upon later reflection, change their tone. Gregory notes, "when they recall to their memory the things that they endured, they become inflamed by the fire of aggravation and begin to look for revenge, and by retracting the meekness they had in their tolerance, transform it into malice."[50] If we develop this desire for revenge, then we have sinned.

This idea of grieving as sin is intriguing. As noted above, Gregory seemed to have difficulty following his own advice; he grieved at his own election to the papacy and in the midst of his own physical ailments. That may merely have been a case of "Do what I say, not what I do," yet to talk of grief as a sin is a thought-provoking theological idea. Sin is not an entirely inappropriate label for grief. As Gregory describes it, the sin in grieving is a lack of patience, an inability to bear our suffering, and an unwillingness to sacrifice for God. As Gregory writes,

48. Lewis and Short, *A Latin Dictionary,* 606.

49. Gregory the Great, *Pastoral Rule,* 111.

50. Ibid., 106.

"Because the only sacrifice that God accepts before his eyes on the altar of good works is the flame kindled by charity."[51] Additionally, according to Gregory, we must not only have the outward appearance of patience and charity in the midst of suffering, we must have those virtues in our hearts, for only then are they sincere.

Gregory accepts the reality of evil and suffering in the world. While much suffering can be considered divine punishment for sin, not all suffering is punishment. Gregory believes we should do what we can to alleviate the suffering of others, and, perhaps even more importantly, we should not behave in such a manner as to add to our own suffering (by grieving or desiring revenge) or another's (by behaving like Job's friends). The reason behind our suffering is not the important thing; what matters is whether or not we use the gift of suffering as an opportunity for amendment of life and spiritual growth. There is the potential for great reward in the midst of suffering, if we choose to accept God's gift and do the hard work of learning and growth.

God's Providence

Like Julian of Norwich (whose views will be explored in the next chapter), Gregory believes God allows and inflicts suffering because it ultimately leads to a greater reward. Gregory believes that even when suffering is punishment and discipline from God, it can ultimately be the source of life. As he writes:

> And because we have followed the flesh, through the sight of the eyes, we are tortured by that very flesh which we preferred to the commands of God. For in it we daily suffer sorrow, in it torture, in it death; that the Lord by a marvellous economy might convert that, by which we committed sin, into a means of punishment; and that the severity of punishment might spring from the same source as that which had given rise to sin; so that man might be disciplined to life by the bitter suffering of that very flesh, by the pride of delighting which he had drawn near to death.[52]

51. Ibid., 105. The Latin used here, *caritatis,* is in line with charity—in the sense of the feeling—i.e., "regard, esteem, affection and love," but not the more modern sense of charity as solely good works for those in need. See Lewis and Short, *A Latin Dictionary*, 292.

52. Gregory the Great, *The Books of the Morals*, Vol. I.iii.

The flesh may be the source of sin, but it also holds the possibility of redemption if we are able to submit to God's will and allow ourselves to undergo the severity of God's punishment. This can lead to a more positive view of the body, because through the bodily experience of suffering we can find new life with God.

In order to gain this new life with God, however, we must maintain a wide perspective. Once suffering is seen in its proper context, no matter how awful, ultimately it will seem only light. As Gregory writes of Job's suffering, "But the temptation tries us less than the reward consoles us; in order that he, who used from the weight of the blow to consider that he had suffered some heavy trial, may learn from the recompense he has earned, that what he endured was but light." Job's consolation is in the fact that all that was lost was restored twofold "through the tenderness of the merciful Judge." The story of Job ends with such material abundance as to suggest monetary compensation for suffering. For Christians, however, life and the body are gifts from God, so what price tag could there be on that which threatens our very existence? Gregory asserts that the reward for suffering is not merely monetary, especially because Job's suffering was not just in loss of property. Job was physically affected and emotionally afflicted by the words of his friends. Job deserved not only to be "consoled by the gifts of Divine mercy," but "cherished also with human love; in order that to him, whom sorrows and adversities of pains wounded on every side, the joys of consolation on every side correspond."[53] Here again is Gregory's affirmation that suffering can be transformational and redemptive because the recompense is gifts of great love and consolation from fellow human beings and from God. This belief is affirmed in one of his homilies, where he writes, "Let no one squander this period of great mercy; let no one cast away the medicine of love which has been offered him. The divine bounty calls us back when we have turned away, and prepares an indulgent reception for us when we return."[54] Here, with the emphasis on love and reward we can see echoes of the biblical parable of the prodigal son (Luke 15:11–32),[55] as well as echoes of the theology of Julian of Norwich. God sends the suffering, but does so because it leads to a great reward.

53. Ibid., Vol. III, 676–77.
54. Ibid., *Forty Gospel Homilies*, 277.
55. Straw, *Gregory the Great*, 109.

Health as Gift from God

Rewards and gifts from God are not limited to the end of suffering. God provides many gifts in the here and now. Gregory advises his readers who are healthy not to misuse the great gift of health that God has given them. The Latin word *incolumes* that is translated as "health" means more than just physically fit, it also addresses our wholeness and security. Health and the body are gifts from God, and are, therefore, to be used for good and not evil.[56] The healthy are to be advised that "if they divert the grace of received health to the use of iniquity, they will become all the worse for their gift and later endure an even greater punishment because they did not fear to use the generous gift of God for evil."[57] The healthy are to be advised so they do not abuse their gift of health. The sick are to be advised to remember they belong to God and even our suffering is a gift from God. It is only because one is a "son of God" that "the punishment of discipline amends them."[58] In examining the Latin, we see the phrase emphasizes both the scourge of punishment and its teaching purposes. There is comfort to be found in affliction, because it is also a sign that a greater reward awaits. As noted above, Gregory writes, "For unless it was his plan to give them an inheritance after correction, he would not concern himself to educate them through affliction." In examining the Latin we see Gregory's emphasis on humanity's status as children of God who are destined to inherit his kingdom, if we learn his ways and follow his rules. This is another element of Gregory's

56. The Latin word *incolumes* used here can be translated as: "unimpaired, uninjured, in good condition, still alive, safe, sound, entire, whole." Lewis and Short, *A Latin Dictionary*, 925.

57. Gregory the Great, *Pastoral Rule*, 113. Gregory begins many of his sections in *The Pastoral Rule* by writing how each group is to be *admondendi*. This word means "to put one in mind of" and also "remind, suggest, advise, warn, admonish." See Lewis and Short, *A Latin Dictionary*, 41. It is interesting to note that Davis uses "admonish" in his translation, while Demacopulous uses "advise." Demacopulous's choice seems less harsh, and does seem to fit with his focus and understanding of Gregory's emphasis on pastor as spiritual director, and one who guides and leads. The Latin used regarding "generous gift" here has connotations of goodness and of something that is lavishly bestowed. See Lewis and Short, *A Latin Dictionary*, 243 and 1036.

58. Gregory the Great, *Pastoral Rule,* 115. The Latin *aegri* does literally mean those who are ill. See Lewis and Short, *A Latin Dictionary*, 54. The Latin *flagella* refers to "a whip or scourge." Ibid., 755. The Latin *disciplinae* has more of a sense of instruction or teaching than of just punishment. Ibid., 587. The Latin used here *castigant* means corrects, chastises, punishes. Ibid., 297.

theology of acceptance. Suffering is to be accepted, even welcomed, because it represents the reality of a greater reward, a belief shared by Julian of Norwich. As with so many of the other Church Fathers, Gregory draws on Scripture passages to support the belief that affliction is a sign of God's love. He identifies passages, such as Revelation 3:19, which reads: "I reprove and discipline those whom I love. Be earnest, therefore, and repent," and Hebrews 12:5, which reads: "And you have forgotten the exhortation that addresses you as children—'My child, do not regard lightly the discipline of the Lord, or lose heart when you are punished by him.'" Hebrews 12 uses the metaphor of a parent disciplining a child to describe God's punishment of humanity, reminding the reader that as with children, even if it may not seem so at the time, the discipline is for good. We can see Gregory's theology of suffering is grounded in Scripture. His work echoes Hebrews 12:11, which reads: "Now, discipline always seems painful rather than pleasant at the time, but later it yields the peaceful fruit of righteousness to those who have been trained by it."[59] In many ways, that verse could be considered a summary of Gregory's theology of suffering.

In Gregory's view, God is clearly the source of all suffering. This does not make God malevolent or sadistic. God sends suffering so humanity may reap the spiritual fruits of its discipline. Humanity does not need to rejoice in the midst of suffering, but we should nevertheless be grateful for the gifts of God—even the challenging and painful ones. The God Gregory believes in is a strong disciplinarian, but one who intends good for humanity through that discipline, and therefore we can have faith that all God gives is for our own good.

Salvation

If suffering comes from God and is, as Gregory believed and as noted earlier, a scourge to cleanse our souls, then to grieve is to reject a gift from God. Gregory writes, "Therefore, let those who are humiliated by the adversity of the temporal life rejoice in the hope of the eternal inheritance, because the divine Dispensation would not curb them for the purposes of instructing them in discipline unless he deigned to save them for eternity."[60] Grief can then be seen as an error or sin because

59. Gregory the Great, *Pastoral Rule*, 115.

60. Ibid., 168. Interestingly, the Latin used here *adversitas* and *humiliat* has a

it is an affront to God and denies God's providence and sovereignty. God has sent suffering as a curb and scourge in accordance with his purposes. To reject God's gift by grieving is not only sinful because it is an affront to God; it is also dangerous, for in so doing we jeopardize our own salvation.

If we do not allow ourselves to be disciplined, if we do not allow suffering as an opportunity to become a more faithful Christian, then there may not be any reward. Additionally, to allow our feelings to turn to malice in the face of suffering is to leave room for the workings of the devil. It is important to note that Gregory held a strong belief in the devil. As Demacopoulos writes, "Gregory's frequent use of phrases like: 'the enemy who lies in wait' or 'the ancient foe' suggests that he embraced supernatural phenomena in a way that Augustine never did."[61] While the devil may have been very real to Gregory, God's power is always greater than the devil's. The superiority of God, however, does not mean everyone is automatically saved. For Gregory, the real possibility of eternal suffering never fully disappears. We might be comforted by the reality of earthly affliction as an indication of salvation, but we must allow ourselves to feel the weight of that affliction. Suffering must inspire reflection and repentance. Even the act of repentance has its own benefits; as Straw notes, "Repentance is cathartic as it draws the soul from fear and sorrow to love and hope. The anxious examination and the grief of repentance slowly dissipate the sinner's feelings of guilt. Released from the burden of anxiety and fear, the Christian feels a new optimism. . . "[62] Suffering is also seen as a tool for spiritual cleansing. Suffering does not completely perfect a person, but it can enable improvements. Gregory believes God "brings the fire of tribulation upon us so that he may purify us from the rust of our vices. But we do not lose the rust of our vices through fire whenever we do not lose the vices in the midst of punishment."[63] We should not be seeking perfection but welcome the tribulation as an opportunity to be cleansed

---

connotation of opposition or being against, and "lowness" or being brought low or humbled. This would seem to be addressing those who have been in opposition and brought low by the challenges of their earthly life—those who have seen suffering as an opportunity for repentance. See Lewis and Short, *A Latin Dictionary*, 49 and 870.

61. Ibid., 21–22 and 105–6.

62. Straw, *Gregory the Great*, 223.

63. Gregory the Great, *Pastoral Rule*, 120–21.

and transformed by God's loving discipline. What seems clear from Gregory's writings in *The Book of The Pastoral Rule* is the fact that he does not want either the minister or the believer to be complacent in his life, especially in times of suffering. It would be a mistake to assume that because Gregory advocates acceptance he is advocating passivity in the midst of suffering. For Gregory, the life of faith even when lived out in a monastery is an active and dynamic one. We are to respond to suffering—not with rage or sadness, but with acceptance and repentance. Gregory's writings and his own ministry as pope to those in need are evidence of this active response.

In highlighting Gregory's views of salvation, we come to further understand the kind of response to suffering Gregory advocates—an active one with awareness of its own significance. This response to suffering is not only about whether we take the opportunity to repent and live more faithfully in the here and now; it is also about our own salvation. While God intends goodness and reward for all, the realization of that reward is dependent on our own actions. If we respond with faith and repentance, then we will reap the benefits of that act. If we use an experience of suffering as an opportunity to sin further or to reject the gifts of God, then we will face the negative consequences. A rejection of God means we may suffer eternal punishment. For Gregory, acceptance and not rejection of God's gifts, including suffering, is the mark of a faithful Christian.

Christ

Perhaps Gregory's strongest argument for acceptance of and patience in suffering is that to do so is to follow Christ himself. There is certainly a long history in the Christian tradition of accepting suffering as a way of imitating Christ. Gregory is quite eloquent and persuasive on this point, so it is a passage worth quoting at length:

> The sick should be advised that to preserve the virtue of patience, it is necessary that they continuously consider the great evils that our Redeemer suffered from those whom he created: that he endured so many horrible insults; that while he was daily rescuing souls from the captivity of the ancient enemy, he was beaten by the men who insulted him; that while washing us with the water of salvation, he did not hide his face from the spitting

of evil men; that while he freed us from eternal punishments by his counsels, he tolerated great punishment; that while he gave everlasting honors among the choir of angels, he endured blows; that while he saved us from the piercing of our sins, he submitted his head to the crown of thorns, that while he filled us with eternal sweetness, he accepted bitter gall; that with him in divinity, he remained silent when adorned mockingly; and so that he might prepare life for the dead, he gave his life unto death. Why, then, is it so difficult to believe that humans should endure suffering from God for the evil that they do if God endured so great an evil in response to his goodness? And who with healthy reasoning can be ungrateful for his suffering if God himself did not go without punishments, even though he was without sin?[64]

This imitation of Christ, or desire to be like Christ, is a potentially double-edged sword. There could be solace found in the knowledge that Christ suffered. Yet Gregory does not lift up the sufferings of Christ as a source of comfort, rather they are meant to be a chastisement and a reminder of perspective.[65] We should not complain about our own suffering because it is minimal and deserved (in light of humanity's sinfulness) compared to the suffering of Christ. An individual's suffering is slight in comparison to the enormity of what Christ suffered, and we should not forget that Christ's suffering was on behalf of humanity. Therefore, the response to suffering, in addition to patience, should be one of gratitude. Suffering offers an opportunity to follow in Christ's footsteps and learn so that we might improve our character.

We could fault Gregory for promoting a focus on (and possibly glorification of) Christ's suffering, because it could potentially lead to the belief that we should accept all suffering and even seek it out for its spiritual benefits. As noted in the chapter title, Gregory refers to grief (the response to suffering) as the "great teacher." The glorification of suffering has certainly been a part of the Christian tradition down through the centuries (and will be discussed further in the chapter on Ivone Gebara). It might seem possible to place some of the blame for that glorification at Gregory's feet, yet it is important to note that Gregory does not tell his followers to go and seek suffering. His admonitions and encouragements are for those already suffering. Given the realities of Gregory's world, there would seem no need to seek suffering; it is

64. Ibid., 117–18.

65. See Gregory the Great, *Forty Gospel Homilies*, 99.

already a given in life. When it does come, suffering is to be considered an opportunity for spiritual cleansing, an opportunity to grow more Christ-like, and an opportunity to avoid further chastisement by God.

For Gregory, Christ is central to thinking about suffering. First, it is important to remember the extent of Christ's own suffering, because when we do so our sufferings pale in comparison. No suffering we undergo could possibly be as great as what was endured by Christ in his passion. Secondly, suffering has the potential to be a noble act, since to suffer is to follow in Christ's footsteps. For Gregory, of course, the significant point is whether or not we use the gift of suffering as an opportunity to also be more like Christ, to be one who strives to do God's will and seek the kingdom of God.

Eternal Life

In *The Book of the Pastoral Rule* Gregory advocates for a balanced perspective—i.e., one is not to be without perspective in the midst of joy nor without hope in the midst of sadness. Gregory writes, "Before the joyful are to be set the sad things that accompany [eternal] punishment, but before the sad the joyous promises of the kingdom should be set. Let the joyful learn by severe warnings what things they should fear, and let the sad hear about the rewards that they may anticipate."[66] This balance may seem harsh. Why should the joyous be reminded of sadness? Why not preserve their joy—is it not fleeting? Yet Gregory is a realist. He seems to know that sadness will return and wants the faithful to be prepared. Additionally, we must remember that whatever joy one might know on earth pales in comparison to the joys of heaven, so we should not lose our focus and become preoccupied by the joys of the earthly world.

Gregory sees the possibility of eternal retribution as an important element in advising one's flock. The possibility of divine retribution was to be used as a check against sinful behavior. Gregory writes that those who fear afflictions:

---

66. Gregory the Great, *Pastoral Rule*, 93. The Latin *laetis* can be translated as "joyful, cheerful, glad, gay, joyous, rejoicing, pleased, delighted, full of joy." See Lewis and Short, *A Latin Dictionary*, 1030. The Latin *tristes* means those who are sad, sorrowful, mourning, melancholy or disconsolate. Ibid., 1901–2.

should be advised that if they desire to be truly free of evils, they should dread eternal punishments, not living in continuous fear of them but growing in the grace of love by nurturing charity. For it is written: 'Perfect charity casts out fear.' And again: 'You have not received the spirit of bondage in fear, but you have received the spirit of adoption as sons, by which we call out: "Abba, Father"' Hence the same teacher says: 'Where the Spirit of the Lord is, there is freedom.' If, therefore, the fear of punishment still prohibits evil actions then no real liberty of the spirit holds the soul of one who is afraid. For if such a one did not fear punishment, he would certainly commit sin. Therefore, the mind is ignorant of the grace of liberty if it is bounded by the service of fear. For good should be loved of its own accord, not pursued by compulsion of punishment."[67]

We can see from this quote that, for Gregory, the goal of suffering is a strengthening of our wills to be able to withstand the temptation to fall into sin. We must have the fear of punishment as prevention against evil, but we must not be overcome by fear, for to do so is to lose our "liberty of the spirit." We must seek to do good for its own sake without actions governed solely by a fear of punishment. While damnation and punishment are not meant to be all-pervasive in our outlook, neither are they to be minimized, as it is clear they were real possibilities for Gregory. As Straw notes, Gregory desires a church where "good Christians always keep the certain uncertainty of death before their eyes before they meet the dreadful Judge. They are conscious that fear is purgative, a cleansing fire burning pride and instilling the penitential disposition necessary to meet the Judge."[68] This focus on the reality of death is also evident in one of his homilies and Gregory uses the occasion to remind his hearers that a focus on death is also an opportunity to live differently. He writes: "Therefore, my friends, direct the eyes of your hearts toward your mortality. Make ready for the Judge who is coming to you by your daily weeping and sorrow. Certain death awaits everyone. . . . Do not pay attention to what you have, but to what you are. . . . Since the hours and their moments are running away, see to it, dearly beloved, that they are filled with what will earn the wages of a good work."[69]

67. Ibid. 118–19.
68. Carole Straw, "Purity and Death," 22.
69. Gregory the Great, *Forty Gospel Homilies,* 155–56 (Homily 20).

A belief in life after death is foundational in the Christian faith, and the focus is often placed on the beauty and joy of the reward of eternal life with God in heaven. Yet for Gregory, the possibility of damnation is just as real. What matters most to Gregory is that we keep our perspective. We must remember our existence is not limited to life on earth and our actions have eternal consequences. There is a stronger emphasis on the reality of eternal damnation in Gregory than in the other thinkers we examine. The others, particularly Julian, do not discount its possibility, but seem to place greater emphasis on the possibilities of divine grace and mercy. In Gregory then, one ends up with a view of eternal life that holds up the hope of heaven for those in the midst of suffering, while also raising the possibility of eternal damnation as a caution against human sin.

SUMMARY ANALYSIS

Gregory starts with an acceptance of suffering. For him, it is a given that humanity has sinned and fallen away from God, and therefore, humanity will be punished with the scourge of suffering in order to be restored to right relationship with God. There is also an acknowledgment in Gregory of the reality of innocent suffering in the world, particularly notable in his *Moralia*. Gregory's life and works advocate reaching out and helping those who suffer, particularly the poor and hungry. He still seems to hold to the belief that all suffering, regardless of its cause, is an opportunity for spiritual education. Gregory understands suffering through the paradigm that all suffering, whether it is punishment for sin or affliction on the innocent, can be considered a purifying scourge. Even if we might try to alleviate the suffering, we should still take the opportunity for reflection and repentance. Overall, in Gregory there is emphasis on acceptance of suffering because of how we can grow from it. Gregory's view is not that acceptance necessarily must (although it certainly could) lead to a negative perspective on life and the world. It is acceptance grounded in faith. It is acceptance that lives out the belief in the sinful nature of humanity (that is therefore deserving of punishment), and in the providence and mercy of God, as well as certainty about life beyond the grave. For Gregory, eternal life is possible through faith and God's grace, and given that, the sufferings of this life begin to pale in comparison to those of Christ. It is an honor to suffer as

Christ did, and we must not forget the gravity of the suffering the sin-less one experienced. Eternal damnation is also a possibility, and that reality should keep us from sin. Gregory, like those who follow him in this work, has elements in his theology that emphasize a greater world beyond this earthly life. He also believes that although he (like others) must do his part to combat evil in his lifetime, the ultimate question of good vs. evil has already been answered. Like Augustine, Gregory be-lieves God's goodness has already triumphed over evil. The battle may still be playing out, but there is no doubt God is the victor.[70]

CRITIQUE

Initially, criticisms of Gregory come easily. He can be criticized for his views on whipping or slavery. In his chapter on servants and masters, Gregory writes that servants should always consider the humility of their position, and "masters should not forget that they share the same [fallen] condition as their servants. Servants should be warned not to despise God by proudly contradicting his ordinances. Masters are to be warned that they offend God if they take pride in the things he has given them or if they fail to realize that they share the same condition of nature with their subjects."[71] To a modern ear there may be a dif-ference between servant and slave. The Latin word used by Gregory *servi*, however, can be translated as either servant or slave, and given the prevalence of slavery in the ancient world, we can assume Gregory was talking primarily to slaves.[72] To a modern world, horrified by the practice of slavery, the idea of slavery being something ordained by God and slaves being "gifted" by God to their masters seems abhorrent. Disapproval for Gregory's theology may (at least on this front) be in-tensified when we note Moorhead's observation that "anyone who reads him [Gregory] at length becomes aware that he has an uncomfortable amount to say about people being whipped, an experience which he believes often turns out to be beneficial."[73] Here Gregory must be given

70. Evans, *The Thought of Gregory the Great*, 64.

71. Gregory the Great, *Pastoral Rule*, 97. The Latin used here *ordinationi* does have the sense of ordinances, rules, orders, customs and regulations. See Lewis and Short, *A Latin Dictionary*, 1277.

72. For definition of *servi* see Ibid., 1683.

73. Moorhead, *Gregory the Great*, 43.

allowance for his time. He lived in a city that practiced slavery. As one whose life and beliefs were governed by Scripture, he could no doubt point to the same biblical passages, in Leviticus and elsewhere, that were used for centuries after his death to justify the practice of slavery as a divinely ordained practice. Yet it is worth noting that, rather than glorify the practice of slavery, Gregory upholds the beliefs of the Christian faith, particularly evident in the writings of Paul and the Pauline tradition,[74] that emphasize the equality of all people in the eyes of God. As noted above, Gregory reminds masters that they share the same created nature with their servants. While Gregory upholds the hierarchy of his society, he also honors those at each level of society and recognizes the shared humanity of all.

Gregory's theology has a high view of God that does not sacrifice any of God's omnipotence or authority, but it seems to leave little room for human action to alleviate suffering, particularly for the poor. This issue highlights a tension in Gregory's life and writings. On the one hand he, like much of the early church, focuses more on eternal life than earthly life. "Like writers before him, Gregory believes death brings true life (*vera vita*); it is the gateway to eternity, and it inspires the virtue that is the life of the soul."[75] A Christian focus on eternal life rather than earthly life has its foundations in Scripture (e.g., John 3:16), and it is one that continues for centuries. Although the focus may not be as strong, a belief in the reality (or at least the possibility) of eternal life is still evident over thirteen centuries later in the writings of C. S. Lewis: "Am I for instance, just sidling back to God because I know that if there's any road to H. [his wife Joy], it runs through Him?"[76] Implicit in Lewis's question is a belief that Joy still exists, and is in some way "alive" for him to meet. Christianity's focus on resurrection and eternal life creates a tension between earthly life and the afterlife. On the other hand, much of Gregory's own work as pope, and some of his own writings, point to the importance of human actions to alleviate some of the suffering we see in the world. Ivone Gebara is a theologian who would applaud Gregory's numerous actions, and occasional statements (see homily quoted below) that point to the importance of working to alleviate suffering, but would criticize him for the statements in which he seems

74. See Galatians 3:28, 1 Corinthians 12:13, Ephesians 6:8, and Colossians 3:11.

75. Straw, "Purity and Death," 16.

76. Lewis, *A Grief Observed*, 79.

to argue for a blanket acceptance of suffering. For Gebara, this work against suffering is the heart of the Christian tradition, and it comes from her own understanding of Jesus's ministry. Gebara believes "[t]he core of Jesus' life was the battle against evil in all its manifestations."[77] Gregory did do much as pope to alleviate the suffering of his people. As John Moorhead notes, "Gregory was also tireless in finding ways to make life more tolerable. In the ninth century a big book could still be seen in the Lateran palace, the headquarters of the bishop of Rome, which showed the names, ages and professions of all those, in Rome and elsewhere, who received largesse from him."[78] Markus also notes how Gregory's papacy was characterized by efforts to help the poor. The money received was "spent on the salaries of clergy and officials, payments to local cemeteries, monasteries, hospices and welfare stations." Markus goes on to cite from the early biography of Gregory by Deacon John, who recalls how Gregory distributed money and food to the poor, generously supported a local convent, and provided for "the infirm and needy in all quarters of the City."[79] We can see from these various testimonials that Gregory did much to alleviate the suffering he witnessed around him. Additionally, he called others to join him in his work to alleviate poverty. In one of his homilies he writes, "Learn, my friends, to look down upon all temporal things, learn to reject ephemeral honors and to love eternal glory. Honor the poor you see; consider that those you see the world outwardly despising are within themselves friends of God. Share your possessions with them, so that finally they may deign to share what they have with you."[80]

There is a tension then, in Gregory's life and work, between a call to accept all suffering and encouragement for his followers to do as he did and reach out and help those suffering, particularly those in need of the basic necessities of food, shelter, and clothing. It is a tension Gregory seems to have lived with, but not one that he seems to acknowledge. Perhaps his lack of acknowledgment is due to the strong emphasis on his theology of divine agency and authority, which certainly fits with Christian tradition. Orthodox Christianity has long held that humanity cannot save itself from its own sins. It is God who is

77. Gebara, *Out of the Depths*, 87.

78. Moorhead, 7.

79. Ibid., 121–22.

80. Gregory the Great, *Forty Gospel Homilies,* 385 (Homily 40).

savior. As Augustine writes in *City of God*, "From this life of misery, a kind of hell on earth, there is no liberation save through the grace of Christ our Savior, our God and our Lord."[81] To modern ears the writings of Augustine and some of Gregory's may seem passive or too cerebral. We may want to ask: Is not the calling of Christians to be out in the world loving fellow human beings? Humanity is not to be complacent in the face of suffering, convinced it has no power, and resigned to suffering as God's will. Yet, Gregory's emphasis on acceptance offers a check on human egotism. Gregory offers a broader view—a reminder that humanity cannot do all things. His emphasis on acceptance may seem like a recipe for despondency and complacency. Viewed another way, and in light of his actions to alleviate suffering, though, this view can be a source of inspiration. It is a reminder not to be discouraged in the face of insurmountable odds. His perspective reminds humanity not to lose heart, not to lose sight of the larger picture, and not to forget that all is in God's hands. Truth be told, centuries have passed since he wrote his words, and there is still great suffering. Wars have not ceased. Humanity is still ravaged by disease and famine. Natural disasters still happen. Gregory's challenging wisdom is still relevant. Christians are still called to live with the tension between acceptance of suffering and a call to alleviate it. Gregory's life and work do offer a model of working to alleviate suffering, while placing emphasis on the spiritual work of accepting the reality of suffering and seeing it as an opportunity for repentance and transformation. For Gregory, suffering offers an opportunity to grow closer to God.

Another area where Gregory's theology can be challenged is in his description of grief as sin. In a more contemporary context where suffering is not always seen as being sent by God, it may be challenging to view grief as sin. To grieve is to be focused on what is lost, to feel sadness, pain, and anger. It is also to feel lost and empty. Those are adequate descriptors of sin as well. Theologically speaking, it could seem appropriate to refer to grief, to the act of lamenting over what is lost, as sin. Pastorally speaking, though, it can certainly seem problematic. Do people who are suffering physically really need to be admonished for their seemingly natural emotional response? Does Gregory's approach put so much emphasis on patience and acceptance that there is no room to feel the pain and anguish of loss? Does his emphasis on avoiding sin

81. Augustine. *City of God*, 1068.

end up promoting the idea that we cannot grieve in any way in response to suffering? Gregory's own life story would seem to indicate an allowance for grief, as he grieved upon his own election and in the midst of his own physical pains, but he seems to be calling his flock to a higher standard in which no one grieves in response to suffering. It can certainly be debated whether this standard is possible or worthwhile. Yet there is wisdom in what Gregory prescribes, for those who grieve add to their experience of suffering. They have an experience imposed upon them to which they add further strife by their own grieving. Additionally, as Gregory's own *Rule* attests, it is a pastor's role to uphold and encourage his flock in faith. From time to time, that may mean advising those who seek to live in sin and grief by pushing them to be patient and accepting in the midst of suffering, while also counseling them not to lose their faith or trust in God and God's will for their lives.

CONCLUSION

Gregory wants his readers to see suffering as a sign of God's investment in the purification of our souls. Gregory reminds us that to live with the expectation of a life free from suffering is to miss out on grief as a gift—albeit a challenging and difficult gift, a gift that can become sin, but a gift nonetheless. Suffering is a gift that, for Gregory, pushes one to engage in reflection, repentance, and amendment of life.

Gregory's high view of the value of suffering and its redemptive qualities does, however, stand in stark contrast to the actions of his life. His own response to the challenges of his election as pope was one of grief. He did not immediately engage in acts of reflection and repentance as he counsels others to do. Additionally, his own work and his exhortations to others encourage working to alleviate the suffering of others—particularly the poor and needy. This means we are left with tension in Gregory's theology. He advocates a response of gratitude and reflection, and yet in his own life he grieved deeply. He advocates acceptance of all suffering, while simultaneously he sought to combat suffering among his people. We are, therefore, left wondering whether it is possible to be committed to the belief that some suffering must be alleviated, if we accept suffering for its educative properties. We also wonder whether it is possible to make room for the grieving process while also valuing the push to repentance that suffering offers. Can we hold the contrasting elements of Gregory's theology together or are they mutually exclusive? Before focusing in on that question, which will be done in the conclusion, there are other theologies of acceptance to be examined; and so we now turn to the writings of fourteenth-century English mystic, Julian of Norwich.

2

Faith through Suffering

An Examination of Julian of Norwich and Her Showings

THIS CHAPTER WILL EXAMINE the *Revelations* of Julian of Norwich, an anchorite in eastern England who wrote a text of hope and joy in the midst of suffering. She lived in the fourteenth and fifteenth centuries in western Europe, centuries of upheaval and uncertainty. There were plagues and wars. It was a time when, as Barbara Tuchman writes, "death was to be met any day, around any corner."[1] Julian's text is one that takes suffering seriously and does not turn a blind eye to its severity or prevalence, and yet also one that interprets suffering in the light of what Julian experiences as God's loving delight in humanity.

Julian's theme of love and hope, which undergirds her entire text, is found most prominently in a parable of the lord and the servant in the fifty-first chapter of *Revelations*. No matter how we may fall, as the servant does in the parable, God desires to bring us to a state of bliss through union with him. Her focus on the love of God emphasizes how humanity's sin, humanity's falling, is not met with wrath, but mercy. Julian puts suffering in the context of divine love. Whereas Gregory the Great argued that suffering should be borne to cleanse our souls, and Julian does not discount the cleansing value of suffering, she believes

---

1. Tuchman. *A Distant Mirror*, 506.

the greatest value of suffering is it awakens us to, and helps bring us more fully into, the depth of God's love. Julian advocates that suffering should be entered into willingly, hopefully, perhaps even joyfully, because she believes God is present every step of the way, and, most importantly, God leads us to the most blessed reward of all: union with him. In Julian's theology, God always reaches out in love to lead us to this blissful union. This chapter, through an examination of Julian's context, her own writings, as well as secondary sources, will lay out her theology as it pertains to and offers insight into the human experience of suffering and grief.

In order to better understand the value of Julian's text, it is worth setting up her work within the context of fourteenth-century Europe. Initially, because of the seriousness of suffering and the pessimism of the times, it seems Julian's distinction is her optimistic tone. Yet, as will be laid out in the coming pages, the situation is more complex than that. Julian is not merely a lone optimist among pessimists. A complex reality of horrible suffering and deep joy is evident both in Julian's writings and in the world in which she lived.

BACKGROUND

Very little is known of Julian's life—not even her real name. The name of Julian is taken from St. Julian's Church in Norwich where she lived as an anchorite for many years.[2] What can be established of her life is mostly from her own writings. Her visions, which form the basis for her text, occurred in 1373 when she was 30, and so it is widely held that she was born in 1342. The presence of her mother and a priest at her bedside during her illness indicate that she had not yet become an anchorite. That she later did would seem to indicate she was from a prosperous family since she was able, following her recovery, to "dedicate herself to devotion."[3] Her life as an anchorite was not one of total seclusion, however. Even in her lifetime, it is written, "she was famed as a mystic and spiritual counselor and was frequently visited by clergymen and lay persons, including the famous mystic Margery Kempe."[4] She is mentioned in a will in 1416, but this would put her in her mid-seventies (a

2. Spearing, *Medieval Writings*, xxx.

3. Julian of Norwich, *Showings*, 19.

4. *Lesser Feasts and Fasts*, 240.

very old age for the time), it is unlikely she lived much longer.[5] An exact date of her death is not known.

Julian's writings report and interpret visions she experienced in the course of a grave illness she suffered in 1373.[6] She was moved by love to write down her visions, because she wanted to share her knowledge of God so other Christians might prosper.[7] She initially wrote down many of her visions with little theological reflection, in what has come to be known as her *The Short Text*. She then continued to reflect on these visions over the course of many years. This fuller reflection on her visions was written down as well and has become known as her *The Long Text*. The parable of the lord and the servant, which provides valuable insight into her theology of suffering, occurs only in *The Long Text*. We could posit many reasons why this is so. In *The Long Text* itself though, Julian seems to offer an explanation. She states that it took her almost twenty years to come to a true understanding of the parable and its meaning.[8] Another possibility has been raised by Elizabeth Spearing, who notes that "the Short Text as we have it may have been composed after the rise and condemnation of the Lollard heresies, influential among women, had made it necessary for a woman visionary to stress as strongly as Julian does that she fully accepts ecclesiastical orthodoxy."[9] This is possible and, as will be seen from the following discussion, there is material in Julian's writing that could be considered radical. The difficulty with this theory is it would only work if the parable were more subversive than other aspects of her text. Given that the themes of the parable, as discussed below, are present throughout her text, it seems difficult to

5. Spearing, *Medieval Writings*, xxxi.

6. It is worth noting that the visions and illness that Julian experienced were something for which she wished. Like so many of her time, she believed that suffering and seeing Christ on the Cross would bring her into a deeper relationship with God. See Aers and Staley, *The Powers of the Holy*, 78. See also Jantzen, *Gender, Power and Christian Mysticism*, 166.

7. Julian of Norwich, *Showings*, 135.

8. Julian of Norwich, *The Showings*, 101.

9. Spearing, *Medieval Writings*, xxxi. The Lollards were followers of John Wycliffe who advocated a dismantling of church hierarchy and promoted reading the Bible in English. For more on the Lollards see: J. C. Dickinson. *An Ecclesiastical History of England*. In her book *Gender and Heresy*, Shannon McSheffrey argues that the beliefs and practices of the Lollards were not particularly welcoming or appealing to women, and that in fact, there was more room for women's spirituality in traditional orthodox religion. See chapters 1 and 6 particularly.

argue *The Short Text* is the more orthodox one. However we choose to explain the gaps between the two texts, it is important to note that it took years for Julian to be satisfied she understood the parable. Julian did not receive, nor does she offer, simple and quick answers to the problem of suffering. What she offers is a process of dwelling with and learning to interpret God's gifts, which slowly leads to new understanding.

THEOLOGY FROM EXPERIENCE

The process Julian offers is one that contains complex theology and a rich message. As Grace Jantzen notes, "Like other women writers, Julian chose to convey her spiritual teachings by recounting her own spiritual experiences and the insights based on them, rather than by any systematic treatise in spiritual theology."[10] Julian is not a systematic theologian, but her method still yields a rich theological understanding of the phenomenon of suffering. Theology formed from experience is neither without merit, nor without precedent in the Christian tradition. St. Paul's letters and Augustine's *Confessions* are both formative evidence of this. To separate experience from knowledge is a modern idea, so it is anachronistic to criticize Julian for basing her work on experience. As Oliver Davies notes, "The very category of 'mysticism,' then, is the product of the modern age when experience had begun to emerge as a free-standing concept."[11] While for some, it is her experience that makes her work compelling and convincing, it is worth noting that her *experience* is not what Julian herself emphasizes.[12] Julian emphasizes her visions and the interpretations granted to her. These are not mere figments of her imagination or understanding conjured solely from her own mind. Julian believes her visions and interpretation are divinely inspired; they are gifts from God.

While it is true Julian is not a scholar, there is no doubt she is learned. As Hildesley notes, "The whole of her *Revelations* is suffused with a profound knowledge of the Bible." Sister Mary Paul asserts "[t]he whole of chapter fifty-one of *Revelations of Divine Love* contains concise and precise theology, echoing many biblical passages." There

10. Jantzen, *Power, Gender and Christian Mysticism*, 147.

11. Davies, "Late Medieval Mystics," 222.

12. Menzies, *Mirrors of the Holy*, 93. See also: Nuth, *God's Lovers*, 100; Watkin, *On Julian of Norwich*, 33.

is, of course, much disagreement among scholars about how well educated Julian was. Turner argues that although Julian "could not have read these authorities in any systematic way, that only goes to show how relatively unimportant formal literacy is in the middle ages from the standpoint of the passing on of a theological tradition. If in a narrow sense Julian does not know these texts, there is a broader sense in which Julian knows their tradition well." There is also a sense in which Julian's lack of formal theological training (although she clearly was steeped in tradition) can be an advantage for her, because she is not constrained by the "rigid logic of scholasticism."[13] In the end, it is significant a woman in fourteenth-century England was able to produce two such theological texts in her own vernacular language. The self-doubt and concern over her ability to teach because she is a woman expressed in her *The Short Text* are not present in *The Long Text*. Julian does assert her own authority as a teacher in *The Long Text*, going from referring to herself as "ignorant, weak and frail" in *The Short Text* to asserting all she writes is for the education of her fellow Christians because that is God's intention.[14] In the space between the two texts, Julian seems to have gained confidence in her own authority. She may not be on par with Augustine or Aquinas as a scholar, but her knowledge of Scripture and ability to think theologically are clearly evident in the text. It is also worth noting the place Julian holds in the Christian tradition and in academia. The various perspectives put forth in this chapter are indicative of the wide range of Julian's influence. Her influence can be seen in modern academic and devotional circles. Julian's status as a theologian, even though her methods and training were a bit unorthodox, seem to have been established by the breadth of her influence in modern scholarship. Julian is a theologian not only because of how she writes, but also because of the perspective she offers. As Spearing notes, "Julian, far removed from the centres of ecclesiastical power, develops a speculative theology that, while never asserting itself in opposition to the Church or questioning its doctrinal tenets, encourages deeper thought about what God's love actually means for humanity and its future."[15]

13. Hildesley, *Journeying with Julian*, 81 and 83; Sister Mary Paul, *All Shall Be Well*, 22; Turner, "Sin is Behovely," 408; Spearing, *Medieval Writings*, viii.

14. Julian of Norwich, *Showings*, 135; Julian of Norwich, *The Showings*, 49. See also Jantzen, *Gender, Power and Christian Mysticism*, 178.

15. Spearing, *Medieval Writings*, xxxii.

THE PARABLE

Julian writes of the parable as being shown to her within a vision. The vision of the parable itself is somewhat simple and brief, but as Julian's own reflections show its brevity may belie the depth of its meaning. Julian sees a lord who is seated and at peace. A shabbily attired servant who desires to do his lord's bidding attends him. The lord sends the servant off on a task, and the servant rushes off, eager to do the task. In his great haste and love for the lord, the servant falls into a valley. He is greatly injured by this fall. He writhes and wails. He is unable to get up or tend to himself in anyway. Julian sees the servant suffers greatly. Not only does he suffer from his own physical torments as a result of his fall, he suffers because of his spiritual pain. In fact, the servant feels seven kinds of suffering: bruising, a heaviness of his body, weakness, blindness of reason (such that he comes close to forgetting his love for the lord), the inability to rise, being alone, and finally, the pain of being in an uncomfortable place.[16] In the extent of the servant's suffering, it is possible to see Julian has a rich understanding of the phenomenon of suffering. It is not limited to physical pain, and it includes the spiritual pain of loneliness and separation. These two types of pain highlight the central elements of Julian's theology of suffering—it is not only about physical difficulties, it is also about spiritual difficulties. It could certainly be argued Julian considers spiritual suffering to be even more significant and meaningful. Ellen Ross elucidates three aspects of spiritual suffering in the writings of Julian: contrition, compassion, and longing. Contrition refers to the suffering that comes from our awareness of our own sinfulness. Compassion refers to the ways in which suffering connects with the salvific, beneficial suffering of Christ, and the way it promotes empathy among humans. Longing refers to a spiritual thirst we have for union with God. The longing is painful because the union has not yet been realized.[17]

In the course of her writing, Julian also identifies four kinds of fear: anxiety, fear of punishment or pain, doubts and faithlessness, and "reverent drede [fear]."[18] These fears are especially present in the midst

16. Julian of Norwich, *The Showings*, 102.

17. Ross, *The Grief of God*, 34–40.

18. Julian of Norwich, *The Showings*, 141. See also Pelphrey, *Christ Our Mother*, 202. Julian of Norwich, *Showings*, 324.

of illness, tragedy, mistakes, and failures. The last fear, the reverent fear, is positive, for it brings about love. Good fear is that which causes a person to seek God; it causes us "hastily to flee from all that is not good, and to fall into our Lord's breast as the child into the mother's bosom."[19] Given Julian's own experience, it could even be said there is value in seeking suffering, so we might experience reverent fear as the gateway to a deeper connection with God. There is a catch of sorts, though. We must also turn to God. For any suffering to be transformational, we must acknowledge God is at work in the world. Julian calls on Christians to make the choice and turn to God, to realize just as the lord never took his eyes off the servant, so too is God ever present for us. We need only shift our gaze out of the ditch. To make that choice, to turn to God, is also to conquer the other two fears (anxiety and doubt), which can certainly be present in the midst of suffering. If our faith is strong, and we turn to God, then anxiety and doubt cease to exist. Whether or not we turn to God is a choice for humanity. According to Julian, we have the option to turn away from God, to refuse the gift of grace and salvation in our lives, and this is an eternal option. For Julian, to refuse God is to follow the devil.[20]

As will be seen in the discussion below, these fears and elements of spiritual suffering—human sinfulness, a connection to the suffering of Christ and our fellow humans, and particularly a longing for union with God—all figure in Julian's theology. In the initial reading of the parable, we are particularly aware of the longing, anxiety, and lack of reverent fear in the servant, who believes there is no one to help him. He is unable to turn his head and see his beloved lord is nearby. In fact, he becomes so overwhelmed by his suffering he forgets his love for his lord.[21] Yet the servant is not abandoned by his lord and in the end is rewarded greatly, far more greatly than he would have been had he never fallen. The lord says: "See my beloved servant, what harm and injury he has taken in my service, for my love, yes, and for his good will; is it not reasonable that I should reward him his fright and his fear, his hurt and his injury, and all his woe? And not only this, but does it not fall to me to give a gift that would be better to him and more praiseworthy than his own health would have been? Otherwise I have offered him

---

19. Ibid., 142.
20. Ibid., 78–9. See also Jantzen, *Julian of Norwich*, 179.
21. Julian of Norwich, *The Showings*, 102.

no grace."[22] After she lays out the vision of the parable, Julian reflects on and interprets the story she has been given. She describes in further detail the beauty of the Lord's clothes and the love he has for his servant. She comes to understand the lord is God, and the servant, who is dressed much more simply, is both Adam (all of humanity) and Christ himself. She sees in the fall of the servant not only the fall of Adam and humanity, but also the fall of Christ into human form and into hell, so he (Christ) might bring about salvation. The parable is not only a meaningful story about a lord and his servant, for, as Julian understands it, it is the story of our relationship with God.

Form of Parable

Julian's parable, like many of the gospel parables, is an engaging story to which her audience could easily relate. It is a literary, metaphorical tool that would be familiar to a society accustomed to learning from the parables of Scripture. The parable also has the aim of training us in the faith; it, therefore, lends itself to conveying a great deal of meaning as a story that can have multiple interpretations and layers.[23] It is worth noting that Julian's parable is not merely a story she invented to teach her readers: Julian's parable is a vision she firmly believes has been given to her by God and that she then transmits to her readers. At first, Julian just shares an account of the parable in her vision, but in the course of her presentation of the parable she also shares her own insights and reflections. She shows her readers through her writings that there are multiple ways to interpret the parable. This does not mean the possibilities are endless, for Julian understands her interpretation to be guided by God and directing her toward truth. Julian also models for her readers the interpretation and application of the parable that is presented.

22. Ibid., 102–3. Julian of Norwich, *Showings*, 268–9.

23. A parable is defined as, "Teaching by means of a comparison; stories of varying length containing a meaning or message over and above the straightforward and literal, with an element of metaphor." See "parables" in *A Dictionary of the Bible, Oxford Reference Online*.

"All Shall be Well": Parable as Emblematic

If Julian's name is known at all in popular culture it is for the quote "All shall be well." It is true that optimism and love permeate Julian's message. Julian herself concludes her writings with an emphasis on the love of God. "Thus I learned that love was our Lord's meaning. And I saw very certainly, in this and in all, that before God made us, he loved us, which love was never abated, no, and never shall. And in this love he hath don all his works, and in this love he hath made all things profitable to us. And in the love our life is everlasting."[24] This is the message of Julian's work: God is Love. It is a message Julian hoped would be shared with many. Her concluding prayer at the end of her showings is that all those who read her writings show their gratitude to Christ for the revelations and for the fact that Christ, as savior and guide, would lead them "to everlasting bliss."[25] Julian also has a strong view of providence, for she believes all of the world and the entire creation are in God's hands.

Yet the reality and seriousness of sin is something with which Julian, like many faithful Christians across the centuries, struggles. Given the events of her time, it is clear that all is not "well" in the world, at least by human standards.[26] The parable of the lord and the servant is significant because it plays a key role in how Julian wrestles with sin and comes to ultimately affirm the belief that "all shall be well." The parable is particularly notable in the context of her writings, given that, according to Margaret Ann Palliser, it "stands at the heart of Julian's theological vision" and, in fact "once one is familiar with the parable, one can see intimations of it everywhere, especially whenever Julian refers to God's courteous love," writes Joan Nuth.[27] Her parable is also seen by many as the key, hinge, or linchpin of her theology.[28] Even though the parable is absent from The Short Text, its theme of God's courteous love (love

---

24. Julian of Norwich, *The Showings*, 155. Julian of Norwich, *Showings*, 342.

25. Ibid. It has been questioned as to whether this prayer is Julian's own writing or later addition of a scribe. Either way it is still emblematic of Julian's message. See: Kerby-Fulton, *Books Under Suspicion*, 297.

26. See also: Jantzen, *Julian of Norwich*, 170.

27. Palliser, *Christ, Our Mother of Mercy*, 37; Nuth. *Wisdom's Daughter*, 31. For example see chapters 4 and 17 in Julian's *The Short Text*; chapters 4, 8, and 39 in *The Long Text*.

28. Skinner, "The Lord and His Servant," 4; Bauerschmidt, "Julian of Norwich—Incorporated," 90; Baker, *Julian of Norwich's Showings*, 86.

which is kind, caring, and gentle—as the love a parent has for a child, and as the lord has for his servant) is evident throughout both texts, so it is still possible to see the parable as emblematic of her theology. Additionally, the parable allows Julian to re-envision her own experience of suffering. Her sharing of that gift, in turn, allows her readers to change their perspectives on their own suffering.

JULIAN'S THEOLOGY OF SUFFERING: AN "ECONOMY OF DELIGHT"

The themes identified in Julian's parable—sin, suffering, bliss, union with God in Christ, as well as the abiding love and mercy of God—are found throughout her text and provide a framework for discussing her insights into the nature of suffering and grief. Ultimately, what Julian seems to propose could be described as an "economy of delight." The term "economy" is used here predominately in its theological sense. Theologically, economy refers to God's interaction with and government of the world. There is also some of the secular sense of economy, in the sense we can think of "delight" as the currency shared between God and us.[29] Julian proposes a worldview that has as its foundation God's love for us, and as its goal a deepening of our love for God by seeking union with God in Christ. It is a world that revolves around delight: God's delight in us and our delight in God. That delight is perhaps most evident in the parable itself. It is seen in the servant's love for and desire to serve his lord, and it is seen in the loving acts of the lord who remains with and cares for his servant in the midst of his suffering. This economy of delight can also be seen as a reaction to the context in which she lived.

Views of Suffering in the Fourteenth Century

Just as for many who had gone before, including Gregory the Great, suffering is a basic reality of Julian's world. It is not a question, it is a given. As Jane Maynard writes, "To fully appreciate Julian's vibrant theology and distinctive spirituality, we must view them against the backdrop

---

29. Harvey, *A Handbook of Theological Terms*, 247; "Economy." *Oxford English Dictionary Online, 2nd Edition*.

of fourteenth-century life, where death was both an omnipresent and 'grim business.' Julian's time was violent and brutal, marked by cruel warfare, brigandage, the torture and persecution of Jews, and extremes of destructive piety. The masochistic rites of flagellants and the fiery execution of convicted heretics, including the Lollards of Julian's own Norwich, testify to the spiritual disruption that accompanied the terrors of the age."[30]

The specter that looms largest in a study of the late Middle Ages is the plague, or Black Death, as it is frequently called. The plague of 1348–1350 is, according to Barbara Tuchman, "the most lethal disaster of recorded history, which killed an estimated one third of the population living between India and Iceland." The plague would return four times before the century was out, and by then, Tuchman writes, "Europe's population was reduced to between forty and fifty percent of what it had been when the century opened, and it was to fall even lower by mid-15th century."[31] Melvin Matthews writes that in Julian's own Norwich, the plague took one-third of the general population and half of the clergy.[32] The threat of death at that time came from warfare as well as disease. The Hundred Year's War stretched from 1338–1453, and even if one lived far from the battlegrounds, the reality of war permeated daily life. By the late fourteenth century, England, as Tuchman writes, "had caught the contagion of lawlessness which the war had spread upon the continent. . . . According to a complaint in Parliament, companies of men and archers, sometimes under a knight, 'do ride in great routs in divers parts of England,' . . . They commit riots and 'horrible offenses' whereby the realm is in 'great trouble to the great mischief and grievance of the people.' Royal justice made no serious effort to restrain them because the King was dependent for military forces on the same nobles who were responsible for the disorders."[33] Additionally, the English people's lives were subject to disruption and deprivation by the King himself. There was a practice, Tuchman writes,

---

30. Maynard, *Transfiguring Loss*, 42.

31. Tuchman, *A Distant Mirror*, xiii and 507.

32. Melvin Matthews. "Two Women Facing Death," 6. It is also important to note that although these numbers and estimates are likely accurate, there is insufficient data for historians to be able to fully calculate the impact of the plague on the population of fourteenth-century Europe. See: Klapisch-Zuber, "Plague and family life," 131.

33. Tuchman, *A Distant Mirror*, 285.

of "purveyance, that is, the King's right when traveling to commandeer supplies for a number of miles on either side of the road, and also for provisioning of the army."[34]

Neither in Julian's time nor in contemporary times need we seek out suffering—it finds us. Just as the servant, who is representative of all of humanity, came to experience suffering in the midst of his desire to do good, it can happen to all.[35] The more important question for Julian is what can come out of suffering rather than why the suffering occurred. To ask "Why does humanity suffer?" is, it could be argued, to force a modern question back into Julian's time. Julian did not ask that question. She, in her desire for illness, her desire to suffer as Christ did, sought deeper insights into God in the hopes that the insight might lead her to a life of deeper faith.

In her discussion of the parable, after witnessing his fall and his great suffering, Julian seeks to understand why the servant suffers, and so she tries to see how the servant might be to blame for what happened to him. It is interesting to note the conjunction between the servant's inability to see and Julian's quest to see. She tries to "perceive in him any fault or if the lord should assign him any blame." She can see no fault, nor does the lord seem to blame the servant for his misfortune. "For only his good will and his great desire was cause of his falling." Not only does the lord not blame the servant for what has happened, the lord looks upon the servant with great compassion and seeks to reward him.[36] This insight highlights a hallmark of Julian's theology. As Lynn Staley notes, "In sharp contrast to her contemporaries, Julian is more interested in seeking to understand God's mercy than she is in explicating his justice."[37]

Julian's emphasis on a reward for suffering fits with the element of the Christian tradition that promotes suffering as spiritually beneficial. Monastic ascetic practices or those of self-flagellation are examples of seeking (what another would deem) unnecessary suffering. Tuchman

34. Ibid., 290.

35. Julian of Norwich, *The Showings*, 104.

36. Ibid., 102–4.

37. Aers and Staley. *The Powers of the Holy*, 144. There Staley writes: "Even the briefest pass through the sermons and the penitential and devotional literature of the late fourteenth century emphasizes what seems to be an inordinate amount of attention devoted to analyzing, warning about, and providing remedies for the many different ways in which men and women can fall into sin."

notes that in response to the plague in the fourteenth century, self-flagellation become a popular and widespread practice.[38] "Organized groups of 200 to 300 and sometimes more (the chroniclers mention up to 1,000) marched from city to city, stripped to the waist, scourging themselves with leather whips tipped with iron spikes until they bled." The practice was not new, and had originally begun as "a form of penance to induce God to forgive sin." It was believed that "by re-enacting the scourging of Christ upon their own bodies and making the blood flow, [they] would atone for human wickedness and earn another chance for mankind."[39]

Although Julian does seek suffering, she seeks it as a way to understand, not as a way of atonement. It seems the parable is not meant to explain why suffering should be sought. In the parable the servant falls in the midst of trying to do his duty, which seems to point to a belief that suffering is a given, a fact of life. A resignation to the reality of suffering has, for the most part, disappeared from the experience of many by the twentieth century. As Robert Thouless wrote in 1924, "[w]e have at the back of our minds a conviction that the universe was created for us to be happy in, and we find it difficult to reconcile the fact that we suffer with our belief in the goodness of God. The mediæval mind had no such tender concern for human suffering."[40]

Pessimism and Optimism in Julian's Day

It is of little surprise that an attitude of pessimism seemed to permeate the age in which Julian lived and wrote. Because, as noted above, "death was to be met any day, around any corner," it became a source of "ghoulish fascination," and the "cult of death" developed.[41] This perhaps took on its strongest expression in the Danse Macabre, or the Dance of Death, which was a series of artistic depictions in which, Philip Morgan writes, "people, generally from all social ranks, are shown as skeletons

---

38. It is worth noting that, according to Samuel Cohn in *The Black Death Transformed,* this practice did not continue, at least as a response to subsequent outbreaks of the plague, into the late fourteenth and early fifteenth century.

39. Tuchman, *A Distant Mirror,* 114.

40. Thouless. *The Lady Julian,* 66.

41. Tuchman, *A Distant Mirror,* 506.

or putrefying corpses leading their living selves toward the grave."[42] Tuchman also argues that preaching "pessimistic view of man's fate was the duty of the clergy in order to prove the need of salvation," and although this was not a new sentiment, it seemed to be more pervasive in the fourteenth century. It might seem from Tuchman's perspective that there was no hope, no joy, no beauty in people's lives, and that the church, which is meant to be the guardian of hope, was just as much a source of trouble in people's lives as the state. Yet Tuchman does argue that while the church was certainly not devoid of problems, in spite of the pessimism of the age and of its clergy the church did still offer something good. It was a source of physical safety and spiritual hope. For the people, Tuchman writes, "the Church was comforter, protector, physician," and it "gave ceremony and dignity to lives that had little of either. It was the source of beauty and art to which all had some access and which many helped create." Church buildings and worship rites brought brightness and joy into people's lives, but for Tuchman, much of the joy was only in the knowledge that a reward awaited the faithful in the afterlife. As she notes, the Christian church in that time was omnipresent and it promoted the "principle that the life of the spirit and of the afterworld was superior to the here and now, to material life on earth."[43]

It is the joy and beauty in the religious life that Eamon Duffy wishes to highlight in his study of late medieval religion. He acknowledges the prevalence of the "cult of death," but does not share the belief that it led to or was a symptom of a pessimistic atmosphere. He writes, "[t]he influence of the cult of the dead was ubiquitous. Yet it would be a mistake to deduce from its ubiquity that late medieval English religion was morbid or doom-laden," and he cites wills that "testify not to a morbid obsession with death but to a vigorous relish for life." Duffy would take issue with Tuchman and other scholars for their emphasis on the pessimism of the age. To emphasize the pessimism of the age is to take a simplistic view, whereas Duffy sees richness and complexity in the late medieval church.[44] Duffy is not alone in his affirmation of medieval optimism; Melvin Matthews calls Julian's vision "deeply affirmative"

42. Morgan, "Of Worms and War," 125.
43. Tuchman, *A Distant Mirror*, xix, 33, 35, and 508–9.
44. Duffy. *The Stripping of the Altars*, 1 and 302–3.

and sees it as "not so unusual in the middle ages."[45] Samuel Cohn also finds optimism in the late medieval and early renaissance eras. Cohn finds many doctors of the time were optimistic about (and successful in) their ability to respond to the plague.[46] Julian's own writings, with continual affirmations of God's love, and the hope of union with God, of course, also provide an affirmation of the reality of optimism in the Middle Ages. Although the overall tenor of her writings is one of optimism, that does not mean she discounts the realities of suffering or sin.

Humanity, Sin, and Evil within Julian's Economy of Delight

Humanity, particularly the physical body, was an important theme in medieval spirituality, particularly for women writers. Perhaps the emphasis on the physical body in the Middle Ages was also due to the increasing awareness of its fragility and the "ghoulish fascination" with death noted above. The physical body may have held fascination and importance because of its temporary nature. For Christians, the fact that the body is only temporary, whereas the spirit (in a new form or new body) lives on after death, has frequently led to a separation and an emphasis on the superiority of the spirit—it lasts and is what is resurrected in new form or new body. Julian does not focus on that separation, nor does she wish to take up a negative view of the body. The body is to be viewed positively, for Adam and Christ are "but one man," and the human body is the form that Christ took "in the Maiden's womb." Therefore, because it is the form Christ took, the body and our own lives are to be held in high esteem. In the midst of her illness, Julian herself experiences a sense of regret that she might die, for she wants more time to live and love God.[47] Matthews also notes that from 1200 to 1500, women came to see their physicality as a source of opportunity for their spirituality. "Julian and her contemporaries deliberately

45. Matthews, "Two Women Facing Death," 17. Matthew's take is rather polemical, as he goes on to note in the passage that the optimism of Julian and the Middle Ages "was cruelly and dishonestly removed from the hearts of Christian people at the Reformation and replaced by a much more cynical and negative view."

46. Cohn, *The Black Death Transformed*, 236.

47. Julian of Norwich, *The Showings*, 40 and 107. For Julian, a negative view of life and of one's body is also wrong because it does not imitate that courteous, generous, merciful love of God that Julian emphasizes as central to her message. See also: ibid., 86; Pelphrey. *Christ Our Mother*, 186.

espoused physicality as a way to share in Christ."[48] Julian herself writes at the beginning of *Revelations* that she "desired a bodily sight wherein I might have more knowledge of the bodily pains of our Saviour," and that she sought to "suffer with Him."[49] She desires not only an intellectual but a bodily understanding of Christ's passion.

Of course, while the body is seen in a positive light, it is also capable of sin and suffering. "Adam fell from life to death into the valley of this wretched world," and so humanity, following in his footsteps, has fallen with him.[50] While Julian acknowledges the wretched state of the world, her emphasis is on the potential for goodness in us. Julian writes, "For in every soul that shall be saved is a godly will that never assented to sin and never shall." Julian writes of two parts to humanity – the higher and the lower. She sees in the "lower part" our capability for sin, and in the "higher part" the aspect that belongs to and is one with God's will.[51] This division highlights an issue raised within the parable. When the servant falls, Julian struggles to see how he is to blame—for she knows him to be a human capable of sin, and yet she does not see blame in him. This poses a challenge for her, for she is not able to reconcile the blamelessness of the servant with the blameworthiness of Adam (and all of humanity). As she writes, "I saw many diverse characteristics that could in no way be attributed to Adam."[52] This challenge is resolved when she comes to realize the servant is not just Adam; he is also Christ. She comes to realize anything blameworthy in the servant is of the lower part, of Adam, of humanity. Anything blameless is of the higher part, of Christ. Julian writes, "The virtue and the goodness that we have is of Jesus Christ, the feebleness and the blindness that we have are of Adam, which two were shown in the servant."[53] In the servant we see both parts, and ultimately for Julian, it is through Christ those two parts are joined together. By this joining of our blameworthiness to Christ's blamelessness, we are saved and brought fully into union with God.

48. Matthews, "Two Women Facing Death," 8.

49. Julian of Norwich, *The Showings*, 39.

50. Ibid.

51. Ibid., 83, 119. Julian of Norwich, *Showings*, 291. See also: Jantzen. *Power, Gender and Christian Mysticism*, 149.

52. Julian of Norwich, *The Showings*, 103. Julian of Norwich, *Showings*, 269.

53. Julian of Norwich, *The Showings*, 107. Julian of Norwich, *Showings*, 275.

Nature and Implications of Sin

Early on, God tells Julian "Sin is necessary [behovabil], but all shall be well, and all shall be well, and all manner of things shall be well." The word "behovabil" can be translated to "necessary," or "it had to be."[54] This certainly fits with Julian's overall theology; sin had to be because through the experience of sin and suffering God brings us to a greater reward than we would have had without sin. In Colledge and Walsh's translation of *Showings*, sin is also described as "the cause of all this pain. . . ."[55] This meaning can also fit with Julian's understanding. On the one hand, in Julian's writings, sin can be seen as a good for the result it brings, but is also important to talk about sin as the source of suffering. Sin is "behovabil," a necessary part of the human experience (because of the fall and the nature of human existence), and along with the reality of sin comes suffering—both physical and spiritual. Without sin and the fall, there would be no suffering. Sin is therefore the source of suffering, but for Julian the path of sin and suffering leads to the great reward of union with God. As she writes, "For we need to fall, and we need to see, for if we did not fall, we would not know how feeble and how wretched we are in ourselves. Nor should we so fully know the marvelous love of our maker."[56] Without sin, we would not know our own wretchedness through which we come to know the marvelous love of God.

Turner adds to this interpretation that while each individual sinful act is not necessary, it is sin as a category that is a necessary part of the human narrative.[57] This interpretation fits particularly well when we include Colledge and Walsh's emphasis (in translation) on sin as the cause of suffering, as noted earlier. The nature of God is one that intends goodness, but the existence of evil and sin in the world is, at least according to Julian, a necessary aspect of the larger narrative of the whole creation. The narrative of the parable affirms this belief. The lord does not stop the servant from falling, so that he might be brought to a great reward. The story of the lord and the servant is the story of humanity and God; as Julian notes, the servant is Adam (representative of

---

54. Julian of Norwich, *The Showings*, 72 and 173 (note 936). Julian of Norwich, *Showings*, 225.

55. Julian of Norwich, *Showings*, 225.

56. Ibid., 125 and 300.

57. Turner, "Sin is Behovely," 421.

all humanity). Julian notes that her revelations contained little mention of evil, which she understands to be one of the aspects we do not gain full knowledge of in this life. Her emphasis on God's goodness puts the focus on the good God brings out of evil rather than on the reasons why evil exists. Julian believes our attempts to fully understand God's will or why things happen will only end up taking us further from that knowledge, which can only be gained through a complete surrendering of our wills to God as the saints in heaven do.[58]

Julian takes the reality of sin and sinful behavior seriously. We do not get to merely forget faults nor disregard failings. Julian writes that she realizes "I shall do nothing but sin."[59] Julian acknowledges humanity is wretched—strong language not easy to gloss over. Julian also emphasizes the issue of human blindness. Just as the servant was blind to the lord's love while he was in the valley, so too are we blind to that love. Not only does sin prevent us from seeing the depth of God's love, it also prevents us from seeing what our true course in life is. It keeps us from the path that leads to union with God, to the everlasting bliss, which is so important to Julian.[60] Yet sin is more than just a wrong action, an error or a mistake. Julian writes that in her vision she comes to understand that sin is "all that is not good."[61] Sin is all that is evil or wrong in the world, and not just the harmful actions of an individual or a group. Of course, individual sinful actions do matter, and Julian affirms the reality of judgment day, purgatory, and hell. She notes that God's compassion "shall cease on Doomsday," and she acknowledges that the devil and all those who share his condition in this life are "reproved of God and endlessly damned."[62] Julian acknowledges that there are those who fall away from God's will and God's grace, that not all follow what God desires.

Sin is necessary for Julian, but like Augustine, it does not have any power or existence on its own. Julian writes, "What is sin? For I saw truly that God does all things, be it ever so little. And I saw truly that nothing is done by chance, but all things are in the foreseeing wisdom

58. Ibid., 78–9 and 103.

59. Ibid., 81.

60. See also Palliser, *Christ, Our Mother of Mercy*, 40.

61. Julian of Norwich, *The Showings*, 72. See also: Bradley, *Julian's Way*, 108; Beer, *Women*, 144; Pelphrey, *Christ Our Mother*, 145; Aers, *Salvation and Sin*, 166.

62. Ibid., 76, 78.

of God" and that "sin is no deed." There is nothing that happens by accident or chance; it only seems so to us.[63] All happens according to God's wisdom, and sin has no substance in and of itself. In *The Short Text*, Julian writes "sin is nothing."[64] Julian does not deny the experience of sin or humanity's ability to sin. She writes, "For a man beholds some deeds well done and some deeds evil. But our Lord does not behold them so. For as all that is, is of God's making, so all that is done has the property of being of God's doing." Here we see not only that what may seem to be sin in our eyes is not so in the eyes of God, but also a strong affirmation of Julian's view that all is in God's hands. God's providence is at work in the world. As Julian reminds her fellow Christians, God's mercy and love are ever so much greater than humanity's sinful acts. She writes, "For as it was shown to me that I should sin, just so was the comfort shown, assurance for all my fellow Christians."[65] This is the message at the heart of Julian's writings. She herself and all of humanity will sin, but she is also shown the comfort and reward that waits, thanks to God's mercy. There are ditches we will fall into, but God, the loving lord, is always watching, and is at work to bring us to a reward that is a reality of endless bliss. Again we see the joyful possibility that exists, because in the servant is found not only the blameworthiness of Adam, but also the blamelessness of Christ. What Julian seeks to emphasize, over and over again, is God's mercy, and God's desire to bring all to that place of bliss. The fall, as it is for the servant, is ultimately the source of our redemption and reward.[66] As Julian writes in the midst of her interpretation of the parable, "God's Son fell with Adam into the valley of the maiden womb, who was the fairest daughter of Adam, therefore to excuse Adam from blame in heaven and on earth; and mightily he brought him out of hell."[67] Julian sees the servant is not only Adam (who is representative of humanity), but also Christ himself, who fell to earth and took human form to bring about the redemption of humanity.

It is important to note there is an intimate connection between the fall and the reward. Like Augustine before her, Julian understands sin,

63. Ibid., 53–54. Julian of Norwich, *Showings*, 137.

64. Julian of Norwich, *Showings*, 145n.

65. Julian of Norwich, *The Showings*, 54 and 83. Julian of Norwich, *Showings*, 198 and 241.

66. See also: Hide, *Gifted Origins*, 126.

67. Julian of Norwich, *The Showings*, 107.

the darkness of the story, cannot be separated from the light, and as in a good piece of art, the darkness is needed to better define the light.[68] It is important to note in the parable the lord rewards the servant "above what he should have been rewarded if he had not fallen."[69] The reward (the good) cannot be fully understood without the fall (the darkness). The link between sin and goodness, in which sin is understood to be necessary to better understand the goodness, can provide an analogy for understanding that suffering is necessary to better understand joy. Sin and suffering are also inextricably linked: sin results in suffering. The fact that suffering is necessary to better understand joy does not mean suffering is always necessary for the existence of joy. It would seem counter to the foundations of Christian theology, and Julian's own emphasis on God's goodness, to say joy cannot exist without suffering. It is possible to affirm, however, the way the reality of suffering helps us to better understand goodness. The servant's reward has a greater *meaning* because he fell into the ditch; the reward does not owe its *existence* to the fall, for the reward is a freely given gift of the Lord.

The message that "sin is the gate to glory" is, for Sheila Upjohn, at the heart of Julian's theology.[70] Upjohn sees in Julian an emphasis on the ends—the goodness God brings out of sin and evil—and not the origins. Yet, the emphasis on the necessity of sin and suffering does raise an interesting question. Even if we accept that, categorically, sin and suffering must exist, does that mean each individual instance of sin and suffering must happen? Julian's theology proposes we must accept the reality of sin, and yet must still work to turn away from the temptation to sin further; for, as noted above, God desires not sin, but bliss for us. The way to that bliss is through union with God, which only comes when we acknowledges our sinful and blameworthy state, as Julian herself did, and when we repent of our sins. It is important to note the parable of the lord and the servant, with its message of love and hope, comes in her text as the answer to her desire to know how it is that sinful humanity can be the recipient of God's love and grace rather than his wrath, which the depth of our sin would seem to deserve.[71]

68. This similarity to Augustine's view on sin leads one to speculate that Julian may have read his works.

69. Julian of Norwich, *The Showings*, 103.

70. Upjohn, *Why Julian Now?*, 31.

71. Julian of Norwich, *The Showings*, 84–85, 95, and 100–1.

While the overwhelming trend in Julian's writing is one of optimism, if we put aside the ends—the reward and the bliss—we are confronted with a dark view of human nature. Julian speaks of her own
sinfulness and her awareness of the pervasiveness of human sin. All
that is good in us belongs to the "upper part" of human nature, which
truly belongs to God. What is good in us comes not from ourselves,
but from God. Yet this dark view of human nature and the emphasis on
its sinfulness does not last in Julian, for ultimately Julian sees the fall
as a happy event. Julian does not view our sinfulness apart from God's
mercy; the two cannot be separated. There is sin and suffering in the
world, but they lose some of their weight and darkness when they are
viewed in light of God's mercy. Sin and suffering are necessary aspects
of our existence because it is out of them we are brought into the bliss of
union with God. Sin and suffering comprise the gateway to bliss.

God's Providence in Julian's Economy of Delight

Just as the lord was intimately connected with his servant, so too is
God involved in individual lives. Julian shows her readers that God is
not a distant figure. Julian's portrayal of God is in line with much of the
Christian tradition, for the lord is intimately involved in the life of his
servant, and a parallel could be drawn to many Scriptural stories, particularly those of the patriarchs in the Old Testament.[72] Additionally,
Julian sees the fundamental goodness of creation: it is made, kept, and
loved by God. Creation inspires relationship: just as God rejoices in us,
so too should we rejoice in being beloved. In Julian there is, therefore,
inspiration to be joyful. The vision Julian offers is one where joy and
delight are the deepest foundational reality of human experience—the
delight of God in us and our delight in God. Delight is the origin and
the destination of humanity, and if we have the ability to see it, it will
be ever-hovering beneath the surface of earthly life. Julian shows that
God's nature is love and that God longs to bring us to bliss.[73]

In the midst of the parable, Julian writes, "And then I saw that
only pain blames and punishes, and our courteous Lord comforts and
succors, and always he is kindly disposed to the soul, loving longing

---

72. Nuth, *Wisdom's Daughter*, 73.
73. Julian of Norwich, *The Showings*, 43 and 104.

to bring us to bliss." Julian does not mean merely feeling happy in our earthly life. For Julian, bliss belongs to God, and the bliss that is humanity's to enjoy is ultimately in heaven. In the sixty-fifth chapter she writes, "For he wants us to pay true heed, that we be all secure in our hope, in the hope of the bliss of heaven while we are here, as we shall be certain of it when we are there." Hers is not a hope that ignores the reality of suffering. Julian is not advocating repression of suffering or challenges, rather a change of focus. We are to focus on God's love for us, and the fact we are precious to God. We are not to focus on our pain or mourning, but rather on the bliss to which God brings us. Julian writes, "For it is God's will we hold on to our comfort with all our might, for bliss is everlasting, and pain is passing and shall be brought to nought for them that shall be saved." That phrase "shall be brought to nought" is significant, for it puts one's suffering in a whole new context, as something that will not last or endure, but as something God will eventually replace with bliss. The blameworthiness of Adam will be replaced with the blamelessness of Christ.[74]

We might ask, "Why does God not just bring us to a place of bliss first without letting us fall?" This is a fair question, but does not reflect Julian's emphasis. The lord will transform the servant's suffering into endless bliss greater than what the servant ever could have known before he fell. As Julian writes, "The lord's meaning descended into her soul: that though the suffering of the servant need be, the lord in his greatness, who loved the servant so much, would truly reward the servant above and beyond what he would have received had he not fallen.[75]

Julian accepts suffering as a given aspect of life. Just as the servant (who is representative of all humanity) fell, we will inevitably fall in the course of our lives. Julian is not alone in this understanding. As Hugh Hildesley notes, "[B]oth St. Paul and Aquinas share Julian's understanding that God allows evil to happen in order to bring about a greater good and that we will, in spite of our best intentions, continue to do the very evil things we least want to do."[76] Additionally, if we were to seek out suffering, we would be doing so under our own agenda. Therefore, we would only learn what we were seeking, not necessarily what God wants us to see. Like seeking death, seeking suffering puts our own de-

---

74. Ibid., 59, 104, 131. Julian of Norwich, *Showings*, 271, 306–8.

75. Julian of Norwich, *The Showings*, 103. Julian of Norwich, *Showings*, 269.

76. Hildesley, *Journeying with Julian*, 140.

sires above God's, and seeks to do our own will and not God's. The call for people of faith is to live lives in accordance with God's desire for unity and bliss rather than lives focused on individual desires which all too often, as Julian notes, are sinful desires.[77] Finally, and perhaps most significantly, to glorify suffering, and to seek suffering for its own sake, would be to misunderstand Julian's message of love. As noted above, God desires our joy, desires to bring us to "bliss," and therefore, does not desire suffering. For Julian the goal is to be joyfully in God's presence, and it is important to remember that God desires that we know bliss. Therefore, the spiritual goal for Christians is to be in a state of joy, not in a state of pain. Given Julian's own desires and experience, however, we have to allow that God allows (and perhaps even condones) suffering if it is sought as a means to a strengthening of our faith, and of entering into that union with God that is bliss.

The (Happy) Fall

Although the goal is joy, that does not mean the journey will be free from pain and suffering. Julian does not view falling as negatively as many do; she belongs in the tradition of *Felix Culpa* (Happy Fault), those who view the fall as a positive and necessary event because it leads to redemption. Hugh White traces this tradition through Milton back to Langland's *Piers Plowman* (a text written a few decades before Julian's *Revelations)*. As White describes it, "The doctrine is, I think, obligatory for the Christian, who is committed to holding that God has the universe under benign control. Without it, the creation of man has to be seen as an error on God's part, something that goes horribly wrong."[78] White's understanding is certainly an accurate description of Julian's theology. She is one who holds that all is under God's control and all is moving toward endless bliss. Julian writes, "And in another manner he showed himself in earth, thus as if he were in pilgrimage, that is to say, he is here with us, leading us, and shall be till he has brought us all to his bliss in heaven."[79] Jantzen also identifies Julian as fitting with the Augustinian tradition of the *Felix Culpa*, along with Thomas Aqui-

---

77. Julian of Norwich, *The Showings*, 95.

78. White, "Langland, Milton, and the Felix Culpa," 336.

79. Julian of Norwich, *The Showings*, 151. Julian of Norwich, *Showings*, 337.

nas and Gregory the Great.[80] Julian's positive view of the fall is evident when she writes, "And I saw that he will we understand that he takes no harder the falling of any creature that shall be saved than he took the fall of Adam who we know was endlessly loved and securely protected in the time of all his need, and now is blissfully restored in great, surpassing joys." She also writes, "we know that when man fell so deep and so wretchedly by sin, there was no other help to restore man but him that made man for love; by the same love he would restore man to bliss and surpassing joy."[81] What is evident in Julian's writings and fits with the tradition of the *Felix Culpa* is the belief in the necessity of sin and the goodness of the fall, because it also contains within it the fall of Christ into humanity and therefore the source of our redemption.

We also see a mixture of joy and suffering in Julian's vision of Christ on the cross, where she has an experience of being "glad and merry as it was possible." She comes to understand suffering does not take away delight; it offers the opportunity to enter more deeply into it. In her vision she sees a blissful Christ who says, "If I might suffer more, I would suffer more."[82] The deep joy of Christ, evidence of the depth of God's love for humanity, is most clearly evident to Julian at the moment of Christ's greatest suffering. God is the agent in the background who moves things to this end.[83] For Julian the predominant characteristics of God are love and mercy, characteristics often associated with motherhood.

God as Mother

A belief in God as Mother is an ancient idea, and one that has strong theological roots. Caroline Walker-Bynum notes that in the writings of

---

80. Jantzen, *Julian of Norwich,* 196–7.

81. Julian of Norwich, *The Showings*, 52, 112, and 218.

82. Ibid., 66.

83. Christians believe God then transforms the terrible evils of Good Friday into the glorious joy of Easter morning. The suffering is allowed to happen, so that a greater transformation might occur. This belief is also echoed in the Old Testament, in the story of Joseph in Genesis. Joseph has been forced to undergo great suffering because of his brothers' jealousy. Life comes full circle, and Joseph has the opportunity to enact vengeance and retribution on his brothers. He does not. Instead he helps them. He says in Genesis 50:20, "Even though you intended to do harm to me, God intended it for good."

earlier "scholastic writers (e.g. Peter Lombard, Abelard, Albert, Thomas, and Bonaventure) . . . the maternal imagery refers to Christ as the Wisdom of God or to the Holy Spirit; this imagery speaks primarily of God as creator of life or illuminator of knowledge. It is on this tradition, more theological than devotional, that Julian of Norwich draws."[84] It was not an uncommon interpretation in medieval times because at that time, as Brent Pelphry notes, "it made sense to think of the saving work of Jesus in terms of a mother's work: in giving us birth, in his sacrifice for us, in guiding us to maturity, and in giving us the gift of life itself."[85]

For Julian, the notion of God as Mother arises from her own reflections on the parable. As she begins the chapter following the parable, she writes, "And thus I saw that God rejoices that he is our Father, God rejoices that he is our Mother, and rejoices that he is our true spouse, and our soul is his beloved wife."[86] Julian goes on to refer to God, Christ, and Mary all as mother figures on numerous occasions in the remainder of the text.[87] She identifies God as Mother in the wisdom of God, as well as in the salvific acts of Christ. Julian writes, "For in our Mother Christ we profit and increase, and in mercy he reforms us and restores us; and by the power of his passion and his death and resurrection, unites us to our substance." Christ as Mother is the active part of the Godhead: "Our Father wills, our Mother works, our good Lord the Holy Spirit confirms." It is also Christ our Mother who, like the lord in the parable, allows us to fall to reach a greater reward. As noted above, Julian writes, "For we need to fall, and we need to see it, for if we did not fall, we would not know how feeble and wretched we are in ourselves. Nor, too, would we know so completely the marvelous love of our maker."[88] As can be seen in these passages, Mother provides a way of describing aspects of God's nature, and of focusing on the motherly work of Christ in saving humanity.

Julian's belief in God as Mother is also connected to the belief that God permits us to fall. The themes of falling and rising are evident throughout Julian's writing.[89] We see this, of course, in the parable, and

84. Bynum, *Jesus as Mother*, 151. See also: Bradley, *Julian's Way*, 135.

85. Pelphrey, *Christ Our Mother*, 162.

86. Julian of Norwich, *The Showings*, 110.

87. Ibid., chapters 57–64 and 83 particularly.

88. Ibid., 121, 122, and 125. Julian of Norwich, *Showings*, 294, 300.

89. Heimmel, *God is Our Mother*, 85.

Julian also writes of falling and rising at various points throughout the remainder of the text. She writes of how "grace works our shameful falling into glorious rising" and how "in falling and rising we are ever preciously kept in one love." In the parable itself, Julian identifies Christ as a mother who "may suffer the child to fall sometimes," but does not ever let any lasting harm come to the child. Julian reminds her readers that Christ is our Mother who is also "almighty, all wisdom, and all love."[90] Just as the servant is not abandoned in the ditch, neither does God abandon us in the midst of suffering: God brings both to bliss. In understanding God as Mother, Julian invites her readers to have a childlike trust in God, even in the midst of an experience of sin and suffering.[91] It is an invitation to trust that we are never alone in falling, and an invitation to trust that God is at work through Christ to bring goodness out of the fall. For John Michael Mountney, Julian's parable offers a window into what God may be thinking. "It is almost as if God says, Look, don't worry about the miseries of sin. . . . In truth you are all my dearest children, why should I want to hurt and be angry with you? You are my crowning joy, so stop complaining, dry your tears, and smarten yourself up to receive the endless bliss I have been longing to give you." As a parent allows a child to fall to learn a lesson, so God allows us to fall, so that we might understand "our need for grace."[92]

To one in the midst of suffering an argument for the spiritual- and character-building value of falling may not seem very comforting. We might be more likely to wonder: What kind of parent just lets a child fall? Are parents not morally obligated to protect and care for children? Yet it is important to note the parenting metaphor for God does not end with letting us fall. As Julian writes, "The sweet, gracious hands of our Mother are ready and diligently about us. For he in all this working exercises the office of a kind nurse, who has nothing to do but attend to the salvation of her child."[93] God does not leave us fallen, but brings us to salvation.

To talk of God or Christ as Mother is also to bring an emphasis to God's compassion toward the servant rather than God's judgment,

90. Julian of Norwich, *The Showings*, 86, 98, 112, 125–27, 141, 144–45, 148, and 150–2.

91. Bradley, *Julian's Way*, 111.

92. Mountney, *Sin Shall be a Glory*, 70.

93. Julian of Norwich, *The Showings*, 126.

which may be another aspect that sets Julian apart from her contemporaries. For Maynard, "Julian's emphasis on God's immanence developed through her image of Christ as Mother counteracts the prevailing view of a transcendent and impassible God who offers judgment rather than compassion in the face of human limitations."[94] Julian's God is the God of her visions and her parable—a God who intimately cares for his servants and whose countenance is one of love and grace.

For Julian, love and joy are also meaning to be found in suffering. In affirming, "all shall be well," Julian affirms all is in God's hands—even if that does not always seem to be the case. Maynard notes that "[A]s a result of her vision, Julian came to believe that the experience of suffering may be transfigured through the presence of love. Thus she understood *that suffering has meaning because love is present in suffering*."[95] So often humanity (the servant) can tend to narrowly focus on the perspective of the ditch, whereas Sister Mary Paul writes "God the eternal, seeing it from quite a different perspective, will not allow the situation to become dangerous: that is, he will not allow his purposes for man to fail, those purposes which have never been limited to a human lifetime or a planet's history."[96] God has not only a broader perspective but also the power to bring those purposes to fruition.

This emphasis on God's power to bring purposes to fruition shows the strength of Julian's belief in God's providence. God is truly Lord of all and like the lord in the parable, God is at work, guiding and leading us to our reward. This strong view of providence means sin and suffering are not entirely counter to God's will. Julian's understanding of sin and the experience of suffering emphasize they can be the means by which we come to our reward. The fact God wills suffering does not make God a "Cosmic Sadist" (as C. S. Lewis discusses in a subsequent chapter) or one who desires the suffering of humanity. It does mean, however, that God allows us to fall because it is through falling we come to the greater reward. In this is Julian's strong view of God's providence: God permits sin and suffering, so that out of it we might be brought to a greater state of bliss.

94. Maynard, *Transfiguring Loss*, 113.
95. Ibid., 128.
96. Sister Mary Paul, *All Shall Be Well*, 25.

Salvation in Julian's Economy of Delight

Because God is compassionate and merciful, God seeks to give salvation to all. On the cross, God gives of his own self to bring about the salvation of humanity. In the crucifixion, God offers the preeminent example of what it means to give of oneself out of love and compassion. God is at work in bringing us to the place of bliss, the place where there is no more falling. We see in Julian, particularly in the image of God as compassionate and merciful, an emphasis not on pain or punishment, but on the ultimate goal and reward. Julian's God is leading us out of the ditch to a place of love and joy. Julian reminds her readers that in "the beholding of God we fall not."[97] In time we will grow in spiritual maturity and come more fully into God's presence. Julian shows her readers that our perspective must be broader: there is more to life than we are aware of at any particular moment. Of course this emphasis does not discount the reality of sin and suffering. As has been discussed, they are necessities, and we do not reach the place of reward and bliss except by experiencing them.

Through Julian's writings it is possible to see Julian's emphasis on the unity of Christ and humanity. As noted above, she understands the servant to be both Adam (all of humanity) as well as Christ. Because the servant is both, God does not look upon us without seeing the face of his own son. It is through this unity and through the willingness of Christ to fall and suffer for us we are brought to heaven by God. As Julian writes, "Thus he was the servant before his coming into earth, standing ready in purpose before the Father as a servant, until that time he would send him to do that glorious deed by which humanity was brought again into heaven."[98] A further example of God's desiring for us and the longing for union with God that permeates Julian's writing is exemplified in the servant's desire to serve his lord. Julian's understanding of the parable and emphasis on union with Christ help to illustrate the overall positive arc of Julian's theology. Julian acknowledges the reality of humanity's feeble and blind state, but couples that with the affirmation that humanity has goodness and virtue through Christ.[99] No

---

97. Julian of Norwich, *The Showings*, 152; Heimmel, *God is Our Mother*, 86. See also: Reynolds, "Woman of Hope," 16.

98. Julian of Norwich, *The Showings*, 107. Julian of Norwich, *Showings*, 275.

99. Julian of Norwich, *Showings*, 275.

matter how blind we may be, no matter how we may stumble, Christ's goodness will triumph. For Julian, the reality of Christ's triumph is not only evident on a broad theological scale, it is concretely evident in the ways in which human beings serve each other and build relationships. For Julian, actions of goodness and compassion belong to the higher part of human nature, the part that is of God.

As noted above, Julian is aware of the lower part of human nature; she takes the reality of sin seriously. She has a profound awareness of her own sinful nature and the propensity of sin. This means she has a strong awareness of humanity's need for salvation. The transformation of the servant (and all of humanity) from the lowly Adam who sinned, to the glorious Christ who is without sin, is not something we can accomplish for ourselves. It requires the descent and saving actions of Christ. The descent of Christ that brings about the salvation of humanity puts the reality of suffering in a different context. Sin and suffering are not permanent states of being for us, nor are they ones from which we must rescue ourselves. The hope and joy for humanity is found in the reality that God is at work through Christ to bring us out of our sinful state.

Christ in Julian's Economy of Delight

An emphasis on the passion of Christ is pervasive in medieval theology. While Julian herself did pray for a bodily understanding of Christ's suffering, it is important to remember that what she sought, first and foremost, was a greater understanding. She was not seeking suffering in and of itself; she sought suffering as a means to a deeper knowledge of God. She also acknowledges spiritual insights that come from suffering cannot be learned on our own, they are only granted as gifts by God.[100] Seeking a deeper understanding of Christ's passion was a common practice in the Middle Ages. As Joan Nuth notes, "Devotion to the passion of Christ was all-pervasive in the Western church by Julian's time, and both visions of the Crucified and debilitating illness were regarded as profitable ways of sharing in Christ's suffering." Nuth also notes that visions of Christ on the cross were pervasive, and they were more likely to be found in the spiritual writings of women, which puts Julian in

---

100. Ibid., 39.

line with her contemporaries.[101] Although it may be that because her understanding of the nature of Christ continues her themes of joy and mercy, Julian ends up with a theology less in line with many of her contemporaries who, as noted above, place a greater emphasis on God's justice.

Christ as Lord and Servant

As noted earlier, in the parable Christ is seen both in the figure of the lord and the figure of the servant. This is significant for it means that the lord, the one who brings the servant out of the ditch to the reward, also knows intimately the pain and suffering of being in the ditch. As Julian shows, the lord exercises his power with compassion and mercy, in the parable, he shows his might by going into hell not to punish, but to redeem a "company of souls."[102] The lord does not seek to exert his power through cruelty, but rather works to bring the servant to his reward. Staley sees Julian's approach as a method of social commentary, noting that "Julian's decision to blur the boundaries between lordship and servantship in her explication of the example cannot be detached from the highly charged and oppositional social language of the 1380's."[103] It was "a time when almost every major figure in England was discussing lords and servants in radically different terms."[104] It may be that Julian is making a social commentary on the power differential of her day, or it may also be that Julian is just following in traditional Christian understandings. As Julian writes, "The merciful beholding of his lovely countenance filled all the earth and descended down with Adam into hell, and by his continuing pity Adam was kept from endless death. And this mercy and pity dwells with mankind until the time we come up into heaven." In bringing about salvation, Christ descends into hell, with mercy and pity that ultimately preserves us from a fate of endless death. This fits with the Christian tradition in which one who is powerful seeks to be transformative and to be empowering to humanity. Christ empowers us and brings us more fully into his presence. In fact, the life, death, and resurrection of Christ are about bringing us into union

101. Nuth, *Wisdom's Daughter*, 11.

102. Julian of Norwich, *The Showings*, 109.

103. Staley, 161.

104. Ibid., 164.

with God. Through Christ's self-giving, the sin, which has blinded us and prevented us from seeing where we belong and the depth of God's love, is conquered. Again we see the blamelessness of Christ replaces the blameworthiness of Adam, and Christ shows death can become life. As Julian writes, even though we may suffer the "sharpest scourge" of sin, and even though that scourge will result in wounds, the wounds do not remain so in God's eyes, where they are in fact seen as "worships [honors]." Julian writes, "And as we punished here with sorrow and with penance, in contrary fashion we shall be rewarded in heaven by the courteous love of our Lord God Almighty, who does not wish anyone who comes there to lose his labors in any degree." For Julian, humanity's life is grounded in God's love and that love has the power to transform wounds into honors, just as Christ's wounds on the cross were transformed.[105]

Right at the moment when she thought life might be leaving him, Christ's expression is transformed into one of joy and happiness, and thereby Julian also felt joy. As she writes, "And just in the moment when by appearances it seemed to me that life could last no longer, and that the revelation of his end must be near, suddenly, as I looked at the same cross, he changed to an appearance of bliss. The changing of his blessed appearance changed mine, and I was as glad and joyful as it was possible to be."[106] God's love is evident to Julian as she sees Jesus on the Cross. Julian understands Christ freely suffers—he suffers out of love for us. As noted above, if he could have suffered more, he would have, which is evidence of the depth of God's love. Additionally, with the perspective of God, Christ is also able to see the joyful reward that awaits. Christ suffers on the cross so he may draw us to himself and grant the bliss of union with him. From the discussion of bliss it is evident this union with God is not limited to heaven; it is possible to experience some of that bliss in the here and now.

105. Julian of Norwich, *The Showings*, 85–6 and 105; Julian of Norwich, *Showings*, 245 and 272; Bradley, *Julian's Way*, 121. See also: Palliser, *Christ, Our Mother of Mercy*, 131; Jantzen, *Gender, Power and Christian Mysticism*, 154.

106. Julian of Norwich, *The Showings*, 65–66.

Desire for Union with Christ

In writing of union with Christ, Julian is reflecting another theme of medieval piety. Becoming one with Christ is, of course, a widely held goal of Christian spirituality in general, and of mysticism in particular. By the late Middle Ages, the emphasis had shifted from understanding Christ as victor or vindicator, to focusing on his suffering.[107] Given the suffering of Julian's time, this is not a surprising development. Christ's suffering became a place of identification and a way into union with him. Gillian Ahlgren argues that Julian's understanding of, and desire for, union with God and Christ is particularly meaningful to Christians because it can translate into our contemporary, everyday life. Ahlgren sees the theme of eros—the desire for union—as a reciprocal theme in Julian's writing; both God and humanity are desiring of the other. Ahlgren believes, for Julian, "Eros is at the heart of all curiosity and desire, all creative activity, all commitments to sustain and enhance life, all attempts to share who we are with others, all community building, and, ultimately, any human evolution toward goodness."[108] What Julian offers then, is not only a traditional expression of the believer's desire for God, but also a way in which desire can translate into our human relationships as well. Julian's message of love is not meant to be limited to our relationship with God, it is a love to be lived out as charity in our relationships with others. As Julian writes, the charity given by God is "is a gracious gift of working in which we love God for himself, and ourselves in God, all that God loves, for God."[109] Humanity is called not only to worship God and care for itself, but also to act with love toward all whom God loves.

Christ is the central figure in Julian's theology. Her initial prayer was for a deeper understanding of his passion, and through that insight she gained more insights regarding humanity and God. Christ is also the central figure in her parable; for, while the servant is representative of humanity, he is also Christ. For Julian, Christ is a source of consolation because an individual's sufferings can never be as great as his. Christ is also the source of joy and hope, for he represents all that is good in humanity and is the source of salvation. It is through Christ

---

107. Matthews, "Two Women Facing Death," 13.

108. Ahlgren, "Julian of Norwich's Theology of Eros," 37–38.

109. Julian of Norwich, *The Showings*, 153. Julian of Norwich, *Showings*, 341.

we are brought into union with God. We need not despair (as the servant did) in the midst of suffering, for in Christ humanity is brought to union with God.

Eternal Life in Julian's Economy of Delight

A belief in eternal life is pervasive in Julian's writings whenever she mentions bliss. In the midst of her parable, she writes how God (seen in the figure of the lord who rewards his servant) is always loving and longing to bring us to bliss.[110] This belief that God leads us to bliss is an essential part Julian's theology. Often Julian talks about this reward, this bliss, as being in heaven. Even though there is emphasis on heaven in Julian's writing, there is still comfort and joy to be found, because there is at least a partial union with God in Christ possible in the here and now. It is possible to both believe in the value of this life and look with hope to the eventual complete union with God in the next. The current union is not as complete as it will be, but it is meaningful nonetheless. According to Julian, there is hope for the hereafter and joy in the present, because while God is bringing us to bliss in heaven, God is also present in the here and now with us, leading and guiding. As she writes, "But he wants us to trust that he is constantly with us, and in three ways. He is with us in heaven, true man in his own person, drawing us up, and that was shown in the spiritual thirst. And he is with us in earth, leading us, and that was shown in the third revelation where I saw God in a point [moment of time]. And He is with us in our soul, endlessly dwelling, ruling, guiding us."[111]

This means that the joy and bliss Julian writes of is not limited to the afterlife. As Kerrie Hide writes, "[s]ustained by [our] union with Christ we can wait peacefully and live in hope-filled expectation that the union depicted in the parable is partially possible in a life centered on Christ and is a foretaste of the joy of heaven."[112] We abide in God because of Christ, and we can be sustained by that union throughout our earthly life, for as Julian noted, God is always present with us.

---

110. Julian of Norwich, *The Showings*, 104.

111. Ibid., 111; Julian of Norwich, *Showings*, 280.

112. Hide, *Gifted Origins to Graced Fulfillment*, 130.

Julian's theology requires a broad perspective. We must be willing to widen our vision beyond the suffering in a particular moment, and we must not forget the reward that awaits a faithful servant: eternal life with God in heaven. As with many of the elements of Julian's understanding of suffering that are developed through her texts, there are objections that can be made. It may not be especially helpful, for example, to say to one in the midst of suffering that they should remember ultimately they will be in heaven with God, for such reassurance seems absent of any hope or joy in the present moment. Perhaps this is precisely because perspective has been lost. We have become like the servant: unable to see beyond our own pain in the moment. Yet the assurance Julian provides is not only that our destiny is someday to be with God in heaven; it is also that God is present even in the midst of our suffering.

Julian's understanding of eternal life does not create a dichotomy between earth and heaven. Eternal life is a reality she affirms. She believes God desires to bring all of humanity to bliss, but, as noted above, we have freedom of choice, and so we have the eternal option to turn away from God and that invitation. The joy that awaits us is not limited to heaven, for the reality of eternal life can begin in the here and now. A partial union with Christ in the present gives us a foretaste of heavenly bliss. With that foretaste and belief in eternal life, we need not despair in the midst of suffering. It is through suffering we come to the reward of eternal life with God, just as the servant did.

SUMMARY ANALYSIS

In her writings, Julian calls Christians to remember that, like the servant, we are held in God's presence, even when we fall because God's presence with us is everlasting. As noted above, God is always us, guiding us, caring for us."[113] Julian offers a renewed vision that can change how people view themselves and their suffering, at least in the context of the broader divine narrative. Julian offers the confident affirmation that the narrative is one that tends to a joyful end because of the strength of God's providence; people do not depart from God's vision or love even when they fall into a ditch.

113. Julian of Norwich, *The Showings*, 110–1; Julian of Norwich, *Showings*, 280; Palliser, *Christ, Our Mother of Mercy*, 99–100.

Like Gregory, Julian believes the moments in which we fall can have a beneficial cleansing effect on minds and hearts. Julian herself prays that she might be "purged by the mercy of God and after living more to the worship of God because of that sickness." Julian hopes that sickness might cleanse her mind and soul and focus her attention to where it ought to be: on God. As the servant's did, our vision can narrow so much in the midst of suffering that we can see nothing but our own pain. Yet a narrowing of vision does not necessarily have to be negative. It is possible to allow suffering to focus our vision not on our own pain, but on what really matters. This is in line with the belief, evident in Julian, that suffering helps us to gain insight into our own nature as both sinful and beloved by God. It would seem Julian, by example, is not only advocating that we live with a transformed vision, but that, as she did, we also seek to communicate and live out that vision, so as to better the lives of others as well. She concludes her revelation by stating that the consolation she found through her visions is "for our endless comfort."[114] While there is a great deal of the first person singular in her text, she also frequently uses the first person plural, which indicates the lessons and comfort she writes of are not for her alone—they are for all Christians.

While the cleansing and educative aspects of suffering are important to Julian, what matters most for her is the belief that all are intended for union with God and union is a state of bliss. This optimistic view is accompanied by a belief in the transformational power of faith. Given that all her visions occurred within the context of illness, Julian is well aware of the pains and challenges of the human experience. Julian takes the reality of sin seriously and understands she and all humanity will sin. Yet for Julian, the fall is a happy fall since we cannot talk about sin apart from the reality of redemption. The servant in her parable is Adam, and he is also Christ. Through Christ's suffering on the cross (which is joyfully borne, according to Julian) humanity is brought to the reality of union with God, the reality of bliss—in the now and the hereafter.

Julian's strong belief in God's providence and her affirmation that salvation comes through Christ does not mean humans are mere pawns. Julian comes to the point of seeing pain and fear as opportunities to grow in our faith. As noted above, opportunity is only realized if one turns to

114. Julian of Norwich, *Showings*, 39 and 155.

God. We may hesitate to do so in the midst of suffering because of fear of wrath or punishment, yet that is not the vision of God Julian paints. Julian again and again affirms God is continually reaching out in love. The lord does not punish the servant for his haste, rather he reaches out in compassion. The lord sees the goodness in the servant and his desire to do the lord's bidding. So too does God see the goodness in us. Therefore, God is filled with compassion, not anger. As Palliser notes, "[p]erhaps the most consoling aspect of the parable of the lord and the servant is Julian's understanding of God's chere [countenance] of pity in the face of our 'falling' into sin: our sins evoke compassion, not wrath from God . . . . There is no need for despair . . . God's steadfast love is infinitely greater than our sins."[115] We may, therefore, have great hope and consolation. While we may fear turning suffering over and the process of letting go, remembering what benefits will come, may make it easier.

If we do choose to turn to God, we open up our life to the power of love, to reverent fear that is the gateway to a deeper connection to God. In giving over suffering, we also realize suffering is a place of connection with God. Through the sufferings of Christ, God connects with us in the midst of our pain. In fact, understanding Christ's passion is not only a way to connect with God, it is a way to deepen relationships with others. Our own suffering can then be a way to reach out to others in their pain. So often sin and pain can be destructive to relationships, but Julian reminds us it need not be this way. Julian emphasizes the unity of humanity, in that all are sinful, but also notes it is possible our sins can even serve to comfort and help other Christians.[116] As Ellen Ross notes, both Julian and her contemporary Margery Kempe "envision a holistic lifelong path on which a growing relationship with the Divine is coupled with deepening love of self and neighbor." This love of neighbor also includes compassion for the suffering of others.[117] As Julian reminds her readers, Christ dwells in humanity; therefore, people are to be his helpers and "learning his teachings, keeping his laws, desiring that all be done that he does, truly trusting in him."[118] Christ's dwelling in humanity calls us to live a life of compassion, as Christ did. It could also be said having compassion and seeing Christ in others increases

---

115. Palliser, *Christ, Our Mother of Mercy*, 231–2.

116. Julian of Norwich, *The Showings*, 148.

117. Ross, *The Grief of God*, 33 and 37.

118. Julian of Norwich, *The Showings*, 120.

our sense of unity with God, and therefore helps give us a taste of God's bliss in the here and now. Julian calls her fellow Christians to live with charity—to love God and each other—as a result of reading her revelations. Because love is the guiding principle of life for Julian, the way to salvation is through loving our fellow Christians. She writes, "in general I am in unity of lovd with all my fellow Christians. For it is in this unity of love that the life consists of all men that shall be saved."[119] This human element in salvation is also emphasized in Bauerschmidt's understanding of Julian:

> *A Revelation of Love* is Julian's rendering of God's invitation to enter into Christ's crucified side, an invitation made to all of God's lovers, an invitation to be broken and regathered into union with God, to become the city in which Christ may reign. Salvation appears as the incorporation of humanity into a new polity, initiated by Christ's self-gift upon the cross and defined by practices which respond to that gift by reenacting it: feeding the hungry, giving drink to the thirsty, welcoming the stranger, clothing the naked, caring for the sick, visiting the imprisoned. As such, salvation is a task to be accomplished in history through the participatory *mimesis* [mimicking] of Christ's compassion, which reveals in history the perfect sociality of the Father's love for the Son in the Spirit.[120]

This is an understanding shared by many theologians, including Ivone Gebara (who will be discussed in a subsequent chapter). Salvation has a human component; it is realized through the daily activities of Christians. This is not to minimize in any way the salvific act of Christ on the cross, but rather to note how foundational act moves Christians toward union with Christ by enacting that same self-giving behavior. That understanding of salvation, provided that it does not minimize the cross, is certainly one that can provide hope in the midst of suffering. Not only will all be well because all is ultimately in God's hands, but there are people all around working to prevent suffering.

119. Ibid., 49–50; Julian of Norwich, *Showings*, 134.
120. Bauerschmidt, *Julian of Norwich*, 97.

CRITIQUE

Wrath of God

Perhaps the strongest critique of Julian is that she does not take the anger or wrath of God seriously enough. David Aers sees her understanding of the fall as a twist on the *Felix Culpa* tradition because in Julian's understanding there seems to be *felix* but no *culpa*.[121] It seems appropriate to ask how we can affirm God is all love when there is much in the Christian tradition to affirm the reality of God's anger. So much of the Old Testament—from the expulsion from Eden to the plagues of the Exodus to the divine anger expressed in so many of the prophets— attests to wrath as one of the divine attributes. It is, of course, possible to see the emphasis on love in the New Testament as a counter to that argument, yet it is worth noting that the Marcionite way of partitioning divine wrath and love between two deities represented in the two Testaments did not become orthodoxy; the New Testament did not replace the Old. The New Testament (particularly the book of Revelation) does not disregard the wrath of God, and the Old Testament also shows the love and mercy of God. The Christian tradition has affirmed the God of the Old Testament is the God of the New. There is certainly much in Scripture to attest to the reality of God's anger, and it is a fact affirmed by theologians as well. A few centuries after Julian, a fellow English Christian, Jeremy Taylor, a sixteenth-century Anglican theologian (who will be discussed in the next chapter) attested that death happens by God's mercy or by God's anger.[122] Bynum would argue that there is a notable absence of the angry side of God in Julian: "Unlike the God of fourteenth-century mystics (Julian of Norwich or Eckhart, for example), the God of these visions [those of Gertrude of Helfta] is tough. He punishes and damns." Bynum also sees Julian in contrast to other mystics who put a greater emphasis on sin and damnation. "But Mechtild, like the great fourteenth-century recluse and mystic Julian of Norwich, is nonetheless uncomfortable with ideas of sin and damnation in a way that Gertrude and Mechtild of Hackborn are not."[123] Perhaps the argument about the seriousness of God's wrath in

121. Aers, *Salvation and Sin*, 166.
122. Taylor and Carroll, *Selected Works*, 472.
123. Bynum, *Jesus as Mother*, 189 and 234.

Julian's writings, though, is one of semantics or one of perception. For Sheila Upjohn, Julian shows her readers wrath is real, but it does not belong to God. According to Upjohn, "Julian's insight, and one that a twentieth-century psychologist would recognise, is that the wrath we see in God is not in him at all, but is a projection of our own anger."[124] This is evident in Julian's parable where she waited to see if she could see in him any fault, or if the lord should blame him in any way. As she writes, "And I looked carefully to see if I could perceive in him any fault, or if the lord should assign in him any blame."[125] Here, it seems clear enough, Julian expects to see God's wrath. She expects the lord to be harsh and to blame the servant for the fall, and in so doing, is an example of the human tendency to see God as vengeful.

Others would say to project human standards onto God is inappropriate. This idea is present in the theology of Gregory the Great as well. "To speak of Him [God], for instance, as angry or compassionate is to apply terms derived from purely human qualities to One in whom these qualities do not exist. At best such words only have a relative meaning. They are steps by which we may mount up to the unchangeable God."[126] Perhaps Julian would agree with this. What Julian learns in the course of the parable, in the course of her revelations, is while she might expect God's wrath, she does not find it. Julian writes that while she sees us as sinful, and deserving of God's wrath, she realizes "our Lord was never angry and never shall be. For he is God—good, life, truth, love, peace. His charity and his unity prevent him from being angry. For I saw truly that it is against the property of his power to be angry, and against the property of his wisdom, and against the property of his goodness."[127] Part of the complexity of Julian's approach is she understands while we may look for God's wrath, what she comes to understand is no matter how we may search, all we will find is God's mercy.

124. Upjohn, *In Search of Julian of Norwich*, 45.

125. Julian of Norwich, *The Showings*, 102; Julian of Norwich, *Showings*, 268.

126. Dudden, *Gregory the Great*, 319.

127. Julian of Norwich, *The Showings*, 95–6; Julian of Norwich, *Showings*, 259; See also: Spearing, *Medieval Writings*, xxxii.

Judgment vs. Mercy

Another place where there is room for argument in Julian's theology is in the breadth of her perspective. Julian has a cosmic perspective. Her affirmation is all *shall* be well, not that it currently is. Taken to its logical extreme, her view could seem to be ignorant of the severity of human sin. If God is all love and mercy, do murder, injustice, etc., really matter? There is no doubt Julian takes the reality of sin seriously, but does her theology, with its lack of divine judgment, end up promoting moral complacency? If so, then Julian's theology would not be one of hope for those in the midst of suffering—it would even seem to be one that would promote sinful behavior, and therefore, greater suffering. It is important to note the servant is not admonished or punished in any way for his haste. Of course, we would prefer sins (at least our own), great and small, be met with mercy rather than wrath. Is that as it should be? Christianity is, in part, a tradition of rules with grounding in the Ten Commandments. As the Roman Catholic practices of confession and penance attest, it is also a tradition that expects consequences for sin. Judgment seems to be missing from Julian's parable and her theology: God is not judge; God is merciful Lord. It is certainly possible to fault Julian for her failure on this front; she is unorthodox in her approach.

Although we can certainly argue for a lack of wrath and judgment in Julian's theology, punishment is not lacking. The servant certainly suffers consequences for his haste. He falls into a ditch. He is in pain and feels abandoned by his lord. Is what is found in Julian, then, possibly a reoriented approach to sin and morality? Does Julian's theology, with its emphasis on God's love and mercy, end up promoting morality by calling us to act out of a new motive? Avoiding sinful behavior and refraining from causing others to suffer is not done out of fear, but rather out of love. Christians are called to respond to God as God reaches out to them—with love. This is where the hope is for Christians. There is hope not only in the image of God as abiding, compassionate Lord, but also in the call to have compassion for the suffering of others, as Christ did, and Julian did. All shall be well because all is in God's hands.

Providence

The affirmation that all is in God's hands raises another question about Julian's theology. Given her emphasis on the fact God leads us and her focus on how the reward for suffering is greater than it would have been if we had not fallen, we wonder whether her doctrine of providence is too strong. Particularly, if all that happens is in accordance with God's purposes, then God does not merely allow us to fall. It seems God *leads* us to fall. This fits with Julian's image of God as the loving parent who permits a child to fall because of the good and the lesson that will come with it. The implication of Julian's view that God leads us to fall and suffer means all suffering is viewed as necessary and good. For Julian, the goodness in suffering comes because it the path to the reward of blissful union with God in Christ. By having such a high view of suffering, Julian's theology seems to promote suffering as something to be sought for its benefits. It seems in Julian's theology we are left with such a positive view that there seems no room for the dark side of suffering. There is no room for questioning whether or not suffering is unjust and whether or not it ought to be combated rather than embraced with joy.

CONCLUSION

In her text, Julian addresses the major theological issues of her day as Jeremy Catto has identified them: "divine omnipotence and human freedom, God's knowledge of creatures and human knowledge, whether the Incarnation was merely a consequence of the Fall of Man, and finally the relation of God's grace to human merit."[128] She acknowledges humanity is wretched, but her emphasis and focus are on the mercy of God. We may expect the sinfulness of humanity to be met with wrath, but all Julian sees is love and mercy. God cares intimately for us; just as the lord never abandons his servant, neither does God abandon us. Through the cross, God intimately knows the reality of human suffering and is present in its midst. Just as the lord reached out to the servant in compassion, so too God reaches out to us.

The image of God as compassionate and merciful, as Mother, is in contrast to the image of God as disciplinarian or harsh schoolmaster that we find in Gregory. Although Julian does value the cleansing and

128. Catto, "Currents of Religious Thought and Expression," 50.

educative properties of suffering, her focus is on suffering as a means to union with God. Her emphasis is on the bliss that awaits us, and on suffering as the gateway to that bliss. Yet we are left wondering whether or not one we can hold, wholesale, to Julian's emphasis on bliss. Can we focus solely on the future intimacy, the future union with God? Does doing so make one blind to injustice and to the suffering in the world that is of human origin? Does such a focus on bliss lead to a seeking of suffering for its reward and also to a devaluing of earthly life? Julian's emphasis puts one's focus predominately on the afterlife, on the reward that waits. This emphasis on the afterlife is balanced by a focus on how we live in the here and now, which is of particular concern to Jeremy Taylor, and it is to his manual, *Holy Living and Dying* we now turn.

3

Jeremy Taylor's Rigorous, Lifelong Approach to Living with Suffering and Grief

IT IS PERHAPS OF little surprise the most famous work of Jeremy Taylor, a parish priest and bishop of the seventeenth century, would be on death and dying. The ravages of the plagues, known also to Gregory and Julian, continued into Taylor's lifetime, most notably the 1665 outbreak of bubonic plague, which took an estimated fifty-six thousand lives in London.[1] For Taylor, as for Gregory and Julian, death is still an ever-present reality. Modern medicine has not yet arrived, and illness and accidents are common, expected realities. Taylor also lived through England's Civil War. Taylor is no stranger to personal tragedy; of his eight children (five sons and three daughters), only his three daughters survived him by many years. His only son to survive into adulthood died within days of Taylor's own death.[2] An understanding of Taylor's views on suffering and grief can be gained through his own writings, both theological and personal, including his treatise *Holy Living and Dying*, the sermon preached at the funeral of Lady Carbery, as well as a letter to his friend Sir John Evelyn upon the death of Evelyn's two sons.

1. Houlbrooke, "The Age of Decency: 1660–1760," 174–75.

2. Stranks, *The Life and Writings of Jeremy Taylor*, 305. Spurr indicates that Taylor's son died after him, whereas Stranks (271–72) indicates that Charles was buried in London on August 2, 1667, eleven days before his father died. Even if that is accurate, it would seem unlikely that this news would have reached Taylor before his own death. Greer sides with Stranks. See Greer, *A Christian Hope*, 212.

Like Gregory and Julian, Taylor has a wide perspective that humbly acknowledges humanity's insignificance and sinfulness as contrasted with divine greatness. Taylor also shares their acceptance of the reality of suffering in our lives. Taylor does acknowledge the human experience of grief, but it does not lead him to express anger or to question divine providence. Taylor believes loss does not mean the end, since even the experience of grief is within the bounds of God's providence. Particularly, Taylor is notable for his acceptance of death. He firmly lives out the Christian conviction (perhaps most famously expressed in 1 Corinthians 15) that death has lost its sting, because resurrection and eternal life are found in Christ. For Taylor, Christ has undone the fall, and death no longer has dominion over humanity. In affirming this belief, Taylor offers good news and hope to all Christians.[3] Like Gregory, Taylor is a teacher, interested in shaping the role ministers have with their flocks. Taylor also takes Julian's concern with the welfare of the average Christian even further and focuses on the practical application of his theology of suffering. His strong interest is in seeing his theology applied. For Taylor, the value of thinking about death is that it inspires us to *live* differently. As Greer notes, Taylor's writings "tend toward a sunny optimism and a confidence in the value of our efforts that are surprising."[4] Death, both our own as well as the deaths of others, ought to be at the forefront of our mind, not because of a morbid fascination, but because doing so inspires greatness in our lives. We are inspired to live a life of obedience and working toward God's glory when the consequences of our mindset and actions are eternal. Living with an awareness of death keeps us humble, obedient, and hopeful, for, as a Christian, death is a point of transition to a far greater life in union with God. Gregory calls his followers to ascetic practices, and values suffering as a scourge. Julian places her emphasis on God's abiding presence in the midst of and the reward we receive for suffering. Taylor, on the other hand, places his emphasis on a lifelong process of edification and deepening piety so that we may live each day to its fullest in God's service and filled with the hope of eternal life.

---

3. Beaty, *The Craft of Dying*, 270.
4. Greer, *Christian Hope and Christian Life*, 212.

HISTORICAL CONTEXT

Before more fully engaging with Taylor's texts, it is important to gain some understanding of the basic story of his life and the times in which he lived. Although Taylor's written works have been well preserved over the centuries, many of the details of his own life have been lost. The preservation of his works is due to the efforts of Bishop Heber, who, two centuries after Taylor's death, edited and compiled the works, along with a brief biography.[5] Unfortunately, not all of Bishop Heber's information about Taylor's own life is reliable.[6] There is still, however, much that can be known about Taylor and his world.

In the context of English history, Taylor lived at a tumultuous time of civil war and ecclesiastical conflict. Even a century after the break with Rome, the Church of England struggled to form its own identity. As John Packer notes, "It was not easy for a national Church to retain its historical connexions with the past and yet build up a unique and independent system of theology that transcended and purified the past."[7] Taylor was a devout high church Anglican, a strong supporter of the king and the church.[8] He and his fellow Anglicans were persecuted, in turn, when the Puritan cause did win out for a time.

While the Puritans were in power, they temporarily abolished the temporal authority of bishops and deprived them of their seats in Parliament. Additionally, church buildings, ornaments and even festival days (including Christmas, Easter, and Pentecost) were under attack from Parliament, and two to three thousand (almost one-third) of the clergy lost their livings for refusing to agree to a covenant in support of Puritan ideals.[9] Disagreements between the king and Parliament led to the trial and beheading of the king. During the conflict, the traditions of the Church of England were kept alive by Archbishop Laud and his followers, including Taylor, who were often known as Laudians or High Churchmen. Officially, notes Moorman, "[d]evout laity were deprived of the sacraments of the Church and obliged to attend Presbyterian

5. Heber, *The Whole Works of Taylor.*

6. Stranks, *The Life and Writings of Jeremy Taylor*, 28–29.

7. Packer, *The Transformation of Anglicanism*, 2.

8. Greer, *A Christian Hope*, 208.

9. Packer, *Transformation*, 5–6; Moorman, *A History of the Church in England*, 238–39.

forms of worship. The observance of Christmas Day was forbidden, and John Evelyn [a friend of Taylor's] ran some risk of being assaulted or imprisoned when he attended a celebration of the Eucharist in Exeter Chapel on Christmas Day 1657."[10]

The Puritans' influence continued throughout the government of Oliver Cromwell, but their power did not last. After Cromwell died in 1658, his son Richard took over as protector, but resigned in 1660, allowing for the restoration of the monarchy. Under the restoration, a new prayer book was reinstated from 1662 onwards, clergy were returned to their livings (which meant the removal of about one thousand Presbyterian clergy who did not choose to be ordained in the Church of England), and the bishops were readmitted to the House of Lords. Much of this was accomplished because throughout the protectorate, Laudian clergy had exerted their influence over Charles II and, as many had become teachers, over the new generation of members of parliament as well. When the tide turned and the loyalist Anglicans were returned to the halls of power, there was a strong effort to restore order and put down any opposition because it was believed that "[A]t all costs a repetition of the disasters of the last twenty years must be avoided."[11] As Packer notes, the tide may have turned, but the conflict did not immediately disappear. He writes, "The change in government did not, and would not, alter the bitter religious wranglings. Power was now in the hands of the other party but the weapons of attack were much the same, a lack of spiritual charity and an insistence on force to bring about the required ends."[12] Although many would laud the return of the monarchy and the re-establishment of the church, the depth of the conflict and the violence practiced by both sides should not be belied. As both Moorman and Packer note, the loyalist Anglicans may have returned to power in part because of the strength and appeal of the thinkers and writers of the time. It is interesting to note that Taylor and his fellow Caroline Divines (e.g. George Herbert, John Donne) have continued to capture the interest of both theologians and ordinary Anglicans for centuries following their death. Their important achievement was to set a tone for intellectual engagement with our faith that is still alive (perhaps in a resurgence) in the Anglican tradition today.

10. Moorman, *A History of the Church*, 246.

11. Ibid., 248–52. See also Packer, *Transformation*, 199.

12. Packer, *Transformation*, 185.

As Stranks notes, the Divines "gave the Church of England a reputation for learning that many years of sloth and ignorance were not afterwards able to destroy. Nor were they learned only, they were filled with a piety which it is the glory of the Church of England to claim as peculiarly her own."[13] Taylor's own piety, his abiding faith and ability to live out his faith over the course of his life, is evident in his works, and is perhaps his best-known attribute.

EDUCATION AND PRIESTHOOD

The year of Taylor's birth is disputed, but what is known is the date of his baptism: August 15, 1613; it would be reasonable to assume he was born the same year. Taylor entered Caius College at Cambridge as a young teenager, so it seems his intellectual gifts were recognized early. Upon completion of his studies, Taylor began to teach. He was then ordained in 1633, before he was even 21, and from early on, Taylor was recognized as a gifted preacher. He even caught the ear of Archbishop William Laud who took a liking to him and appointed him a Fellow of All Souls College at Oxford.[14]

Professionally, Taylor moved on from academia to serve as a chaplain for Archbishop Laud and then Charles I, and then became a parish priest in Uppingham. Taylor and Phoebe Langsdale were married on May 27, 1638; their first son, William, was born and died in 1642. In the mid 1650s, after the death of Phoebe, Taylor remarried, to Joanna Bridges. Taylor had a total of five sons, only one of whom survived into adulthood, and three daughters who all survived him.[15] Taylor was imprisoned by the Puritans on more than one occasion and considered himself to have been under persecution by them for eighteen years.[16] Taylor confirmed his status as a high church Anglican with the publication of his first book, *Episcopacy Asserted,* in which he held to the importance of bishops for the church and kings for the country. Fortunately

---

13. Stranks, *Life and Writings*, 24.

14. Ibid., 27, 31, and 44. See also John Spurr, "Taylor, Jeremy."

15. Stranks, 50, 52, and 163–64. See also Spurr.

16. Spurr states at least two occasions, while also noting that, "Tradition and over-enthusiastic scholarship may have exaggerated the number of occasions on which Taylor was imprisoned, but the fear and insecurity were all too real." See also Huntley, *Jeremy Taylor and the Great Rebellion*, 56.

for him, in a time when many royalist clergy were persecuted, Taylor's next appointment in Wales allowed him to live in relative comfort, and to become close with the Earl of Carbery and his family. This friendship no doubt had significant influence on Taylor, as *Holy Dying* is dedicated to the Earl and was inspired by his wife. Taylor wrote both the texts for *Holy Living* and *Holy Dying* while living in Wales, the former published in 1650 and the latter in 1651. The two are often bound together, which seems to have been Taylor's intention.[17] It was also at this time Taylor preached the funeral sermon for the wife of the Earl of Carbery, which also provides insights into his views on suffering.

Lady Carbery was his friend and patron (along with her husband), so her death affected him personally. Taylor's grief was all the greater as he lost his own wife around the same time, probably in 1650 or 1651, although the exact date of her death is unknown. The pain of these losses is evident in his dedication to Carbery. Themes of personal piety and devotion guided most of his writings over the years although some of his works, such as *Unum Necessarium*, a work on sin and repentance, which was published in 1655, were also theological treatises. All in all, Taylor would go on to publish over forty works in his lifetime, and his collected works occupy fifteen volumes.[18]

Personal Loss

During that year of 1655, Taylor again suffered grief in his family life, losing his two young sons. In a letter to his friend John Evelyn he writes:

> I have passed through a great cloud which hath wetted mee deeper than the skin. It hath please God to send the small poxe and fevers among my children; and I have, since I received your last, buried two sweet, and hopeful boyes; and have now but one sonne left, whom I intend, if it please God, to bring up to London before Easter; and then I hope to wait upon you, and by your sweet conversation and other divertisements, if not to alleviate my sorrows, yet at least to entertain myself and keep me from too intense and actual thinkings of my trouble. . . . But for myself, I bless God I have observed and felt so much mercy in this angry dispensation of God, that I am almost transported,

17. Stranks, *Life and Writings*, 55, 61, 66–67, and 104.

18. Ibid., 109, 142, 145, and 300.

I am sure highly pleased with thinking how infinitely sweet His mercies are when His judgments are so gracious. [19]

Stranks sees in this letter the "real quality of Taylor's religion."[20] These few lines would seem to provide an adequate summary of Taylor's theology regarding grief and suffering. He does not ignore it, but rather views it in a wider confidence, never losing his faith in God's ultimate goodness. We can also see his practical approach. He acknowledges the depth of his grief. He has been drenched and is liable to sink into his grief if left to his own "thinkings" about his troubles. He trusts his friend will be a happy distraction for him, and he seems to know his presence will keep him from falling into greater grief. Although he describes losing his sons as an "angry dispensation of God," he seems ultimately to view God, and even the event of loss itself, as gracious and merciful. His trust in God is so complete that the death of his own sons is evidence of God's mercy. In the end, Taylor knows the way forward through grief is to focus on the mercy of God and the gifts in his life, and he encourages of his readers to this practice in *Holy Dying*.[21]

Bishop in Ireland

Following the death of his children, Taylor moved to London for a time. Then in 1658 he went to Ireland as chaplain to Lord Conway and his family at Portmore. In August of 1660 Taylor was made Bishop of Down and Connor in Ireland, and in 1661 his title was expanded to include the Diocese of Dromore as well. It is worth noting that although a bishopric is certainly an honor and a reward in many ways, Taylor was not entering a simple situation. Ireland had suffered under numerous wars in the mid 1600s. The Articles of Kilkenny that brought the wars to an end also put forth a massive land re-distribution program that resulted in making many Irish landless and forced into poverty. Taylor's diocese also contained numerous Presbyterians who found the mere existence of a bishop anathema. Taylor certainly had his work cut out for him, and on top of being appointed bishop, he was also made Vice-Chancellor of Trinity University in Dublin. As Taylor worked to

19. Heber, *The Whole Works*, lxi-lxii. Throughout this chapter spelling is kept as it is found in the edition from which the quotation of the text is taken.

20. Stranks, *Life and Writings*, 170.

21. Taylor, *Holy Living and Dying*, 173.

establish his authority in his diocese, he had to contend with his own ill health and with many Presbyterians who were in staunch opposition to that authority. The Presbyterians desired to be dealt with as a group, but Taylor persisted in seeing them as individuals gone astray; he was firm in his conviction and would not budge. Some have gone so far as to say Taylor was guilty of persecution, and, given that he treated others as he had been treated during the Civil War, it seems fair to say that he was.[22] Spurr, in fact, describes him as "belligerent" in his intolerance of the Presbyterians who seemed to threaten his authority.[23] It seems Taylor's conviction of the necessity of bishops overrode his tolerance of various denominations, which was expressed in *The Liberty of Prophesying* (which urged toleration of non-established religions). Taylor would not compromise on his belief in the importance and authority of bishops and therefore viewed the Presbyterians as schismatic. Taylor stuck to his principles, and also strongly believed the Presbyterians, who had been responsible for the destruction of the monarchy, were a threat to peace. He refused to recognize the authority of Presbyterian ministers and removed them from livings they held. The Presbyterians tried to fight back, but their efforts at radical change failed when their petition was refused by Parliament in Dublin, and most returned to worshipping quietly in their own in small groups.[24]

Taylor's personal sufferings were further increased in March 1661 when he buried another son, Edward. Despite the challenges and his own ill health, Taylor remained active and committed to his dioceses. He re-built the cathedral at Dromore in 1661, partially funding it himself. Yet his personal distress was further increased by a quarrel with a friend's son over the friend's estate. In the summer of 1667 Taylor became ill and on August 13 he died. Per his request, Taylor was buried in the cathedral at Dromore.[25] Interestingly, it was nearly two centuries (1827) before a marker was placed over Taylor's tomb—perhaps a sign that he was not particularly beloved in his diocese.[26]

During his time as bishop, Taylor faced a great many challenges both personal and professional, and this may have spurred him to write

22. Stranks, 172, 184, 190, 216, 222, 224, 232, 240–41, and 245.

23. Spurr.

24. Stranks, 72–73, 241–42, and 249.

25. Ibid., 244–46 and 270–73.

26. Williamson, *Jeremy Taylor*, 174.

requesting a different diocese or removal from the burden of his authority. In fact, Taylor went so far as to write, "It were better for me to be a poor curate in a village church than a bishop over such intolerable people."[27] Those with authority, however, had objected to the wideness and inclusiveness of his views in *The Liberty of Prophesying* and *Unum Necessarium* (a call to repentance that contained views on original sin that some considered semi-Pelagian because Taylor does not consider humanity by nature sinful). Taylor believed humanity shares in Adam's loss (i.e., humans are mortal and fallible), but humanity does not inherently share Adam's guilt. Taylor believed "God's grace must be persuasive in character and universal in its scope" and people have the ability to make moral choices of lasting significance. This fits with his response to suffering, the process is meant to be one of edification and piety, by our own effort and God's persuasive grace. The authorities who objected to his views and universalist tendencies in *Unum Necessarium* had prevented him from receiving an English bishopric initially, and continued to do so.[28]

That is the context and the outline of the life of Jeremy Taylor. There are notable similarities between Taylor and Gregory. Both were bishops in challenging times, skilled writers, and committed to their flocks who also suffered greatly in their personal lives. It is perhaps no accident the combination of events and traits leads both men to offer sound and sage advice to those who suffer. Taylor's own advice on this front is laid out predominately in his works, *Holy Living* and *Holy Dying*, which will now be examined.

THEOLOGY OF SUFFERING IN THE WRITINGS OF TAYLOR

Like C. S. Lewis, Taylor is perhaps better known as a writer than as a theologian. Samuel Taylor Coleridge thought so. He described Taylor with Shakespeare as two whose "virtue is all in all" and called him "a poet everywhere except in verse."[29] Yet even if his fame is as a writer

---

27. Ibid., 139. See also Stranks, *Life and Writings*, 259.

28. Stranks, *Life and Writings*, 149–151, 215–16, and 259; Greer, *A Christian Hope*, 213. See also Spurr.

29. Brinkley, *Coleridge on the Seventeenth Century*, 258 and 261.

(particularly of devotional material), he is very much a theologian, and he is a theologian who knew the realities of grief firsthand.

There are glimpses in his writings of Taylor's own personal experience of grief as a husband and a father. We might in fact wish for a further window into his own thoughts and theological reflections on his personal experiences of grief. Taylor, however, rarely writes of his personal experiences within his published works, and there are only small glimpses in his letters. There do not seem to be any sermons from the funerals of his own family. This is not entirely surprising, given that neither the burial rite in the 1559 nor the 1662 Book of Common Prayer provides for a sermon in the liturgy. This fact seems to be a reflection of the growing secularization of death in the sixteenth and seventeenth century. Because Protestants no longer held to the doctrine of purgatory, funerals were no longer about doing something for the dead; they were for the living. As Gittings notes, "Protestants of all persuasions agreed that the fate of the soul was sealed at death. The actions of the living could not affect the dead. . . . The logical outcome of this theological stance was that funerals, having ceased to have any spiritual function for the dead, should be merely secular social events surrounding the practical task of disposing of a corpse." This is a rather strong statement, and perhaps it goes a bit far. Funeral rites, as religious rituals, were not done away with in the sixteenth and seventeenth centuries, but perhaps the desire for greater simplicity may have prevailed and may account for the brevity of the burial service in the 1552 *Book of Common Prayer*. The service only consists of prayers and a single reading, and by the mid-seventeenth century an act of Parliament put the focus in burial on civil honors and did not require the presence of a minister. It is true that in the seventeenth century there was a growing custom of adding a sermon (for an additional fee) to the service, particularly if the deceased was a notable individual, and this would explain the existence of Taylor's sermons at the funerals of other bishops and Lady Carbery.[30] These were exceptions to traditional burials, though, so it is not surprising that no sermons exist from the funerals of Taylor's own family. It is, of course, possible he did preach at those services, but the sermons were not preserved. Thankfully, the works that have been preserved do offer a window into Taylor's thinking and perspective.

30. Gittings "Sacred and Secular" 147, 153, and 158.

Holy Living and Holy Dying: An Overview

Taylor's two works, *Holy Living* and *Holy Dying* were widely read in subsequent generations, and by 1700 twenty authorized editions had been published.[31] These works, *Holy Dying* particularly, are viewed by Nancy Lee Beaty as a climax of the *ars morendi*, a medieval tradition of devotional manuals to instruct Christians on how to die well. Beaty sees *Holy Dying* as having at its core "the old conduct-book, in which a sympathetic pastor guides Everyman to heaven through the straits of death by directing his behavior and ministering to his piety with the voice of authority."[32] Taylor's two works are almost identical in style. They are divided into chapters and then into sections, with each chapter closing with prayers to help a person act on the aforementioned instruction. The works are highly regarded. H. R. McAdoo praises them thus: "It is part of the excellence of Taylor that he succeeds in making a stoutly uncompromising Christianity both attractive and reasonable to men."[33] The works are manuals meant to be used by the laity.[34] Given Taylor's two works together run over five hundred pages, their readers would need to be thoroughly literate and have a great deal of discretionary time, so the manuals were likely intended only for the upper classes. Taylor is a teacher who has high expectations of his students. As Beaty notes, Taylor's readers must "accept Anglican theology and ecclesiastical polity" and also have "a measure of intellectual ability and cultural training which one cannot demand of the bona fide Everyman."[35] Taylor expects an audience of like-minded Anglicans who value the nexus of Scripture, ecclesiastical tradition (and experience) and human reason.[36]

The likelihood of the upper class nature of the intended audience seems to be further supported by the dedication of both works to

31. Williamson, *Jeremy Taylor*, 63.

32. Beaty, *Craft of Dying*, ix and 197.

33. McAdoo, *The Structure of Caroline Moral Theology*, 154.

34. Manuals like *Holy Living and Holy Dying* were common and popular at the time. Taylor's is perhaps the most famous. See Gittings, "Sacred and Secular," 156 and Ralph Houlbrooke, "The Age of Decency" in *Death in England*, 178.

35. Beaty, *Craft of Dying*, 221.

36. These are traditional elements of Anglicanism, with roots at least as old as the works of Richard Hooker (1533–1600), and are certainly a part of the writings of the Caroline Divines. See Beaty, *Craft of Dying*, 201. On Hooker see *Lesser Feasts and Fasts*, 426.

Richard Lord Vaughan, Earl of Carbery. Each dedication is instructive, but it is the dedication to *Holy Dying* that is most notable, for it is written after the death of the Earl's wife and after the death of Taylor's own wife.[37] It is, perhaps, the best way to begin a discussion of these works. In the dedication Taylor writes:

> My Lord, both your Lordship and myself have lately seen and felt such sorrows of death, and such sad departure of dearest friends, that it is more than high time we should think ourselves nearly concerned in the accidents. Death hath come so near to you, as to fetch a portion from your very heart; and now you cannot choose but dig your own grave, and place your coffin in your eye, when the angel hath dressed your scene of sorrow and meditation with so particular and so near an object: and therefore, as it is my duty, I am come to minister to your pious thoughts, and to direct your sorrows, that they may turn into virtues and advantages.[38]

Here it is possible to see the centerpiece (and a succinct summary) of Taylor's theology: his conviction that sorrows can be turned into "virtues and advantages." Taylor hopes people at all stages of life (the younger, the better) will make use of his manual so as to prepare themselves for a holy death. Taylor disdains the Roman practice of deathbed repentance, and believes on our deathbed we can only practice what we have already learned; therefore, our learning should begin early, an exhortation consistent with Taylor's somewhat Pelagian view of grace. Taylor believes a person can work toward salvation, and he strives to lay out in his works the recipes for a holy life and a holy death.[39]

It is through these recipes that we can come to understand Taylor's theology of suffering and grief. First, Taylor asserts that we are to be patient in suffering and "prepared to suffer affliction for the cause of God" because to do so is to be a person of faith. We are also to live with an awareness of the brevity of our earthly life and with awareness that our eternal life depends on how we live. Taylor does seem to set a high bar for his readers, yet he offers them specific instruction in how to live so they are not greatly challenged by misfortune. Taylor instructs, "Virtues and discourses are, like friends, necessary in all fortunes; but

37. Taylor, *Holy Living and Dying,* 292.
38. Ibid., 292–93.
39. Ibid., 293.

those are the best, which are friends in sadness, and support us in our sorrows and sad accidents: and in this sense, no man that is virtuous can be friendless; nor hath any man reason to complain of the Divine providence, or accuse the public disorder of things, or his own infelicity, since God hath appointed one remedy for all the evils in the world, and that is a contented spirit . . . ." Like Nicholas Wolterstorff, Taylor recognizes that grief comes when reality does not meet our hopes and expectations, those moments where there is "disagreeing between the object and the appetite." The edification that Taylor advocates is a reorientation of our expectations.[40]

Taylor establishes his advice under three instruments of "Holy Living: Care of Time," "Purity of Intention," and "Practice of the Presence of God."[41] Because of his emphasis that even the practice of holy dying should be an act of holy living, it is possible to see Taylor's instruments at work in both texts. The themes of these instruments: time (both earthly and eschatological), attitude and practice can, therefore, provide a structure for gaining a better understanding of Taylor's texts and the recipes within them. These themes fit within the broader theological themes (as they relate to suffering) I will examine: humanity, sin and evil; God's providence; salvation; Christ; and eternal life.

Humanity, Sin, and Evil

Taylor's theology regarding suffering, and his general guidance for living, can be summed up in the oft-quoted passage from the Gospel of Matthew about the lilies of the field, which Taylor himself quotes in the midst of his discourse on contentment.[42] In Matthew, Christ tells his followers to, "Consider the lilies of the field, how they grow; they neither toil nor spin, yet I tell you, even Solomon in all his glory was not clothed like one of these" and admonishes followers not to worry, but to "strive first for the kingdom of God and his righteousness, and all these things will be given to you as well. So do not worry about tomorrow, for tomorrow will bring worries of its own. Today's trouble is enough for today."[43] Taylor wants his readers to put their stock in their faith, in their religion, and not in flimsy

40. Ibid., xii–xiii, 3, and 91.
41. Ibid., iii.
42. Ibid., 114–15.
43. Matthew 6:28–29, 33–34.

or temporal things. If readers first seek the kingdom, then the more material matters of life will take care of themselves.

Practice of an Awareness of Death

An important element of the practice of holy living is to live with an awareness of death. Taylor begins *Holy Dying* by making his reader sit firmly with the reality of death, and this focus on death represents a change from previous literary practices. As Stranks describes it, "The refusal to see death as a macabre monster, a black figure hurling poisoned darts, or as the majestic subduer of tyrants and kings, was a breakaway from a literary convention which had been observed by too many and lasted too long."[44] Taylor reminds his readers that death cannot be separated from life. The passing of the day is a death, and the changes in the human body as it ages are reminders of death. "Thus nature calls us to meditate of death by those things which are the instruments of acting it; and God, by all the variety of his providence, makes us see death every where, in all variety of circumstances, and dressed up for all the fancies, and the expectation of every single person." Taylor does not let his reader forget death is everywhere. He knows many happy moments are "soured by some sad instance of a dying friend"—death is not something from which we can escape. This can be a disquieting fact to people whose will to live is strong. It does not sit easily with many to be reminded our fate is that of worms and serpents, a fate of death and decay, at least where our physical body is concerned.[45] Taylor does not trivialize death or make it mundane. He is, rather, reminding his readers that death is part of life—whether we think of it or not, it is a part of our daily existence. Perhaps Taylor's views on the fall and original sin have some bearing here as well. Since death is the consequence of the fall and awaits all, and since death is not to be hated or feared, Taylor provides a matter-of-fact view of death.[46] As noted earlier, Taylor believed humanity shares "Adam's loss, but not his guilt."[47] For Taylor death can even become positive because it also means an end to suffering, and an awareness of it can help us to transform our lives.

44. Stranks, *Life and Writings*, 112.
45. Taylor, *Holy Living and Dying*, 301–5.
46. Hughes, *The Piety of Jeremy Taylor*, 31.
47. Stranks, *Life and Writings*, 150.

Although Taylor spends much time in *Holy Dying* dwelling on the challenges and miseries of life, he does not leave his reader to wallow there. He invites his readers to move from that "place of sorrows and tears, of great evils and a constant calamity." Of course, Taylor knows it is physically impossible to avoid the evils of the world, so he advocates this movement in a metaphorical sense. Suffering cannot be kept at bay, but we can at least reframe our minds, and change how we think about suffering and death to, metaphorically at least, remove ourselves from the terrible realities of the human condition. This transformation of approach does not happen overnight. It is a lifelong endeavor that requires fervent prayer seeking divine aid and guidance, so that we may be able to be patient in the face of suffering and also strong enough to resist the devil's temptations. We must continually examine our soul to prevent sin and to repent of sins committed. There is, however, a significant caution: preparation to die well should not be a selfish act concerned only with our own fate. We must also practice charity because "Charity is the channel through which God passes all his mercy upon mankind." As we prepare for death, we must think not only of our own wellbeing, but that of others as well.[48]

Miseries of the World

The difficulty in reading Taylor is that while most of the time he has an optimistic or at least a hopeful bent, there are moments when he makes statements that seem very dark indeed. He says, for example, "As our life is very short, so it is very miserable; and therefore it is well it should be short," and later in the same section, "The prosperity of this world is so infinitely soured with the overflowing of evils, that he is counted the most happy who hath the fewest; all conditions being evil and miserable they are only distinguished by the number of the calamities." Statements such as these seem devoid of hope. They are firmly grounded in the miseries of the world and indicate Taylor's strong awareness of the depths of human suffering in the world. Yet suffering does not have the last word, at least for Taylor and his fellow Christians. Suffering is not limitless or insurmountable; there is a limit, a divine limit that puts an end to it once and for all. That limit is death. As Taylor writes, "God is

48. Taylor, *Holy Living and Dying*, 330, 335, and 343.

pleased to put an end to all these troubles and to let them sit down in a natural period, which, if we please, may be to us the beginning of a better life." In order to experience the end of suffering, we must make the choice to seek the kingdom of God rather than allow ourselves to be in love with the thorns of earthly life. There does seem to be a possibility for the experience of suffering to endure, at least for those who choose the thorns over the kingdom, but Taylor does not allow himself to be overwhelmed by his own suffering or that which he has witnessed, and he wishes the same strength for his readers. His readers are called to remember that suffering and grief is temporary, whereas God, the source of all that is good, is everlasting. This reality can provide hope and comfort in the midst of suffering, because as Taylor notes, "no evil is immortal."[49]

Sin

Taylor does not, however, wish for his readers to be comfortable with the miseries of the world. Taylor reminds his readers that life is not meant to be easy—nowhere is humanity promised a life of ease, and so we should not expect it.[50] As a Christian who takes seriously the consequences of the fall and the reality of sin in the world, we should rather be surprised by carefree moments than vice versa. Taylor does see a benefit in considering all the miseries of the world: it serves "to sweeten the bitter cup of death." Although it may seem an odd conclusion, there is hope in this statement. For Christians who believe in eternal life, Taylor urges his readers, death is not such a terrible thing after all. Death is positive, because it brings to an end our suffering and grief, and marks a transition to a heavenly life, an eternal life with God. As Taylor writes, "Death is that harbour, whither God hath designed everyone, there he many find rest from the troubles of the world." Taylor cautions, however, that despite the fact death is positive, we should never seek death or suffering out since to do so would be to reject the blessed gifts of God. Taylor, in significant contrast to how Gregory lived, does not even advocate much use of ascetic practices such as fasting: "All fasting is to

49. Ibid., 111, 322, 326, 328, and 329.

50. Ibid., 328. As noted above, Taylor does not believe humanity to be inherently sinful, but that does not mean he denies the human capacity for sin. That capacity is quite real, and Taylor's calls for the need for repentance in *Holy Dying* is evidence of that.

be used with prudence and charity: for there is no end to which fasting serves but may be obtained by other instruments." In fact, Taylor reminds his readers that Christians are to take care of their bodies "that we may the better exercise the labours of virtue." Additionally, we are not exercising the virtue of patience if we seek death; to be patient we must be "content to live." We are not to seek suffering, grief or death; they will come, and when they do, they are to be seen as opportunities for spiritual growth.[51]

Practice of Living a Holy Life

Taylor's understanding of the value of sickness and suffering has practical implications, for it is meant to help us *live* a more holy life. Taylor believed sickness and suffering could help "to keep sin from our souls or to drive it thence." Taylor saw suffering, particularly bodily suffering, as a way to cleanse us from sin, and for him the emphasis is on the edification that may result from the cleansing. Taylor writes that an individual should be resolved that sickness "may serve the ends of the spirit, and be a messenger of spiritual life, an instrument of reducing [one] to more religious and sober courses." Sickness, then, can be seen as a tool, a method for transformation in our lives. It is to prompt a person to "set his house in order," make a will, engage in acts of charity, seek forgiveness of those he has wronged, and give thanks for his blessings. These acts, and indeed the whole process of living a holy life, are not meant to be solitary; Taylor encourages his readers to seek the guidance and assistance of a minister. The minister can begin by hearing confession and setting one on the road of repentance and spiritual recovery. In addition to a minister, our family and friends can also assist us with the spiritual task at hand. Part of this task would be to affirm the faith, that all is in God's hands, and the actions required of a Christian who desires to die well: prayer, repentance, conversion to new life. Family and friends are also specifically encouraged by Taylor to pray for the one who suffers.[52]

---

51. Ibid., 191, 327–8, 383, and 409.
52. Ibid., 259, 441, 452–6, 462, and 465.

Practice of Joy and Repentance in the Midst of Grief

As noted above in his letter to a friend, in facing the death of his own children, Taylor puts great value on the children still living. Taylor finds comfort and joy in the great mercies of God, and he believes doing so was an important part of the Christian response to grief. In writing to his friend John Evelyn upon hearing of the death of Evelyn's two sons, Taylor begins by acknowledging the depth of a father's grief, "the causes of my real sadnesse in your losse are so just and so reasonable, that I can no otherwise comfort you but by telling you that you have very great cause to mourne." Yet in typical Taylor fashion, he does not leave it there. He goes on to tell Evelyn to find comfort in the knowledge that his boys are now "two bright starres" in heaven, and to encourage Evelyn to "master" his grief because that is the mark of a true Christian. We do not wallow; we move forward with great faith. Importantly, Taylor does not discount the reality or the severity of a parent's (or any loved one's) grief, but he also does not see it as an excuse for laziness regarding our own spiritual lives. Rather, he sees mourning as a test of character. Taylor hopes to visit Evelyn the following week that he may be a witness to Evelyn's "hristian courage and bravery."[53] For Taylor the challenge of suffering and grief is one to be met with our full strength of character. It is an opportunity, too, for repentance and spiritual growth. As Taylor writes in the preface to his funeral sermon for Lady Carbery, "My lord, I pray God this heap of sorrow may swell your piety till it breaks into the greatest joys of God and of religion: and remember when you pay a tear upon the grave, or to the memory of your lady (that dear and most excellent soul) that you pay two more: one of repentance for those things that may have caused this breach; and another of joy for the mercies of God to your dear departed saint, that He hath taken her into a place where she can weep no more."[54]

This prayer is significant because it shows Taylor's belief not only that suffering is an instrument of character growth, but it is a way to reach the greatest joys. Because grief can inspire great piety, because it can put our focus properly on heavenly things, it can even be considered a necessary and important part of the Christian experience. For Taylor, as for Gregory and Julian, there is no question as to whether or

53. Heber, *The Whole Works*, lxxv–lxxvi.
54. Heber, *The Whole Works*, 427.

not we will experience grief in the course of our lives. The question is how we respond. For Taylor, as for Gregory and Julian, our response to the reality of grief must be to seize it as an opportunity for spiritual growth, to allow the experience of grief to teach us the shortness of life, and the value of the gift of having faith in God's goodness and mercy. If we can respond in this way to experiences of grief, then we can grow more Christ-like.

One of the strengths of *Holy Living* (and many other of Taylor's works), and probably a large part of his wide appeal, is he not only engages in theological discourse, he also offers practical guidance for those in need and those who wish to deepen their faith. *Holy Living* concludes with pages upon pages of petitions, prayers of thanksgiving, and sentences from Scripture. Not surprisingly, many of the prayers echo the psalms. Most are designed for use by someone who is ill or in distress. Like the rest of Taylor's writings, the prayers are eloquent (and often long). They are also emblematic of Taylor's theology, with both the call to repentance and the call to remember God's mercy. There is an acknowledgment of the severity of affliction and a reminder that all is in God's hands and will be brought to good.[55]

It would certainly be possible to argue Taylor has a negative view of the human condition. He focuses on the miseries of the world, believes humanity lives in a fallen world, and he knows all have the capacity for sin (although he does not believe in a literal inheritance of sin from Adam). If this were all there were to Taylor's views on humanity and suffering, he could certainly be considered a pessimist. For Taylor, however, there is also great cause for joy in life. While we are to accept the reality of sin, suffering, and death in the world, an awareness and experience of these can lead to transformation of life. As for Gregory, the experience of suffering can be a catalyst for reflection and repentance. For Taylor, the important realization is the call to a lifelong practice of reflection and repentance. We are to strive always to live a more holy life. The resources of our faith will enable us to cope with the challenges of life, and in the midst of suffering we can always have trust in the mercy and guidance of God.

---

55. Taylor, *Holy Living and Dying*, 252–89.

Providence of God

In addition to offering inspiration, Taylor directs his readers to his understanding of God's providence. We are to have patience and hope in the midst of suffering, not only because there are so many valiant examples to follow, but also because God has promised "to be with us in our trouble, and to be with us in our prayers, and to be with us in our hope and confidence." We are also to have hope because all is in God's hands: "God having in this world placed us in a sea, and troubled the sea with a continual storm, hath appointed the church for a ship, and religion to be the stern; but there is no haven or port but death." There is, of course, great hope to be found in the knowledge we are in God's hands, and again it is a balanced hope. It is a hope for the future, for eternity, and also a hope for our earthly lives, for the here and now. There is also a potentially troubling note here. There is a strong providential, paternal note in Taylor's theology, a strong belief that God allows or even causes bad things to happen because they serve his good purposes somehow. As Taylor writes, "Remember that thou art a man and a Christian: as the covenant of nature hath made it necessary, so the covenant of grace hath made it to be chosen by thee, to be a suffering person: either you must renounce your religion, or submit to the impositions of God and thy portion of sufferings." Some may object to the idea that God is the source of our suffering, and yet, like Julian, Taylor finds hope behind that statement. Taylor's conviction of God's goodness and guidance is strong. He admonishes his readers, "Never say I can do no more, I cannot endure this; for God would not have sent it if he had not known thee strong enough to abide it." In this view, God does send suffering, but he does so with full knowledge of what we can bear. God may be the cause of the storm, but we can also trust that God is guiding us to a safe harbor. Taylor's theology is expressive of Psalm 139, which emphasizes that there is nowhere we can go to get away from God. Early in *Holy Living*, Taylor admonishes his readers to remember this Psalm and its message often. His readers are to remember that no matter where we are, we are in God's hands. We are to be content in that knowledge.[56]

---

56. Ibid., 23, 364–65, 383. See also p. 357 where he discusses the valiance of women and children in the midst of suffering. Also discussed later.

Attitude of Freedom from Jealousy

The challenge in the contentment Taylor advocates is to accept it fully, without jealousy. There is a great temptation to grieve over our life in comparison to another's. Taylor reminds his readers "it is a huge folly rather to grieve for the good of others than to rejoice for that good which God hath given us of our own. And yet there is no wise or good man that would change persons or conditions entirely with any man in the world." Taylor believes those who would desire to change places would only desire that which is good in another's life and are therefore seeking after a fantasy that cannot be. What is possible is to find contentment in our own lives.[57] Here is his strong paternalistic view. All is in God's hands, and God is the source of our suffering. The benefit of this view is it can comfort. If God is merciful, good and just, and is responsible for ours suffering, then there can be no doubt that it leads to some good end. That can, however, be a bitter pill to swallow for one in the midst of terrible grief. In the face of a tragic national or deep personal loss, it can be difficult to understand how the death of thousands in a single day or the death of a young child can possibly serve the benevolent purposes of God. From that place of heart-wrenching loss, God can seem cruel. What kind of God takes children before they have really begun to live? What kind of God allows plagues and civil wars? In the face of those losses, God may seem distant and spiteful. Taylor, however, like Gregory, understands God as fully in charge of the world; perhaps an analogous image would be that of an unyielding schoolmaster who instructs pupils for their benefit. All that happens comes from God and is ultimately for good.

In contentment free from jealousy, we are to be content with what we have been given, even if it includes suffering. Taylor also reminds his readers that to be jealous is to covet the things of this earthly world, and a Christian's mind is to be ultimately focused on heavenly things, on that place where there is no suffering. To be free from jealousy is not to be without desire, but it does mean a lack of attachment to earthly things.

57. Ibid., 97–98.

Attitude of Hope

In addition to being free from jealousy, Taylor's Christian should be hopeful. Hope is a willingness to believe even when all evidence seems to the contrary. The essence of Christian hope is captured in the following statement of Taylor's: "To rejoice in the midst of a misfortune or seeming sadness, knowing that this may work for good, and will, if we be not wanting to our souls. This is a direct act of hope, to look through the cloud, and look for a beam of the light from God . . ." Our sorrows can be moderated by the process of edification and if we keeps our hope grounded in God—not in money or friends or other worldly satisfactions. We are not to expect fulfillment from that which is temporal, but rather we are to expect it from God. Our hope is also to be moderated by our "state, person, and condition." We are not to hope for extravagance. For instance, if we are farmers our hope is for a good harvest, not for "a rich kingdom, or a victorious army." Hope is also to be sustained. Hope is not fleeting or temporary. It may not seem an easy virtue to maintain, particularly in the face of challenges or loss, but Taylor encourages Christians to keep their hope by holding fast to what he believes are God's promises, as well as remembering past experiences of blessing and "divine favours." Taylor seems to argue that we can have faith because blessings have come before, they will again. Past experiences of God's goodness and mercy are proof God is good and merciful, and will continue to be so. They are foretastes of what is to come, and we can trust more will come. Even in times of doubt and despair, we have a strong record on which to rely for strength and comfort. Taylor is not advocating a simple optimism that views the world through rose-colored glasses. Taylor urges his reader to be grounded in faith, to trust in God and in God's goodness. Taylor firmly believes "God hath obliged himself by promise that we shall have the good of everything we desire; for even losses and denials work for the good of them that fear God."[58] Like Julian, Taylor advocates a belief that God works all things toward good. This does not mean all is good, but all of life—its trials and joys— is being brought to a good end by God. Like Julian, Taylor's theology acknowledges the reality of suffering, but also contains the conviction that the ultimate end of our life is good because our end is in God.

58. Ibid., 168–69, 171, and 173.

Like Gregory and Julian, Taylor has a strong view of God's providence. Taylor believes God is good and merciful. Taylor sees God's mercies and gifts of blessings present everywhere, even in midst of times of grief or sadness. Even times of suffering or loss are not devoid of God's goodness. Taylor trusts so completely in God's goodness that even those things that might seem negative (such as the loss of a child) are still to be counted as a good. Taylor believes God does all things for good, even those things that might not seem so from the human perspective. The strength of trust Taylor has in God's providence leads to an attitude of hope and to freedom from jealousy. Because all is in God's hands working for good, we can always have hope and we need not be jealous of anyone else. We can, therefore, trust in God and devote ourselves to living a holy life.

Salvation

Earthly Time

Taylor reminds his readers of the importance of living in the present moment, for truly that is all that is certain: "Enjoy the blessings of this day, if God sends them, and the evils of it bear patiently and sweetly; for this day only is ours: we are dead to yesterday, and we are not yet born to the morrow." Taylor laments those who are constantly wishing to be in a different state than where they are—those who are young wishing to be older and vice versa. Without losing our focus on the hereafter and its reminder of the fragility of life and the importance of salvation, we are to live in the present moment in such a way as to deepen our relationship with God. Taylor's goal, after all, in *Holy Living* (and most of his works) is to help Christians lead more faithful lives. Religion, Taylor argues, is the best remedy against the evils of life. It is the sanctuary that will keep our soul from shipwreck, although, he notes, it does not protect us from the storms of life.[59]

59. Ibid., 101 and 104.

Attitudes of Contentment and Patience

For Taylor, we are also not to be seeking after a different type of life; instead we are to be content with our station. As he writes, "Here, therefore, is the wisdom of the contented man, to let God choose for him . . ." There is a challenge here to choose God's will rather than seek our own will and desires for our destiny. It does raise the question of how much of a role an individual has in the future and whether or not submission is always the right course of action in the face of challenge or disappointment. These are worthwhile questions, which will be dealt with more later. For now, it is worth considering Taylor's compelling argument for the value of an even countenance that accepts life as it is. As Taylor notes, "But no man can be happy that hath great hopes and great fears of things without, and events depending on other men, or upon the chances of fortune." As Christians, our hopes and fears should be with God. For Taylor, seeking after God and seeking to follow Christ by submitting our will to God is how we develop a character of contentment.[60]

With his advocacy of patience and contentment it could seem Taylor does not wish Christians to be active and engaged. Yet there are times Taylor does advocate human agency and engagement. In a letter to Lady Annabella Howe, who expressed concern over the relationship between reason and faith, he writes: "Madam, if you dare trust your reason, you may proceed to action; if you dare not, what will you be guided by?"[61] Taylor does not mean, therefore, for humans to be automatons or merely passive beings. In another letter he encourages the recipient, who is facing difficulty, "I am confident in imitation of your Great Master you will bring good out of evil."[62] Taylor does allow for a degree of human agency. Yet the question remains, to what extent is this human agency to be marshaled to fight against suffering in addition to being used in support of our own piety and virtue? Taylor did not support the human agency that toppled the monarchy and the hierarchical governance of the Church of England, but he did support agency within the bounds of tradition, as evidenced by his manuals and his encouragement of people to improve their own spiritual lives. It is also important to remember Taylor's focus is not on the political upheavals

60. Ibid., 93–4.
61. Jeremy Taylor to Lady Annabella Howe, Letter. 29 August 1657.
62. Jeremy Taylor, Letter. 29 August 1657.

of his day, but rather on the individual piety of his readers who are living in the midst of those upheavals.

Quality of Time

In Taylor's estimation, the measure of our life is not in length but in quality. Taylor laments if people "spend in waste what God hath given us in plenty, when we sacrifice our youth to folly, our manhood to lust and rage, our old age to covetousness and irreligion, not beginning to live till we are to die . . . then we make our lives short."[63] What Taylor seeks is to help us begin to live, to fully live, long before our deaths. Taylor contends that it often takes a brush with death, an awareness of our own mortality, to inspire us to take stock of our lives and make changes. In pushing us to accept the reality of death, Taylor begins the process of transformation, changing our perspectives and awareness. In more Christian terms, Taylor calls us to repent of our old ways and convert to a new mode of living, one which, as noted above, is daily aware of the reality of death.

A Lifetime of Preparation

A consistent theme in Taylor's writing is the importance of living a holy life, with emphasis on *life*. We are not to live a holy week or a holy year; our efforts are to be life long, patterning our whole life in light of the reality of death. As he writes in his funeral sermon for Lady Carbery, "Go home and think to die, and what you would choose to be doing when you die, that do daily."[64] In fact, McAdoo believes Taylor's whole moral theology can be summed up in the brief sentence: "Be wise and begin betimes [before it is too late]."[65] Beaty also identifies the core of Taylor's argument as equating holy dying with "the very nature of Christian life itself." As Beaty further reflects, "The equation of 'life in Christ' with 'the Way of the Cross' is of course fundamentally Pauline; but surely no devotional writer before Taylor had developed St. Paul's theme with anything approaching the complexity of understanding, still less artistic

63. Taylor, *Holy Living and Dying*, 316.
64. Heber, *The Whole Works*, 437.
65. McAdoo, *The Structure of Caroline*, 55.

imagery that we find here." Beaty sees Taylor as managing to maintain the essence of medieval Christianity while incorporating the changes of the Renaissance and Reformation without letting go of the pastoral concern at the heart of his works.[66] This approach is perhaps a large part of what makes Taylor "one of the most influential of the 'Caroline Divines.'"[67] Seeking Christ and a deeper relationship with him is central to the Christian tradition. What is notable about Taylor then, is that he offers a distinctive, Anglican approach to that quest, and a manual for how to live out a holy life framed with an emphasis on death. According to Taylor, we are to live each day as if it were our last. As *Holy Dying* concludes: "It remains, that we who are alive should so live, and by the actions of religion attend the coming of the day of the Lord, that we neither be surprised nor leave our duties imperfect, nor our sins uncancelled, nor our persons unreconciled, nor God unappeased; but that, when we descend to our graves, we may rest in the bosom of the Lord, till the mansions be prepared where we shall sing and feast eternally."[68] A focus on death is to inspire us to die well, not only literally, but also figuratively. Beaty sees in Taylor's text "the relationship between holy dying and holy living [are kept] in such delicate suspension that the reader somehow finds himself not only well prepared for dying literally when the time comes, but freshly motivated to die figuratively in a new Christ-centered life."[69] It is the central theme of Taylor's work that preparation for death should inspire us to live differently, to live a life that is inspired by the promise of salvation offered in Christ.[70]

Given that Taylor's emphasis is on how we live our whole life, he is particularly critical of the idea that a simple, brief act of repentance on our deathbed is sufficient. He considers it an act of vanity. We are to spend our lives striving to be Christian, striving to live as God intended. The practice of repentance and amendment of life is to be a daily one, not a once in a lifetime event. As Taylor states, "resolving to repent upon our death-bed is the greatest mockery of God in all the world, and the most perfect contradictory of all his excellent designs of mercy

66. Beaty, *Craft of Dying*, 216.

67. *Lesser Feasts and Fasts*, 332.

68. Taylor, *Holy Living and Dying*, 525.

69. Beaty, *Craft of Dying*, 241.

70. Taylor, *Holy Living and Dying*, 421–23.

and holiness."[71] Stranks notes that, "*Holy Living* contains one of the first attacks Taylor made upon the idea that a death-bed repentance is sufficient to save a man who has consistently disobeyed God throughout his life. This was a crusade that he never gave up."[72] Additionally, Williamson sees *Holy Dying* as an "anti-Catholic tract" in its denial of the Catholic practices of extreme unction and absolution of the dead.[73] Our commitment to God, to a faithful life, is to be lifelong. It is not as genuine if it is only inspired at the last minute by fear of death or damnation. The higher calling is to spend our whole *life* seeking to be more faithful.

Like Gregory, Taylor believed our actions not only have immediate consequences, they also have eternal consequences. How one lives out one's *whole* life matters. We are to respond to the challenges of grief and suffering with hope, with faith and with perseverance. We are not to despair or wither with grief. We are to be strong—always. What is notable about Taylor is his dislike of deathbed repentance. He did not believe we could make up for a sinful life in a last-minute act of contrition. Taylor believed we are to live a holy life, always striving to be more Christ-like, because our salvation depends on it.

Christ: Patient Endurance as a Response to Christ's Suffering

We are also called to be patient in the face of sickness and suffering. Interestingly, as inspiration for this patience, Taylor writes of the patience of children in illness: "For there is no sickness so great but children endure it, and have natural strengths to bear them out quite through the calamity, what period soever nature hath alloted it. Indeed they make no reflections upon their sufferings, and complain of sickness with an uneasy sigh or a natural grown, but consider not what the sorrows of sickness mean; and so bear it by a direct sufferance, and as a pillar bears the weight of a roof. But then why cannot we bear it so too?"[74]

We are not to complain in the midst of suffering because there is no doubt "you, or I, or some man wiser and many a woman weaker than us both, or the very children, have endured worse evil than this

71. Ibid., 292 and 424.

72. Stranks, *The Life and Writings*, 106.

73. Williamson, *Jeremy Taylor*, 69.

74. Taylor, *Holy Living and Dying*, 356.

that is upon thee now."[75] Women and children, then, are examples of strength in the midst of pain and suffering. This is a significant statement in an era when women and children were often relegated to the background. It is likely a momentary glimpse into Taylor's personal life. It would seem likely he had even witnessed in his own family, and in his parishes, fortitude and courage exhibited by women and children in the face of illness. Here, we could see the admiration of a husband, father and priest who had so recently watched people dear to him struggle valiantly for their lives.

The act of enduring has a strong place in the Christian tradition as a response to suffering. The example of women and children is, of course, coupled with the preeminent example of enduring suffering: Christ on the cross. As it is for Julian and so many others, the remembrance of Christ's sufferings on the cross is seen by Taylor as valuable in the midst of pain. Taylor's understanding of the crucifixion finds comfort in the knowledge that our own sufferings are not as great as Christ's.[76] Just as he reminds his readers that there are women and children who suffer more, he reminds them of the depth of Christ's suffering. This may seem of little comfort, but we can see in it an effort to provide his readers with a broader perspective, a reminder that things are perhaps not as terrible as they might seem. Our sufferings are not as terrible as what Christ endured, and in our own suffering we come into a greater understanding of and a deeper relationship with Christ. Suffering offers a positive opportunity, then, to enter more fully into union with Christ, a theme of much of Christian theology and spirituality, particularly that of mystics like Julian of Norwich, with deeper roots in Christian neo-Platonism. Christians are meant to seek fullness, unity, even if it is beyond our reach on earth. This seeking of union is foundational to Christian theology, and it is strongly evident in Caroline theology as well. According to Edmund Newey, for the Caroline Divines "participative union with the Creator God [is] the origin and the end of all created human being[s]."[77] This is most evident in Taylor's sermon *Via Intelligentiae*, which was preached in 1662.[78] Taylor writes:

75. Ibid., 357.

76. Ibid., 366.

77. Newey. "The Form of Reason," 4.

78. Ibid., 15–18; Heber, *The Whole Writings*, 363–391.

> For when our reason is raised up by the Spirit of Christ it is turned quickly into experience; when our faith relies upon the principles of Christ, it is changed into vision; and so long as we know God only in the ways of man by contentious learning by arguing and dispute we see nothing but the shadow of Him and in that shadow we meet with many dark appearances little certainty and much conjecture but when we know Him . . . with the eyes of holiness and the intuition of gracious experiences with a quiet spirit and the peace of enjoyment then we shall hear what we never heard and see what our eyes never saw then the mysteries of godliness shall be opened unto us and clear as the windows of the morning and this is rarely well expressed by the apostle, 'If we stand up from the dead and awake from sleep then Christ shall give us light.'[79]

A fuller understanding of God and a deeper life of faith happen through learning, but only when that learning is grounded in and unified with the Spirit of Christ. Additionally, to suffer is to share in the divine inheritance because "God chastens every son whom he receives." [80] Suffering, from this perspective, can be a sign of divine favor. Suffering can also be seen as a noble service to God. We should bear it with grace and patience because it might be the last opportunity we have to serve God in this life.

Like Julian, Taylor sees suffering as an opportunity to enter more fully into union with Christ. We grow in faith and in closeness to Christ through suffering if we keep our focus on Christ. We are to keep our vision outwardly focused on Christ, because, as for Gregory, Christ offers Taylor the preeminent example of how to suffer and the consolation that no suffering can be as great as his. We should, therefore, model Christ's behavior of patient endurance. Interestingly, Taylor holds up women and children as ones who have exemplified this endurance. Like Christ they demonstrate how to live in the midst of suffering. The strength of others, particularly Christ, is meant to be a source of inspiration and strength in the midst of one's own suffering. We are also to remember, as Christ's own story shows, suffering does not last. Yet it is interesting to note in contrast to Julian, who looks to union with Christ as the blissful reward for our suffering, Taylor's view is less ecstatic and focuses on Christ merely as the premier moral exemplar to one in the midst of suffering.

79. Heber, *The Whole Writings*, 379.
80. Taylor, *Holy Living and Dying*, 366.

Eternal Life

In Taylor's viewpoint, Christians are to have a very long sense of time, and their ultimate focus is to be on eternity. If we believe in salvation, in eternal life, then all those earthly goods—and our suffering—pale in comparison. "But if thou believest thou shalt be saved, consider how great is that joy, how infinite is that change, how unspeakable is the glory, how excellent is the recompence, for all the sufferings in the world, if they were all laden upon the spirit?" In Taylor's eyes, the ultimate reward awaiting the faithful in heaven so far outweighs any suffering we might endure on earth that there is no comparison. As with Julian's parable, there is a great reward awaiting the servant who suffers, if only we can expand our vision to see it. Of course, given Taylor's extreme dislike of the practice of deathbed repentance, the great reward was not a universal one. Taylor shares Gregory's belief that punishment awaits those who are wicked. As Taylor writes, a dying man who has sinned greatly should be fearful of "future pains," "an angry God," and the fact that he will spend eternity with "the damned and accursed spirits." There is further cause for despair because on the final judgment day the damned "shall be brought forth to change their condition into a worse, where they shall feel more than we can believe or understand."[81] Taylor, like Gregory, seems to hold this possibility of damnation as a deterrent to sin. There is all the more reason to live a holy life, not only because of the consequences in the here and now, but most importantly because our actions have eternal consequences.

Like Julian and those who have gone before, Taylor's emphasis on the afterlife may seem to demean human, earthly existence. For Taylor, however, the glories of the afterlife do not make the here and now devoid of meaning. Of course, full knowledge of the reward for our faithful obedience to God is not possible in our earthly life, but we can take the blessings of this present life as a comfort and a foretaste of what awaits the faithful. In fact, Taylor believes our current blessings can also be a source of hope in the midst of tribulation. As he writes, "there is no man but hath blessings enough in present possession to outweigh the evils of a great affliction."[82] To those in the middle of a crisis, these may seem idle words, but it is important to note they were lived out with firm

---

81. Taylor, *Holy Living and Dying,* 366.
82. Ibid., 99.

conviction by Taylor in his own life, even in the midst of great tragedy. As his letter at the death of his sons (quoted earlier) attests, he was one who could always find mercies for which he was grateful, even in the midst of great pain. Despite the losses he suffered, it seems he never stopped trusting in God, in providence, and in the value of earthly life. Greer finds in Taylor a belief in Christian hope whose object is "firmly located in the age to come" but also a "reality in which it is possible to participate in the here and now."[83] This participation happens through God's grace that brings heaven to earth and through the human act of repentance, which turns our focus heavenward.[84]

Attitude of Detachment

As Taylor writes, "He that would willingly be fearless of death, must learn to despise the world: he must neither love any thing passionately, nor be proud of any circumstances of his life."[85] A belief in detachment has a long history in the Christian tradition, where its implications are not isolation, but heightened attention. As Rowan Williams notes, "Detachment is not seen as a way of escaping from the unappealing or frustrating present, but as a way of being more fully where one is." For Williams, detachment is also about changing the focus of our desires from the things of the world to desiring a deeper connection with God.[86] Taylor's theology is certainly in this line. As noted above, he advocated contentment—being content with the circumstances of our lives. Beaty, in fact, argues that Anglican piety is one that is "'in the world but not of it' in a uniquely tempered way."[87] She writes "It is 'in the world' to a degree unacceptable to the ascetic tradition, for it sees all life as sacramental, as infused with God's glory or truth or grace; yet it is not 'of it,' for it accepts self-discipline as a necessary condition for keeping heart and soul (and mind as well) 'ever ready up to Godward.' It therefore resolves the conflict between faith and works by identifying

---

83. Greer, *A Christian Hope*, 7.

84. Taylor, *Holy Living and Dying*, 229 and 254.

85. Ibid., 388.

86. Williams, "Christianity and the Ideal of Detachment," 8 and 13.

87. Beaty, *Craft of Dying*, 204.

the response of faith *with* works, including not only action in the world, but also prayer and self-conquest."[88]

Beaty's description of Anglican piety certainly seems to fit with Taylor's efforts. Much of Taylor's text is devoted to helping people keep their focus on God and their ultimate union with God, and on the world in that light. Additionally, in arguing for the practice of detachment, Taylor may be advocating a willingness to let go, a willingness to trust that we will meet again those we truly loves – God, family, and friends—beyond the grave. In his sermon at Lady Carbery's funeral, Taylor writes, "Remember that we shall converse together again: let us therefore never doe any thing of reference to them which we shall be asham'd of in the day when all secrets shall be discovered, and that we shall meet in the presence of God."[89] Taylor's attitude of detachment, then, is tempered by the reality of that future meeting. We are not, of course, to be overly attached to the material goods of the world: our position in life, our monetary gains, etc., for those things are all temporary and perishable. Clinging to those superficial items will only cause us to fear their loss, and therefore to fear death. We must be willing to let go of earthly goods and acknowledge that in the grand scheme they are insignificant in comparison to heavenly things. We can trust that that which is most meaningful—life and love and the relationships that sustain them—are what are to be held on to because they exist beyond they grave; they are treasures that can be stored up in heaven. We need not fear death because all that truly matters does not die.

This means Taylor is quite matter-of-fact about the reality of death, even the death of children. As a result, Taylor may seem brusque or callous to the suffering of those who grieve, particularly parents. Yet if, in addition to his belief in heaven, we take into account the realities of the age in which he lived, as well as the realities of his own life, then it is possible to see his writings as the efforts of a parent and a theologian trying to live with his loss. Even after having lost some of his own children, Taylor writes, "If I have lost one child, it may be I have two or three still left to me." For Taylor, his joys outweigh his sorrows. He also writes that we ought to "consider that all the world must die, and therefore to be impatient at the death of a person concerning whom it was certain and known that he must die, is to mourn because thy friend

88. Ibid., 204-5.

89. Heber, *The Whole Works*, 436.

or child was not born an angel." In terms of the death of children, Taylor finds consolation in the knowledge that they died sweet and innocent, before they could be corrupted by the world. Consolation, for Taylor, is also to be found in the knowledge that one who has died has "gone to God," and therefore this should not be a source of grief and despair, but rather one of comfort and gladness at their "good fortune."[90]

Taylor believes firmly in eternal life and finds great comfort in the midst of the death of his children in the knowledge that they are with God. He offers his belief in eternal life with God to his readers as a source of comfort and hope in the midst of grief or loss. We need not grieve because a loved one (assuming he lived a faithful life) is with God and will be seen again in heaven. The strength of his belief in eternal life leads Taylor to advocate that his readers live life with an attitude of detachment. Taylor's detachment does not mean we are aloof to the world, but rather we are not attached to the material world because we know that all that is truly valuable in life is that which lives on for eternity with God. Earthly life is still to be valued because the blessings and mercies of God are present in it, but we are also to remember they are only a foretaste of what is to come.

SUMMARY ANALYSIS

There can be no doubt Jeremy Taylor was a gifted pastor and theologian whose life and works aided many in distress. As Hughes writes, "His writings suggest that he had a real understanding of the ways of the human heart and a man of sympathetic insight may find himself at one with those whose temptations are not his own."[91] Taylor calls his readers to a better life, into deeper relationship with God and an increase

---

90. Taylor, *Holy Living and Dying*, 98, 118–19, and 120–21. What lies behind Taylor's belief that children who die have "gone to God" is his controversial belief regarding original sin. Taylor does not hold to a traditional understanding of original sin; he does not believe Adam's sin is biologically passed down from generation to generation. As Spurr writes, "For Taylor, God does not damn anyone solely on the grounds of an inherited sin, but for the actual sin they voluntarily commit." Children are by nature innocent and most likely have not committed any great sin, and therefore will go to heaven. As noted earlier, Taylor does believe humans inherited the consequences of Adam's sin (i.e. death and the capacity for sin) but that human beings are not inherently sinful.

91. Hughes, *The Piety of Jeremy Taylor*, 15.

in their own piety. Taylor offers his readers a new way of living, one that asks them to focus on eschatological, rather than earthly, time. If we do this, we will see our own sufferings pale when contrasted with the possible joys of eternal salvation, and pale in comparison to the sufferings of Christ. We are to trust death is a mercy, for it means an end to suffering and an entrance into eternal joy. This does not mean our earthly life is devoid of joy, but rather we can view the joys of life as foretastes of what awaits. Additionally, Taylor's focus is on the mercy and grace of God who is ever present in the midst of suffering and can be trusted only to send that which we can bear. Taylor's strong view of God's providence shows one need not despair in the midst of suffering, which has come from God for the increase of our piety and our edification. Taylor also advocates that his readers live by adopting the attitudes suited to a Christian living a holy life. We are to be content with what we are given, not jealous of others or attached to worldly goods. We are to always to have hope, and particularly, in the midst of suffering, we are to exhibit patient endurance. These attitudes are not meant to be lived only in challenging times; Taylor's call is to a holy *life*, and the work he calls his readers to is meant to be lifelong. We are to live always with an awareness of death (not to be morbid, but so that we may make the most of the present), and to be diligent in the practice of prayer. We are to strive daily to be more pious and faithful. Taylor did not put any stock in the practice of deathbed repentance, and given Taylor's Pelagian tendencies, this comes as little surprise. For Taylor, one must live a holy life, not only because it is good and right, but also because it is the way to salvation.

CRITIQUE

Taylor's theology offers a predominately hopeful outlook that takes seriously the reality of human sin, and yet always affirms the reality of God's mercy. The integrity of its author, the challenges of his life and his own unbending faith are evident throughout. Yet, there is also cause to push back on Taylor's method and views. He does take the reality of human sin seriously, but predominately from a self-critical viewpoint. He views sickness and suffering as opportunities for self-examination and cleansing. He certainly believed if more people heeded his call to live a more holy life, the world would be a better place. His emphasis

on personal self-examination does, however, seem to avoid an awareness of corporate or institutional sin. Taylor focuses on building up our
personal piety, on the cultivation of sober virtue and an almost stoic
response to suffering—whether it is our own or that of others. This
means there is also little emphasis on acknowledging the ways our sins
may have contributed to the suffering of others. As noted above, Taylor
does advocate making amends with those we have wronged; and this
is important, but does not go far enough. We might wish Taylor had
asked for internal scrutiny and repentance of the institutions of his day.
To twenty-first-century eyes and ears, it may seem insufficient to ask
the wealthy not to be attached to their property. What about asking
them to repent for the ways they have trampled on the lower classes?
What about a greater awareness of the issue of collective or corporate
sin in society? Taylor, does, of course, encourage acts of charity and
perhaps it was his belief that this was the way to correct the economic
imbalances of his society. It must be remembered, however, that Taylor
is a part of the establishment. He may never have been wealthy, but he
kept company with lords and ladies, and was at one time chaplain to the
king. Given that members of the aristocracy were his patrons, and that
most of his works, in particular *Holy Dying*, were dedicated to them, he
may not have felt it his place to lay such strong criticisms upon them
or their way of life. Additionally, Taylor's focus was on one's individual
life of faith and piety. He did not see efforts at social change as an out-
growth of personal piety. Taylor believed strongly in the providence of
God. Each person is given a lot, and it is the duty of each Christian to
live out life as best as each can. It is not a person's duty to seek to change
circumstances or, as noted above, to be jealous of others whose lives
seem better.

One symptom of Taylor's moralizing tone and his strong emphasis
on cultivating our own virtue and stoicism, is the sheer length of his
manual. While his emphasis on the lifelong nature of the task of holy
living in and of itself may have necessitated five hundred pages, such
length shows what a high standard he has set for his fellow Christians.
We wonder how would it be to actually strive to live as Taylor instructs?
Is there enough encouragement to keep going when we fail? Taylor sets
forth a challenging goal, something for which to strive, and he himself
affirms that life is not meant to be easy. In terms of the question of
encouragement, Taylor may fall a bit short on this front. Although he

does seem to have strong faith in the mercies of God, his repugnance for the practice of deathbed repentance does lead us to wonder how compassionate Taylor is toward human failure.

Taylor is not a systematic theologian, but rather one who focuses on personal piety.[92] Even so, we wish for a greater effort to grapple with the challenging questions raised by his theology. He seems too concerned with accepting what comes, without question. There is no sense of questioning or frustration evident in his writings, no anger at God. This is surprising given that the Scriptures, particularly the stories of Israelites grumbling in the wilderness and the Psalms, would seem to provide license for Christians to express their anger at their difficult circumstances, and even at God. Taylor would not, therefore, be departing from tradition were he to express anger. Yet it is also interesting to note that even the psalms of lament end with an affirmation of God's goodness and mercy. It seems, finally, that Taylor lives at the end of the psalm. Unlike C. S. Lewis, for whom the response to suffering is a process that includes deep grief, Taylor is consistently able to reaffirm God's goodness and mercy. This point offers an opening for criticism that Taylor is often too quick to jump to the positive. The fact that in response to the death of his sons he chose not to grieve, but to focus on those still living seems the paramount example of this. Taylor's approach would seem to prevent Christians from doing the important work of grief—of living with and working through it? The intensity of our feelings at the loss of a loved one or the experience of a tragedy cannot easily be brushed aside, but if we are truly going to reach that sense of contentment which Taylor advocates, do we not also need time to grieve? In his rush to assurance, Taylor seems to forget to leave room for the all-important time of tears. Of course we should not wallow in grief, but neither should we skip over it. It is certainly simpler to believe God is the source of all, and even those things which seem evil or cause grief are in fact somehow working toward God's good purposes. Yet this seems to put Christians in the difficult position of always seeing suffering as positive because they believe it to be ultimately directed and in God's hands. This, in turn, raises the question of passivity in the face of suffering.

Particularly given his profound awareness of human sin, it seems Taylor should also draw a distinction between suffering that is merely endemic to the human experience and that which is of human origin.

92. Ibid., 153.

For Taylor, however, all suffering is existential, and, like Gregory, he believes suffering is sent by God, as a part of the human experience that we must accept. It is not the place of children to question the wisdom of the divine parent. The difficulty is that this view can lead to complacency, to a lack of interest in fighting back against unnecessary or unjust suffering. Perhaps Taylor's views that life is short and miserable (as noted earlier), and his abiding faith in the possibility of eternal life lead him to believe that it is not necessary to differentiate between endemic and unjust suffering. Perhaps Taylor is so aware of the human tendency to commit sin that he feels all suffering is just. Yet he is also the man who counsels reconciliation and charity. Given that, it would seem he leaves some unanswered questions. If we are to seek to help others, and thereby prevent unnecessary and unjust suffering, how are we to reconcile that charity with a belief that all suffering is from God?

CONCLUSION

Together with Gregory and Julian, Taylor offers a broad perspective that has a long vision in which human suffering begins to seem small in the face of eternal realities. It is a valuable perspective that requires a willingness to face the stark and harsh realities of death, suffering and grief, without ever letting go of our faith in God's abiding presence and the possibilities for a brighter future. Taylor's work is notable because it transforms that theological framework into a recipe for life. Christians are not only to think differently as a result of their encounters with suffering and death, we are to *live* differently. Yet his focus on personal piety and his emphasis on cultivating an almost stoic response to grief do not leave room for a deeper, passionate faith. The piety Taylor advocates seems to cut one off from the possibility of distinguishing types of suffering and seeking to combat unjust suffering. In addition, his almost stoic response to grief does not allow one the space to grieve fully. We are left wondering whether we can truly engage in the lifelong cultivation of personal virtue and piety, while also being attentive to the realities of unjust suffering and our own need to fully grieve the losses we experience. While Taylor shows his readers a way to live with suffering, C. S. Lewis shows his readers how to express the depths of grief and anger that seem to be lacking in Taylor, and it is to the work of C. S. Lewis we now turn.

4

Permission to Grieve

C. S. Lewis and a Personal History of Sorrow[1]

LEWIS UPHOLDS MANY OF the doctrines held by those who have gone
before him. Like Gregory, Julian, and Taylor, he believes humanity lives
in a world where suffering is a reality. He believes in the goodness of
God, and, like Julian, he believes God reaches out to humanity to bring
it out of suffering and ultimately to union with him. Like them, Lewis
also knows full well the realities of pain and suffering in this world. In
his case, the loss of his mother at an early age, his service in the trenches
during World War I, and the death of his beloved wife, Joy, after a brief
marriage, all acquainted him with the pain of human existence. Like
Gregory, Lewis acknowledges the cleansing and focusing power of suffering. He shares Julian's belief in a good end to suffering, and he also
shares Taylor's effort to focus on the positive in the midst of suffering.
Where Lewis differs from his predecessors is in his moments of pushing
back. He expresses doubts and forceful anger toward God that are not
evident in the works of Gregory, Julian, or Taylor. Through that pushing
back amidst the fiery furnace of grief and loss, Lewis came to a deeper
and stronger faith than that which sought a simple solution to the
"Problem of Pain" (the title of his early essay on suffering). In the end,
the strength of Lewis's faith and the hope he has to offer are those of one
who has spiritually wrestled with and explored the depths of his own

1. Taken from Lewis's own description of his work in *A Grief Observed* (hereafter
AGO), 68.

grief and suffering to come to a new understanding of God. Peter Kreeft notes that part of the greatness of Lewis is his ability to "understand *end* experience through theology" and "theology through experience."[2]

In this chapter, we will examine Lewis's life and writings, with a particular focus on his marriage and the loss of his wife Joy that is chronicled in *A Grief Observed* and reflected upon in *Letters to Malcolm*. These two works merit focus because, like *The Book of the Pastoral Rule, Showings*, and *Holy Living and Dying*, they offer a theology that is deepened by profound personal experience with pain and loss. In order to more fully understand Lewis's theology, it is necessary to look at other works of his as well, but because *A Grief Observed* and *Letters to Malcolm* chronicle a change in his beliefs, as well as model a way to live with suffering, they are central to an effort to understand Lewis's theology of suffering and grief.

BIOGRAPHY

Clive Staples Lewis was born in 1898 in Belfast, Ireland. His brother Warren was three at the time. Lewis himself notes that his parents came from different backgrounds, and exhibited contrasting temperaments. As Lewis writes, "I was aware of the vivid contrast between my mother's cheerful and tranquil affection and the ups and downs of my father's emotional life, and this bred in me long before I was old enough to give it a name a certain distrust or dislike of emotion as something uncomfortable and embarrassing and even dangerous."[3] Having this distrust of emotion instilled at such a young age makes the raw, emotive writing of *A Grief Observed* all the more significant.

The pivotal event of Lewis's childhood occurred when Lewis was ten and his mother died of cancer. Lewis goes on to note that his father "never fully recovered from this loss."[4] Lewis could not have known when he wrote those words that in a few short years he would be in his father's shoes, but we wonder whether part of Lewis's determination to keep his faith in the midst of his own loss is because of the suffering of his father. Lewis lost both his parents, in a sense, when his mother

---

2. Kreeft. *C. S. Lewis*, 28.

3. Lewis. *Surprised by Joy* (hereafter *SBJ*), 4.

4. Ibid., 18.

died. During the course of their mother's illness and death, Lewis and his brother came to rely more and more on each other, and even began to lie to their father. As Lewis writes, "Everything that had made the house a home had failed us; everything except one another." His mother's death not only took away his previously good relationship with his parents, it also took away his security and happiness. "With my mother's death all settled happiness, all that was tranquil and reliable, disappeared from my life. There was to be much fun, many pleasures, many stabs of [spiritual] Joy; but no more of the old security. It was sea and islands now; the great continent had sunk like Atlantis."[5]

Sadly, the reality of trauma in Lewis's childhood did not end with his mother's death. Hardly a month after her death he was sent away to school in England. Lewis himself describes the school as a concentration camp.[6] The headmaster was a Rev. Capron who was known for his wild outbursts of temper. One of Lewis's biographers refers to Capron as "a certainly brutal and probably insane tyrant of a headmaster."[7] The violent outbursts of Capron, which were further exacerbated by his wife's death, gave Lewis "a fresh reason" to "fear and hate emotion." Once Capron's school was closed, Lewis moved on to join Warren at the preparatory school at his college in Wyvern. In spite of his strong relationship with Warren, Lewis describes his time at Wyvern as one of "aching and continuous weariness" that is on par with his time in the trenches of World War I.[8]

Lewis's great joy in learning did lead to happy moments at Wyvern.[9] The overall experience, however, was so negative that Lewis continually wrote his father begging to be taken from the school, even going so far as to threaten to shoot himself.[10] Then his father transferred him for his final years of schooling to be a pupil of William Kirkpatrick in preparation for entrance into university. For Lewis, the time under Kirkpatrick's tutelage was ideal. As Lewis writes, "For if I could please myself I would always live as I lived there."[11] There are those, however,

---

5. Ibid., 19 and 21.
6. He titles his chapter on his time at Capron's school "Concentration Camp." Ibid., 22.
7. Sayer, *Jack*, 54.
8. Lewis, *SBJ*, 33 and 96.
9. Ibid., 118.
10. Gresham, *Jack's Life*, 23.
11. Lewis, *SBJ*, 141–43.

who believe the death of his mother, the distant relationship with his father, and the cruelty of his school life had sent Lewis into a state of depression that lasted for "the first half of his life."[12]

Lewis's love of learning continued to be fostered as he moved from Bookham to Oxford in 1916. We could really say that Oxford would be his home for over fifty years, interrupted first by World War I and second by the years he spent commuting to teach at Cambridge. Lewis obtained undergraduate and graduate degrees in English Literature and went on to become a fellow of Magdalen College. Despite all his time at Oxford, however, he never became a full professor there, and he was only given a chair at Cambridge in 1954.[13] During these Oxford years, three periods stand out as having particular relevance to Lewis's understanding of suffering and grief: his army service in WWI, his conversion to Christianity, and his marriage to Joy Gresham.

World War I

Lewis enlisted in the Army in 1917 and arrived in the trenches on his nineteenth birthday.[14] In his own writings he does not speak much of the war. According to Lewis, "The war itself has been so often described by those who saw more of it than I that I shall say here little about it. Until the great German attack came in the Spring we had a pretty quiet time. . . . Through the winter, weariness and water were our chief enemies." He does, however, acknowledge the horrors of the trenches, writing of "the frights, the cold, the smell of H.E., the horribly smashed men still moving like half-crushed beetles, the sitting or standing corpses, the landscape of sheer earth without a blade of grass, the boots worn day and night till they seemed to grow to your feet."[15] Gilchrist notes that Lewis's writings in the time after the war "all show signs of distinct trauma," and argues that he suffered from post-traumatic stress disorder.[16] Given the horrors of the war, this diagnosis is not surprising, and Lewis's stepson notes that for many years both Lewis and his brother suffered from nightmares of the trenches. In addition to the psycho-

12. Nicholi, *The Question of God*, 111.

13. Wilson, *C. S. Lewis*, 245.

14. Ibid., 188.

15. Lewis, *SBJ*, 195–96.

16. Gilchrist, *A Morning After War*, 153.

logical injuries, Lewis did not escape the war physically unscathed. He suffered from trench fever, which took him out of action briefly. Lewis was ultimately returned to England after being hit by shrapnel in April of 1918. He was still recuperating when the Armistice was signed in November.[17]

During his recuperation in a London hospital, Lewis was most frequently visited by Mrs. Janie Moore. Mrs. Moore was the mother of Paddy Moore, a young man whom Lewis had befriended early in his training. Before heading to the front, Lewis had spent his leave with the Moores, who lived in Bristol at the time, because, despite his efforts, he was unable to get his father to come to England during his brief leave.[18] Lewis and Paddy made a pact with each other that if either one did not survive the war, the survivor would look after the other's family. Paddy Moore went missing in early 1918 and was declared dead several months later, so the burden fell to Lewis. Lewis lived with the Moores in various arrangements from 1918 until Mrs. Moore died in 1951.[19] It is worth noting that Lewis took his obligation seriously despite the numerous times it proved to be a financial and emotional burden. As Green and Hooper note, "Mrs. Moore seems to have been highly possessive and selfish—or thoughtless—to an astonishing degree. Lewis was expected to help with the housework and run errands for her, even when they were able to employ two resident maids, a daily and a handyman-gardener."[20]

Conversion to Christianity

Although Lewis is thought of as one of the great Christian apologists of the twentieth century, it is important to remember he was not always a Christian. He grew up in a Christian family, but by adolescence was "desperately anxious to be rid of my religion."[21] It would not likely

17. Gresham, 51 and 56; Lewis, *SBJ*, 189.

18. Gresham, *Jack's Life*, 49. As Gresham notes Albert's lack of visits to England, and Lewis's time with the Moores created a "rift" that was "never properly healed" (41). See also Sayer, *Jack*, 127.

19. Gresham, *Jack's Life*, 50–54 and 142.

20. Green and Hooper, *C. S. Lewis*, 66. See also Wilson, *C. S. Lewis*, 64–69, 75–76, 83, 92, 121–2, 140–3, 222–5; Gresham, *Jack's Life*, 117–130.

21. Lewis, *SBJ*, 61.

come as a surprise to many that the horrors of the trenches seemed only reinforce to Lewis's atheism. It was not until Lewis was a professor at Oxford that he became a convert, first to theism and then to Christianity. He credits his own studies, particularly in philosophy, as well as the efforts and conversations of many colleagues with his conversion.[22] In the end, of course, Lewis's conversion was also a matter of almost tangible experiences during the late 1920s. He describes being aware he was "holding something at bay, or shutting something out," and of feeling the "unrelenting approach of Him whom I so earnestly desired not to meet." Lewis writes, "In the Trinity Term of 1929 I gave in, and admitted God was God, and knelt and prayed: perhaps, that night, the most dejected and reluctant convert in all England." Lewis still felt fearful although he intellectually understood he was discovering the "source from which those arrows of Joy had been shot at me ever since childhood." Lewis's father died in September of 1929, and Sayer, in noting the profound effect his father's death had on him, recognizes that Lewis's sense of his father's abiding presence helped him believe in immortality and "helped persuade him to join a Christian church."[23]

Marriage

Although he had no idea of it at the time, it was Lewis's conversion to Christianity that would ultimately bring him times of emotional happiness and emotional distress: his marriage to Joy Gresham. During World War II Lewis wrote *The Screwtape Letters* and gave numerous talks on Christianity for the British Broadcasting Corporation (BBC), both of which significantly contributed to his popularity as a writer and an apologist. As his fame grew, so did the volume of letters he received.[24] Lewis was a diligent letter writer (often with help from Warren) and took pains to answer all his mail. In 1950, he began his correspondence with Joy Davidman Gresham, a married American writer and an adult

22. Ibid., 225. Colleagues, including Hugo Dyson and J. R. R. Tolkien, who with others later formed a group known as the Inklings that met regularly for decades to review each other's writing and discuss ideas among friends. For more on the Inklings see: Duriez, *The C. S. Lewis Encyclopedia*, 96–100.

23. Sayer, *Jack*, 224–37.

24. The following relies on the account of this time as found in Wilson, *C. S. Lewis*, 235–93.

convert to Christianity. (Her parents were Jewish, but not practicing). Unlike many of the other letters he received, letters from Joy were not mere fan mail. Joy had an avid mind; like Lewis, she loved a good intellectual argument, and so their correspondence flourished.

Joy left her husband, and they divorced shortly thereafter. She came to England in 1952 and met Lewis at Oxford for numerous visits including spending Christmas at the Kilns. Lewis was helping support Joy financially and paying for her boys' schooling. In 1956, when the British Home Office refused to allow Joy to remain in England, Lewis married her, seemingly as a legal courtesy to allow her and the boys to remain in England. His love for Joy began to blossom at this time; there was, however, a great difficulty for Lewis. Although they were married in the eyes of the state, the Church of England still forbade remarriage after divorce, and the Bishop of Oxford would not grant his permission for Joy and Lewis to be married in the church. For Lewis, particularly, he felt he was not truly married until he was married in the eyes of God and the church. There became an increased urgency in their desire to have their marriage blessed by God, because in the spring of 1957 Joy (who was initially hospitalized for a broken leg) had been diagnosed with terminal bone cancer. Ultimately, the need was met by a clergy friend of Lewis's, who agreed to perform a marriage ceremony while Joy was in the hospital Miraculously, Joy recovered and was walking again. This began a time of great happiness for the two. As Lewis remarked to a friend, "I am experiencing what I thought would never be mine. I never thought I would have in my sixties the happiness that passed me by in my twenties." They enjoyed many good times together before she died on the July 13, 1960. That day began the months that are so intimately chronicled in *A Grief Observed*.

In the remaining years of his life, Lewis continued to teach and write. There were happy times, but his health was failing. As Banks notes, "During the last years of his life, his body was more that of a man in his mid-seventies than early sixties."[25] In fact, Lewis's health had never been good. He suffered from nightmares, poor digestion, and headaches. Lewis suffered a heart attack in June 1963, from which he briefly recovered to enjoy two happy months at The Kilns with Warren. Lewis died peacefully at The Kilns on the November 22, 1963.[26]

25. Banks, "C. S. Lewis on Pain," 146.
26. Gresham, *Jack's Life*, 76 and 79. Wilson, *C. S. Lewis*, 295–98.

THEOLOGY OF SUFFERING AND GRIEF
FROM THE WORKS OF C. S. LEWIS

It can certainly be argued that Lewis lives on, and perhaps even enjoys greater popularity decades after his death than he did in his own lifetime. This is, of course, due to the wide appeal of his writings, particularly his fiction and his apologetic texts.[27] This section aims to examine those works that offer particular insight and help illuminate Lewis's beliefs about suffering and grief in relation to his understanding of humanity, sin, and evil; god's Providence; Christ and salvation; and eternal life.[28]

The Problem of Pain

In surveying Lewis's works on suffering, it is most logical to start with *The Problem of Pain* (published in 1940), as this is a theological work that focuses particularly on the question of suffering. As its title indicates, it endeavors to provide an answer to the problem of suffering. Briefly put, Lewis's solution has two parts. First, suffering is a result of the fall and a consequence of human freedom, which means that much of the world's pain is of human (not divine) origin and so can be easily explained by the actions of sinful human beings. Second, Christian doctrine states that suffering, while not a good in and of itself, can produce good.[29]

27. As noted above, it is beyond the scope of this work to offer a complete survey of his works, particularly since good overviews of his thought and work already exist. See Duriez, *The C. S. Lewis Encyclopedia;* Hooper, *C. S. Lewis;* Vaus, *Mere Theology;* and Clark, *C. S. Lewis.*

28. In a discussion of Lewis's works on suffering, it is important to acknowledge a recent work, *C. S. Lewis and Human Suffering, by Marie Conn, which provides an examination of Lewis's own theology around the issues of grief and suffering throughout his lifetime.* Conn's method is to not only examine the grief Lewis suffered with the loss of his wife, but to consider at the whole span of his life and the losses he suffered as a child and a young man. She begins with the loss of his mother and his years as a young atheist. She then moves into a discussion of his book *The Problem of Pain*, which she sees as his effort to deal with suffering on an intellectual level. Conn also spends multiple paragraphs discussing Harold Kushner's *When Bad Things Happen to Good People* and the Book of Job, which are relevant but end up detracting from Lewis's own work. Then she moves to a discussion of *A Grief Observed*. This would seem to be the heart of the book, but unfortunately Conn does not go into sufficient depth with Lewis. The chapter is too brief—only seven pages. One would expect that she would have spent more time on that work in particular.

29. Lewis, *The Problem of Pain* (hereafter *PP*), 63, 86–87, 110, and 118.

Intellectually, it may seem that Lewis has solved the problem of pain. He has explained its origins and reconciled the seeming incompatibility of a sovereign God and a high view of human freedom. The solution seems logical, simple and straightforward. Lewis does what he sets out to do: "to solve the intellectual problem raised by suffering."[30] Yet it is not a solution that holds up for Lewis. Over the course of Lewis's life and writings, he changes his view of God's sovereignty. Note that in *The Chronicles of Narnia*, Aslan (the Christ figure) says to one of the children, "You would not have called to me unless I had been calling to you."[31] Here the emphasis is not on the human choice; the initiative lies with God. This view that puts a greater emphasis on God's sovereignty, is one Lewis affirms at the end of his life. In his final interview, Lewis did not see his own conversion as a moment of personal decision. While it was felt to be a free action, it also did not seem possible to choose any other way. As Vaus notes, Lewis "is not, in the end, interested in reconciling human free will and God's sovereignty along logical-causal lines. He is the C. S. Lewis who is sure in his own case that his decision for Christ was not all that important. What is important is that he was 'decided upon.'"[32] It would seem the experiences of Lewis's later life led him to change his emphasis regarding his own theology and his own views on human freedom.

It is interesting to note *The Problem of Pain* begins with the assertion that the issue of pain, the issue of suffering, is an intellectual problem of which there can in fact be a simple solution. There may be an intellectual problem or disconnect that we encounter in the midst of suffering, but dealing with that problem may not help us to answer the more important question of how to *live* with suffering. Lewis discovers in the face of overwhelming grief that an intellectual solution does not take our grief away and is not an adequate comfort. Not everyone would agree *The Problem of Pain* is inadequate. Robert Banks, in fact, argues *The Problem of Pain* is not a book made up solely of "reasoned arguments" and argues that by use of "picturesque metaphors, striking analogies and familiar illustrations, he presents a Christian vision of reality, one that is inextricably linked to the overarching biblical story of Creation, Fall, Redemption, Sanctification, Judgment, and

30. Ibid., xii.
31. Lewis, *The Chronicles of Narnia* (hereafter *TCN*), 558.
32. Vaus, *Mere Theology*, 60–61.

Re-Creation."[33] However, while this may be an accurate portrayal of Lewis's technique, in the end we are still left with a solution that does not adequately address the question of how to live with the magnitude of human suffering in the world. Lewis himself acknowledges the inadequacy of his approach in his preface. Interestingly, in doing so, he provides insight into his own understanding of suffering. He writes "for the far higher task of teaching fortitude and patience I was never fool enough to suppose myself qualified, nor have I anything to offer my readers except my conviction that when pain is to be borne, a little courage helps more than much knowledge, a little human sympathy more than much courage, and the least tincture of the love of God more than all."[34] In that statement Lewis acknowledges that suffering requires virtue, community, and a relationship with God. *The Problem of Pain* does provide a way to think about suffering, but it does not provide much to help us to live with it.

Lewis's solution emphasizes pain on an individual level because "There is no such thing as a sum of suffering, for no one suffers it."[35] It could be argued no one actually experiences a sum of suffering, we only experience our *own* suffering. Yet later, Lewis acknowledges his own suffering in losing his parents and wife to cancer, and he underwent his own suffering in witnessing the suffering of his wife.[36] So there would seem to be a tension between Lewis's stance in *The Problem of Pain* and his later experiences. In *The Problem of Pain*, he seems to place his emphasis on the suffering we experience as our own, but later his account of suffering broadens to emphasize the pain experienced in witnessing the suffering of others. While we cannot experience a sum of suffering, it is important to acknowledge the human experience includes both individual suffering and relational suffering (that which is experienced by witness the suffering of others).

33. Banks, "C. S. Lewis on Pain." 144.
34. Lewis, *PP*, xii.
35. Ibid., 116.
36. Lewis, *AGO*, 12.

A Grief Observed

Almost immediately following Joy's death, Lewis did what he had always done: he wrote.[37] He filled four notebooks with a chronicle of his own grief. As one of his biographer's records it, "[h]e started about two weeks after Joy's death and stopped just over a month later. He wrote, he said, about himself, his dead wife, and God 'in that order,' creating a kind of 'map of sorrow' as 'a safety valve' to prevent a 'total collapse.'"[38] The writing out of his thoughts and feelings enabled Lewis to "get a little outside" of his grief. Lewis begins his text with a now well-known statement: "No one ever told me that grief felt so like fear."[39] This opening statement sets the tenor for the whole of the book. It is unlike any of his other works. It is not a "work" at all, or at least it did not originate as one. It was just his personal journal, a way to record and sort out his thoughts. It was not meant to be published or probably even read by others. Lewis was, understandably, reluctant to publish the notebooks. He did, however, with the urging of his friend Roger Lancelyn Green, under the pen name N. W. Clerk, (*Nat Willk Clerk* in Anglo-Saxon, which means "no one knows the writer").[40] It was not until after Lewis's death that the pen name was replaced with his own.[41]

Lewis captures well the roller coaster of emotions that is the experience of grief. There are the commonsense moments when we are sure things will get better, followed by tears and agony as a memory returns. He notes the physical reality of grief, saying "And no one told me about the laziness of grief. Except at my job—where the machine seems to run on much as usual—I loathe the slightest effort." One of the great challenges of grief is interacting with other people. Lewis notes that he wants people around, but does not want to have to talk too much. The difficulty in relationships, Lewis finds, is the sense of awkwardness and embarrassment. People do not know what to say; there is nothing good to say, and

Elijah
Rest

---

37. Many of the sentiments of *A Grief Observed* are also echoed in his letters at the time. See Hooper, *C. S. Lewis,* 1160–89; Lewis. *C. S. Lewis's Letters in Latin,* 101–19.

38. Banks, "C. S. Lewis on Pain," 147.

39. Lewis, *AGO,* 1 and 10.

40. Gresham, 158–9.

41. Interestingly there have been occasional implications over the years that *A Grief Observed* is a work of fiction, but the overwhelming evidence seems to indicate it to be Lewis's own account of his experience. See Lindskoog, *Sleuthing C. S. Lewis,* 158–59.

people are troubled that a grieving person is, as Lewis puts it, "death's head"—a reminder that everyone is mortal. As noted above, Lewis is also aware of the cumulative aspect of grieving. His grief is not only for his wife, but also for his parents, both of whom also died of cancer.[42]

Beginning in the second section of the book, Lewis realizes how selfish his notes seem—as though Joy's death "mattered chiefly for its effect on myself." He desired to broaden his vision and perspective, but he gradually realized it is the nature of grief, particularly early on, to be internally focused. The realization raises a fear because, although he thinks about Joy all the time, he is afraid the Joy who is in his thoughts will become more and more disconnected from the Joy he knew. And so he mourns all over again for the loss of her physical self. He tries to conceive of what kind of existence she might now have and what it means to be "with God," but that spiritual existence does not meet his physical desire for her presence.[43]

As religious people often do in the midst of grief, Lewis seeks out comfort in his faith, but he does not easily find it. He writes, "Talk to me about the truth of religion and I'll listen gladly. Talk to me about the duty of religion and I'll listen submissively. But don't come talking to me about the consolations of religion or I shall suspect you don't understand."[44] This last sentence is a significant criticism—not of God necessarily, but of religious tradition. In the early immediacy of Lewis's grief, the consolations of religion hold no meaning for him. Lewis's statement seems to criticize all those who offer theological writings to comfort those in the midst of suffering. It could certainly be read as a criticism of some the other thinkers I present (although not of Gregory, for his writings were more about chastisement than consolation), as well as of this book itself. He raises the question of whether religion can truly offer any comfort to those who suffer. Lewis finds that platitudes or statements of assurance offer neither comfort nor hope. His pain is raw and deep, and he does not want to hear soothing statements that seem to ignore the depth of his pain. In response to his criticism it

42. Lewis, *AGO*, 1–3 and 11–12. Albert Lewis died in September 1929. Green and Hooper note that, "Both Warren and Clive felt Albert Lewis's death far more than they had thought possible" (97). It is significant that his death, while enabling them to buy their own home, also meant the loss of their childhood home, which no doubt added to their grief.

43. Lewis, *AGO.*, 18–19 and 27.

44. Ibid., 28.

seems worth noting that there may be some truth to what he has to say. In Lewis's experience in the depths of grief, consolation (in the sense of soothing, attempting to diminish, or explain away the depth of suffering) is not helpful. Lewis himself wishes for an easy answer, but realizes there is none. Here it seems important to distinguish between consolation and hope. Hope is grounded in faith in the ultimate goodness of God. That kind of faith demonstrates a trust in God that does not seek to understand why something terrible has happened, but persists in trusting that, as on Easter morning, life and love will have the last word. Consolation seeks to explain away questions rather than live with them. It seeks to put an end to pain by explanation. Christian hope, on the other hand, acknowledges the depths of pain but persists in trusting the pain will not last. It is that trust—and, therefore, hope—Lewis offers in his own writings (particularly the *Chronicles)* and it is that hope that ultimately sustains him through his own grief. He may have no patience for consolation, but he does not run away from religion; his text is full of questions but is not devoid of hope.

Even in the midst of his searching and pain, we see glimmers of hope. At the conclusion of section two, Lewis writes, "One flesh. Or, if you prefer, one ship. The starboard engine has gone. I, the port engine, must chug along somehow till we make harbor. Or rather, till the journey ends." He goes on to acknowledge that the end of the journey may be rough, as it was for Joy and for his mother, but in his image of a ship continuing on there is hope and there is evidence that grief has not overwhelmed him completely. His vision is beginning to open and to broaden.[45]

As Lewis begins to come out of the depths of his grief, he realizes part of him is not ready to move forward. He suggests there is a strange sense in grief that the depth of our pain is somehow proportional to the depth of our love, so not grieving greatly or for a long time must be indicative of a lack of love for the one who died. He does not want to feel better, and there is "a feeling that one is under a sort of obligation to cherish and foment and prolong one's unhappiness." As Lewis himself realized as the cloud of grief began to lift, however, the depths of grief do not bring us closer the dead, but rather take us away. In fact, it is in the moments where the sorrow is least strong that he is most aware of Joy's presence.[46]

45. Ibid., 39.
46. Ibid., 62 and 64.

Lewis's journey of healing continues as he begins his fourth note-book. He writes it will be the last because it is the last empty one he has, and he refuses to purchase new ones for this purpose. He had sought, in his entries, to make a "map of sorrow," but he comes to realize sorrow is not a place or a state, but rather a process, and so he has written a history of that process. His optimism continues. His focus has shifted from himself to God, and he realizes that is where his focus should have been all along: on God. When his focus is on God, he is no longer paralyzed by grief, and, in fact, feels more connected to Joy. Lewis's hope and optimism are further evident in his affirmation of Julian's conviction that "all shall be well."[47]

Letters to Malcolm

The sense of peace in the midst of grief that closes *A Grief Observed* is also evident in *Letters to Malcolm*, a text that is a collection of fictional letters, this time to a friend who, over the course of the correspondence, is coping with a loved one who has a serious health issue. Because the text was written after Joy's death, and perhaps because it is fiction, and therefore, can be a bit removed from personal experience, it could even be argued that *Letters to Malcolm* provides a better articulation of Lewis's conclusions than *A Grief Observed*, with its raw emotions unmitigated by time. In *Letters to Malcolm*, Lewis seeks to be patient in the midst of suffering. Lewis writes, "The petition, then, is not merely that I may patiently suffer God's will but also that I may vigorously do it. I must be an agent as well as a patient. I am asking that I be enabled to do it. In the long run I am asking to be given 'the same mind that was also in Christ.'" This is no longer the angry, fearful Lewis who writes the opening pages of *A Grief Observed*, rather it is the Lewis who is more at peace with the reality of suffering. Again he writes of the fruitful nature of suffering, comparing it to planting seeds that must die before new growth can happen.[48] In this, we can see echoes of Taylor's letters in the midst of his own suffering. Yet it is not as though Lewis has returned to his previous sense of faith and confidence. He has been touched and transformed by his grief. In writing to "Malcolm," who is facing the health crisis of a loved one, he remembers well the fear and the anxiety, the torment of false hope.

47. Ibid., 68, 71–72, and 75.

48. Lewis, *Letters to Malcolm* (hereafter LTM), 26–27 and 40–41.

Humanity, Sin, and Evil

The Screwtape Letters, a fictional collection of letters from a senior devil to his nephew on the best ways to lead a human over to Satan's side, offers a straightforward statement of Lewis's understanding of evil. In his preface he writes, "The proper question is whether I believe in devils. I do. That is to say, I believe in angels, and I believe that some of these, by the abuse of their free will, have become enemies to God and, as a corollary, to us. These we may call devils. They do not differ in nature from good angels, but their nature is depraved. *Devil* is the opposite of *angel* only as Bad Man is the opposite of Good Man. Satan, the leader or the dictator of devils, is the opposite, not of God, but of Michael."[49] In this we understand that while evil has reality for Lewis, it does not have ultimate power comparable to God's power. Satan is not God's equal, only that of the Archangel Michael. Evil, therefore, may be present in human life, but it cannot be stronger than God's goodness. Evil and temptation may not always be as literally personified as they are in *The Screwtape Letters*, but it is important to acknowledge that for Lewis they are real. As Lewis notes, he needed to look no further than his own heart to know how "temptation works."[50] Certainly, the existence of devils does not entirely explain the reality of suffering in the world, but they serve as a reminder of the suffering caused when humans give in to temptation.

Lewis believes much suffering is a result of human sin, and devils play a role in this by tempting humanity to sin. As Marie Conn notes, Lewis "felt that most of our suffering comes from other humans,"[51] so in a discussion of suffering a focus on the origins and nature of human-caused suffering is important. As noted above, one of the aspects of the solution in *The Problem of Pain* is that much suffering in the world is caused by human action. Lewis does believe humanity is capable of great sins, but he does not have a wholly negative view of humanity or human nature. He does not believe in the doctrine of total depravity and sees much good in the world. Lewis believes in the doctrine of original sin because he considers humanity to be "members of a soiled species," but he does not believe all suffering is, therefore, punishment

49. Lewis, *The Screwtape Letters*, vii.
50. Ibid., xiii.
51. Conn, *C. S. Lewis*, 41.

for that fact.[52] For Lewis, the fall serves, therefore, to explain how humanity has such a capacity for sin and to explain the reality of sin and evil in the world.

The reality of evil is also affirmed in the *Chronicles of Narnia*, Lewis's much beloved children's stories, which were published from 1950–1956 (ten years after *The Problem of Pain*, but in the years before *A Grief Observed*). We read of the White Witch or the Queen of Charn and feel we have had an encounter with evil; it's inevitable. Yet what is perhaps most illuminating about the *Chronicles* is how Lewis chooses to deal with the issue of evil. It does not last, and it does not win out. The *Chronicles* tell the Christian story: the story of redemption and salvation. The *Chronicles* also provides insight into how Lewis's understanding of God was enriched in the years after writing *The Problem of Pain*.

It might seem that someone who believes strongly in devils and who affirms the reality of evil and the sinful tendencies of humanity would paint a very dark picture of the world. Yet Lewis does not. He acknowledges the darkness—in the world and in all of humanity—and he also affirms hope in the goodness of people and of God. The darkness of the world, the fact humanity lives in a fallen world, means humanity will suffer both from the nature of the fallen world and from the sinful actions of our fellow human beings. What Lewis affirms throughout his writings, and in his own experience, is the fact that the goodness and power of God are ultimately greater than any evil or human sin that might result in suffering.

God's Providence

In *The Problem of Pain* in particular, there is a great emphasis on human freedom. This emphasis means Lewis does not conceive of a world where God is intimately intervening in human affairs to stop bad things from happening, because in Lewis's mind such a world would be one where "wrong actions were impossible" and "freedom of the will would be void." This does not mean he disregards the sovereignty or goodness of God. Lewis believes human freedom, divine power, and divine goodness are not incompatible. He writes, "To be God—to be like God and to share His goodness in creaturely response—to be miserable—these are the only three alternatives. If we will not learn to eat the only food

52. Lewis, *PP,* 61 and 81.

that the universe grows—the only food that any possible universe ever can grow—then we must starve eternally." Again we see the emphasis on human freedom: there are alternatives, and we have a choice. The picture of God in *The Problem of Pain* is that of a more distant God because the emphasis is on the choices humanity makes. Lewis writes, "Pain insists upon being attended to. God whispers to us in our pleasures, speaks in our conscience, but shouts in our pain. It is his megaphone to rouse a deaf world."[53] While this does speak of a God who is connected to and involved in human affairs, it does not speak of God as a companion or friendly guide in the midst of pain. God is shouting at humanity, an action in contrast to the gentle guidance of Aslan portrayed in *The Chronicles of Narnia* (discussed further later in the section on Christ and Salvation).

God in Grief

Lewis also comes to understand God somewhat differently through his writing of *A Grief Observed,* perhaps because he spends much of the book questioning the messages of the Christian tradition in the light of his own grief and the depth of his own pain, and, like Job and the psalmist, questioning God. First, he wonders where God is, and "Why is He so present a commander in our time of prosperity and so very absent a help in our time of trouble?" Lewis does not come to the place of questioning God's existence, but, as he identified in *The Problem of Pain*, the experience of suffering raises questions about the nature of God and humanity's relationship to him. Lewis's fear, in fact, is that his suffering will lead him to a very negative view of God. Lewis finds little comfort in the knowledge that Joy is "in God's hands." He wonders, "Do they suddenly become gentler to us the moment we are out of the body? And if so, why? If God's goodness is inconsistent with hurting us, then either God is not good or there is no God: for in the only life we know He hurts us beyond our worst fears and beyond all we can imagine." Lewis wonders whether God is, in fact, not the benevolent God most Christians talk about, but rather some kind of "Cosmic Sadist" who seems gracious while "He was really preparing the next torture." Lewis acknowledges he is seeking a way out. He is seeking an explanation that

53. Ibid., 24, 47, and 91.

will somehow take the pain away. "Aren't all these notes the senseless writhings of a man who won't accept the fact that there is nothing we can do with suffering except to suffer it? Who still thinks there is some device (if only he could find it) which will make pain not be pain."[54]

In the course of his writing, Lewis begins to see the clarifying effects of suffering. He realizes Christianity does not promise a life free from it: "I've got nothing I hadn't bargained for." Yet he comes to understand our suffering takes on a new level of meaning when one is faced with its reality in personal experience. Our faith and our understanding of God change as a result of suffering. Lewis writes, "Only torture will bring out the truth. Only under torture does he discover it himself." The difficulty with this realization that our faith is strengthened by suffering, is it returns to the conclusion that God is either a "Cosmic Sadist" or the "Eternal Vivisector."[55] Here is a seemingly ever-present conundrum for Christians: how do we continue to believe in the goodness of God in the midst of suffering?

Lewis does realize his desire to label God as a Cosmic Sadist arises from his desire to fight back for the pain he is enduring. He seeks the obtuse pleasure of trying to hurt God as much as he feels he has been hurt by him. That pleasure, of course, is not productive or long lasting, and he discovers healing does not come by inflicting more pain. Lewis goes on to note how pervasive and long lasting his grief is, particularly physically. He compares his grief to the steady barrage of trench warfare and the continuous circling of a bomber. These comparisons are, no doubt, grounded in his own personal experience in World War I. Like a soldier, he also wonders if there is an end in sight. He can acknowledge it is better to believe suffering can be cleansing and strengthening, but he also wants to be assured there is an end to the suffering, even if it is only at death. Lewis begins to see an end, at least to his physical suffering. He realizes a good night's sleep and a sunny day can bring a bright spot into his darkness, and in that bright spot, as his grief is lightened, he is actually able to remember Joy the best.[56]

This bright spot leads to a realization in his relationship with God as well. He feels no longer is the door "shut and bolted," that perhaps it was his own frenzy of grief that slammed the door, and perhaps he

54. Lewis, *AGO*, 4–5, 31, 35, and 38.

55. Ibid., 42-44.

56. Ibid., 45–50 and 52.

was behaving like "the drowning man who can't be helped because he clutches and grabs." He also returns to a more positive view of God, crediting "the merciful good sense of God" with the fact he has in no way lost his memory of Joy or his sense of her abiding presence. In fact, he comes to a rather startling conclusion: "God has not been trying an experiment on my faith or love in order to find out their quality. He knew it already. It was I who didn't." He realizes God knew his capabilities and the strength of his faith all along, but somehow his pain had made him blind to his own gifts. The bright spot and the realizations only mean the worst is over. Lewis likens himself to a man who has had a leg amputated, saying, "At present I am learning to get about on crutches. Perhaps I shall presently be given a wooden leg. But I shall never be a biped again."[57]

Lewis does believe in a purpose for all beings, that each has a destiny, and that destiny is in God's hands. He writes, "If there is Providence at all, everything is providential and every providence is a special providence. It is an old and pious saying that Christ died not only for Man but for each man, just as much as if each had been the only man there was. Can I not believe the same of this creative act—which, as spread out in time, we call destiny or history?"[58] There is a shift here in Lewis's emphasis to a greater sense of God's involvement in each individual life. It is certainly a change of emphasis to talk about Christ's dying for oneself instead of Christ's dying for all. There is an intimacy to Lewis's account of providence from the *Chronicles* that is not present in *The Problem of Pain* where God is using pain as a megaphone (a harsh way to rouse someone). In the *Chronicles*, Aslan is the companion of the children, and in *A Grief Observed*, Lewis comes to understand God as one who says "Peace, child; you don't understand."[59] The distance between God and humanity decreases over the years as Lewis writes. This intimacy, which also shows an emphasis on the importance of each individual life means life has meaning and, perhaps more importantly, suffering has meaning. There is also consolation for Lewis, as for many, in the intimacy of the incarnation. All the challenges and sufferings of life are "from before all worlds, known by God from within." This belief

---

57. Ibid., 54 and 59–62.

58. Lewis, *LTM*, 55.

59. Lewis, *AGO*, 81.

is part of what leads Lewis to share in Julian's belief that "all will be well," for in the incarnation the light has swallowed up the darkness.[60]

No longer is God seen as the Cosmic Sadist. Instead, God is the source of all goodness and the remedy for our suffering. This does not mean Lewis denies the wrath of God, but rather he never lets it be separated from God's love and forgiveness. Humanity does experience the wrath of God, particularly when humanity has gone astray, but it is important to remember, as Lewis notes, anger subsides and can be transformed into forgiving love. Lewis writes, "That is how friends and lovers are truly reconciled. Hot wrath, hot love. Such anger is the fluid that love bleeds when you cut it. The *angers,* not the measured remonstrances, of lovers are love's renewal. Wrath and pardon are both, as applied to God, analogies; but they belong together to the same circle of analogy – the circle of life, and love, and deeply personal relationships."[61] Therefore, to talk of God's anger is also to talk of God's love. The possibility and experience of God's wrath seem much less terrifying with the reminder that with repentance, forgiveness follows anger.

The sovereignty and power of God are significant aspects of Lewis's theology. Over the course of Lewis's life and writings we come to understand the importance and intimacy of the divine-human relationship for Lewis. God is not a distant figure up in the clouds ruling the universe. Lewis's God is one of intimate relationships who cares deeply for humanity and seeks to strengthen that bond. In the midst of his own grief, Lewis certainly questions God's power and intentions, and for a time he wonders if God is a Cosmic Sadist, but that view does not hold. Lewis returns again to his belief in a loving God who reaches out to humanity with grace and mercy. Lewis comes to accept he cannot fully understand God's ways or plan, but he also firmly believes he can maintain trust in God's goodness and love for humanity. That love is perhaps most evident in Christ and in God's salvation of humanity.

Salvation and Christ

For Lewis, like Gebara, there is a sense in which salvation is found in the midst of daily living. As noted above, the bright spots of a good night's sleep and a sunny day can help relieve the burden of his grief. Of

60. Lewis, *LTM*, 70–71.

61. Ibid., 96–97.

course, for Lewis there is more to his understanding of salvation than just his own experience in the midst of grief. In fact, in the theology and writings of Lewis, the discussions of salvation and Christ are so intertwined that they cannot be separated. In *Letters to Malcolm,* Lewis writes that he sees fear and anxiety felt in the midst of suffering not as sins, but as afflictions, and he counsels that when they can be seen as afflictions then they are "our share in the Passion of Christ." Pain and suffering are now a familiar road to him. They can still be a challenge, and renewed by encountering others who are suffering, but that fact does not trouble him. He finds comfort that he and Malcolm are in a "shared darkness"—a darkness where Christ is also present. This is neither unfamiliar territory, nor the wrong place to be. Lewis reassures Malcolm that they are "on the main-road." Christ is not only the companion on that road, but also the guide.[62]

Aslan the lion in *The Chronicles of Narnia* personifies the nature of Christ. As Vaus notes, "In the character of Aslan, Lewis combines the tenderness and strength that he believed were so perfectly combined in Christ." Additionally, Vaus labels Aslan as the Redeemer, in giving his life for Edmund, and as the Sustainer, for the ways in which he comforts and provides for the characters throughout the stories. Even when Aslan is not a part of the action of the story, he is "behind the scenes, guiding each character who is one of his followers and providing for their needs." Aslan is also the "coming one" who brings about the end of Narnia in many passages that echo the prophecies of Isaiah and Revelation.[63] Through the character of Aslan we can gain an understanding of how Lewis viewed the life and work of Christ. It is interesting to note his emphasis on care and compassion. This seems to echo Julian's understanding of Christ as the one who suffers for humanity out of love and would have suffered more if he could. As quoted above, Aslan is strongly connected to his followers; he calls to them as he did to Jill and Eustace. In the *Chronicles* we particularly see this compassion in Aslan's willingness to die for another, but we also see his strength and his fierceness. A lion can be a gentle animal, but he is not always one. As Mr. Beaver describes, Aslan is not "safe. But he's good."[64] This is an important element to understanding Christ—a reminder that following

62. Lewis, *LTM*, 41 and 44.
63. Vaus, *Mere Theology*, 89–90.
64. Lewis, *TCN*, 146.

him is not always easy or safe; it is a risky endeavor, but we need not worry, for he is *good*. Ultimately, he is the compassionate companion and guide who is the source of salvation. It is also important to note the connection between Aslan and suffering. Like Christ, Aslan does not simply die, he suffers and his suffering is caused by the ways in which people have given into temptation; in fact, his suffering absorbs the suffering of others who otherwise have had to face the full consequence of their own and others' sins. In addition, Aslan actually *inflicts* suffering of a different kind, such as when he strips the dragon's skin off Eustace (see below), in order to purify his followers. Aslan/Christ is also the one who brings humanity and the world to fulfillment.

Lewis's understanding of Christ and salvation is, perhaps, most evident in his portrayal of Aslan in *The Chronicles of Narnia*. It is through the character of Aslan we come to see God is intimately connected to human suffering, because Aslan/Christ undergoes great suffering to bring about salvation. Aslan/Christ can also be understood as the companion and guide who leads humanity through earthly life and into the joyous beyond. We see in Lewis's writings an affirmation of the incarnation and the passion—an affirmation that God fully understands the depths of the human experience. Along with this is an affirmation of the glorious reward that awaits the faithful at the end.

Eternal Life

In *The Problem of Pain,* Lewis deals with the issue of suffering in an eternal context, addressing the question of hell. The possibility of eternal suffering, which in Lewis's mind is the possibility of eternal separation from God, is real because of human freedom. Ultimately, those who refuse God's continual offer of relationship and forgiveness will be left alone for all eternity.[65] As *The Great Divorce* (1946) also shows, Lewis believes that even if we have rejected God at some point in our lives, we are again offered the possibility to accept his offer. A belief in the eternal option to accept or reject God is a view he shares with Julian, which reveals the great emphasis he placed in his early writings on human freedom.

---

65. Ibid., 130.

The Narnia stories are important to understanding Lewis's beliefs about eternal life and also because they provide a clear indication of Lewis's Platonic worldview. For Lewis, what we see and know in the midst of this human life is merely a shadow of what is to come. This is most evident in the passage quoted below regarding the intensity of all things in the "new Narnia" where everything is more beautiful, more fragrant, more everything than it was in the children's previous life.[66] There is a depth and richness in the new Narnia; what they knew before pales in comparison. In this, Lewis solidly affirms a belief in the ultimate insignificance of earthly life, for what awaits is far greater and far richer than anything we have known on earth. It is interesting to note how Lewis chose the genre of children's fantasy deliberately because it "seemed the ideal form for the stuff I had to say." Additionally, Lewis wrote the text with the explicit purpose of addressing the issue of suffering:

> I thought how stories of this kind could steal past a certain inhibition which had paralysed much of my own religion in childhood. Why did one find it so hard to feel as one was told one ought to feel about God or about the sufferings of Christ? I thought the chief reason was that one was told one ought to. An obligation to feel can freeze feelings. And reverence itself did harm. The whole subject was associated with lowered voice; as if it were something medical. But supposing by casting all those things into an imaginary world, stripping them of their stained glass and Sunday School associations, one could make them for the first time appear in their real potency? Could one not thus steal past those watchful dragons? I thought one could. . . .[67]

Lewis certainly seems to succeed in the endeavor. The *Chronicles* are fanciful children stories. They do not shy away from the realities of suffering and grief,[68] yet the overwhelming trend of the book is posi-

66. For further study on Plato's philosophy and Narnia stories see Murrin, "The Dialectic of Multiple Worlds." For a broader discussion of Lewis and philosophy see Beversluis, *C. S. Lewis and the Search for Rational Religion* and Smith, *Patches of Godlight.*

67. Sibley, *Through the Shadowlands,* 72–73.

68. It is interesting to note, however, that Lewis uses the story to undo a bit of his own grief. He realizes what must have been his own fantasy as a small boy early on in the *Chronicles* in *The Magician's Nephew.* He tells of the boy Digory who brings an apple back from Narnia to save his dying mother, who then makes a miraculous recovery.

tive. This may seem odd, given the battles, losses, and deaths that occur within the stories and the fact the main characters themselves die in the end. There is certainly grief and suffering in the stories, and yet, as in the broader Christian story, suffering never has the last word. In the end there is joy, even in death. Interestingly, Lewis has been criticized for the imbalance of evil in his stories. As Robert Smith writes, "one does not read far into Lewis's novels without realizing that the conflict is inherently out of balance. The forces of evil are never more than momentarily strong; the outcome is never seriously in doubt."[69] Given the terrible death of Aslan, the evil of the White Witch, and the battles the children must fight, we cannot say evil does not have real force in the stories and on the reader, but if there is a kernel of truth in Smith's criticism, it could be evil does not last in Narnia. It is not a strong criticism, for the *Chronicles* are Christian allegory, providing a portrait of Lewis's strong Christian faith and exhibiting his belief that God's goodness always has the last word. This belief is most evident in the concluding pages of the *Chronicles*. The children have crossed into a new Narnia, one that is "a deeper country, every rock and flower and blade of grass looked as if it meant more."[70] The children are joyous at the beauty of the world and the reunions with loved ones, and yet they are also fearful and reticent. When they finally encounter Aslan, he says to them, "You do not yet look so happy as I mean you to be." Lucy replies, "We're so afraid of being sent away, Aslan. And you have sent us back into our own world so often." Aslan then explains that there is no returning from this place. There was a train accident. They died. They have come to stay with him for always. This may seem a terrible way to end a children's story: everyone died. Yet Lewis points out to his readers that this is *not* the end of the story. He is firm in his Christian conviction (and Platonic viewpoint) that earthly life is only the beginning. He writes, "But for them it was only the beginning of the real story. All their life in this world and all their adventures in Narnia had only been the cover and the title page: now at last they were beginning Chapter One of the Great Story, which no one on earth has ever read: which goes on for ever: in which every chapter is better than the one before."[71]

69. Smith, *Patches of Godlight*, 213.

70. Lewis. *TCN*, 760. A similar vision of heaven is articulated by Lewis in the closing lines of *Letters to Malcolm*, 124.

71. Ibid., 766–67.

The children have, of course, arrived in heaven. We know from his earlier writings that Lewis has a strong belief in both heaven and hell. The closing passages of the *Chronicles* are idyllic, but they also raise the question of whether everyone goes to heaven. Lewis does not seem to be a Universalist. He holds to the reality of human freedom, and that freedom includes the ability to reject God. The children choose to follow Aslan. Lewis chose to become a Christian, although he acknowledges God's influence on that choice. While Lewis may not be a Universalist, and *The Great Divorce* certainly shows that he believed some people never choose God, it seems his own experience of conversion contains a hope for universalism. There is the hope God will act, as in Lewis's life, to help us to say yes.

The hopeful message of *The Chronicles of Narnia* is told in the simple format of a children's story, and, perhaps because of that, it comes through quite strongly. In reading the Narnia stories, we cannot help but find joy and comfort. The messages of love and hope are clearly broadcast, particularly in the final pages. Lewis leaves his readers with an important message: we need not fear suffering or death, for they do not endure. There is something far more wonderful that awaits. Consolation in the afterlife has long been a theme of the Christian tradition, and it is certainly one open to criticism. To one in the midst of suffering, a far off reward may seem to be little consolation. Lewis did not have to wait long before the joyful tenor of his theology was tested by his wife's illness and death.

Not surprisingly, some of the questioning in *A Grief Observed* addresses the question of what Joy's life is after her death. Lewis wonders, "Am I, for instance, just sidling back to God because I know that if there is any road to H., it runs through Him?"[72] This leads him to question whether God's terms are that the only way to meet Joy again is in loving God so much it no longer matters whether or not he meets her. Interestingly, these later questions are like musings. They have lost the bitter sting of his inquiry. The raw anger and emotion have lessened, and they are curious, not hateful questions. The response is still the same. Still God seems silent, but the tenor of the silence has changed, or at least Lewis's perception of the tenor has changed. As he writes (and is quoted in part above), "When I lay these questions before God I get

72. Lewis, *AGO*, 79. In *A Grief Observed*, Lewis uses "H." (an abbreviation of her first name Helen) throughout rather than the familiar "Joy."

no answer. But a rather special sort of 'No answer.' It is not the locked door. It is more like a silent, certainly not uncompassionate, gaze. As though He shook His head not in refusal but waiving the question. Like, 'Peace, child; you don't understand.'"[73] Lewis ends his notebook, and the book, with this same sense of peace. He recalls Joy's final statement (to the Chaplain), "I am at peace with God," and acknowledges it would be wicked to bring the dead back from that place of peace. He ends with a line from Dante's Inferno: *Poi si tornò all'eterna fontana* [then she turned towards the Eternal Fountain].[74] He has some peace now, for he knows that she is at peace in the presence of the eternal source of all.

Lewis is also notable for his belief in purgatory. While Anglicans traditionally reject this Roman Catholic belief, Lewis maintains it as a necessity, and it is another element of his theology that is evident in *Letters to Malcolm*. Lewis desires a cleansing of the soul before entrance into heaven.[75] He knows himself to be an imperfect, sinful being, and so it must follow that before we can enter into heaven all those sinful bits must be purged. We must be cleansed. Particularly illustrative here is the passage in *The Chronicles of Narnia* where Eustace (the boy who has become a dragon) is turned back into a boy by Aslan. Successive layers of dragon skin are painfully peeled off and he is made to swim in a bath that initially stings, but then in a moment all is well and he is his own self again.[76] There is an appeal in the images of sloughing off skin and being cleansed, but whether purgatory is really required, as Lewis believes it is, can be debated. Rowan Williams argues that this stripping away of what stands between us and God does not require purgatory; rather, it is merely a part of a Christian belief in judgment. He writes, "the hope is that if we have accustomed ourselves to living with Christ in this life something has been 'constructed' that allows us to survive the terror of meeting the truth face to face: the truth has come to be, in some degree, 'in us,' to use the language of St. John's first letter. At one level, we are left naked and undefended, with nothing of our own to appeal to or hide behind; yet we trust that we are gifted with the clothing, the defence we need."[77] Williams offers a picture of

73. Ibid., 80–81.
74. Ibid., 89; Dante, Paradiso Canto XXXI:64–93.
75. Lewis, *LTM*, 108–9.
76. Lewis, *TCN*, 473–75.
77. Williams, *Tokens of Trust*, 145.

judgment that sounds remarkably similar to Lewis's, particularly to the story of Eustace and the dragon skin. Williams's understanding suggests a belief in purgatory is not necessary in order to have the cleansing Lewis desires. There is an Anglican approach, according to Williams, that provides the cleansing Lewis believes is required as a natural part of the process of entering into eternal life with God.

We might be tempted to focus on the beauty of the closing pages of the *Chronicles* as a summary of Lewis's belief in the afterlife, but as a survey of other works of his shows, there is much more to his belief than the beautiful heaven in which the children join Aslan for the final time. Lewis stands out in the Christian tradition, at least among Anglicans, for his belief in purgatory. This belief is certainly connected to his belief in the sinful nature of humanity; he feels his own sinfulness demands purgatory's cleansing. Lewis also believes in hell, which is a more universal belief in the Christian tradition. One of the ways in which he upholds his belief in human freedom is to affirm, like Julian, that humanity has the eternal option to turn away from God. There is little emphasis on fire or punishment in Lewis's hell; rather, we get a sense of emptiness, the reality of truly being left alone by God. That might seem a terrifying reality, but it is important to remember that for Lewis there is a choice. We have the option to turn away from God and the option to turn toward God. What Lewis affirms, along with Gregory, Julian, and Taylor, is that if we turn to God, particularly in the midst of suffering, then we can have great hope, for God seeks to reward faithful servants.

SUMMARY ANALYSIS

In *A Grief Observed*, Lewis, like Taylor, provides Christians with a way to live with the reality of suffering. In contrast to Taylor, Lewis shows it is acceptable and appropriate to rail at God in the midst of grief. Lewis provides a model for how to move through the grief process. What is new in Lewis is the freedom to question, the freedom to express the depth of our anger and anguish. Lewis does, however, share with Gregory, Julian, and Taylor the hope and comfort of those whose faith has grown stronger because of their suffering. Yet the extent to which his beliefs and understanding of God were shaken by his experience of grief sets him apart. He comes to his beliefs not only as one who has suffered, but as one who has been angry at God. For those who find others, particularly Taylor, lacking in depth of feeling, Lewis shows how experiencing the depths of grief does not prevent us from gaining understanding or maintaining our hope. Lewis shows those who are crying out in the depths, as he did, it is possible, over time, to move to a place where the pain is less acute, the questions are calmer, and God's seeming silence is a source of comfort rather than despair.

Overall, the theology Lewis comes to is one that emphasizes our intimate relationship with God, and it is one focused on the individual's experience of God, Christ, evil, and salvation. It certainly seems one that could enable us to live with an experience of suffering. We wonder, however, if it is too intimate? Does the emphasis on God as a personal being and on our own experiences result in limiting and diminishing God? Does a theology grounded almost entirely in our personal experience mean we develop a loss of cosmic perspective and blindness to attributes of God that we have not experienced? It remains to be seen whether Lewis's theology and emphasis on the personal can stand the test of time or was merely convenient in the midst of his own experience of grief and loss.

Like those who have gone before, Lewis ultimately offers a faith strengthened through the trials of grief. Although he fears his faith to be a "house of cards," he discovers it is far stronger than that.[78] He realizes his beliefs and his experiences of God's presence can sustain him and they do not ultimately crumble. They are shaken, no doubt; Lewis is open and vulnerable about his fears. He questions God. He wonders if God is only a Cosmic Sadist who seems to delight in persecuting humanity, but he does not maintain this line of questioning. Like a lover after a quarrel, he forgives God for the pain in his life, or at least being willing to live with it. Like his predecessors in this work, Lewis accepts the suffering he must endure. Unlike his predecessors, Lewis does not arrive easily at the place of acceptance. It is not his starting point by any means. A process that is certainly arduous and challenging is required for Lewis to share a posture of acceptance.

It could certainly be argued that, intellectually at least, Lewis did share his predecessors' view for much of his adult life. *The Problem of Pain*, in providing a logical framework through which to understand the reality of suffering, does seem to promote an attitude of acceptance.

78. Lewis, *AGO*, 42.

Yet this posture is sorely tested when Lewis undergoes the anguish of his wife's death. The anguish brings out fear and anger, physical and emotional pain. Initially, it does not seem possible for Lewis to hold onto an acceptance of suffering. To do so would seem to say to God that suffering and Joy's death were acceptable. Yet things change for the better for Lewis (but not returning as they were), because he makes the choice to *live* with pain. The emphasis being on *live*—he continues to live his life: working, praying, finding glimpses of happiness. Like Gebara, as we shall see, there is a sense in which salvation is both a distant reality (accomplished by Christ on the cross) and an everyday reality. Salvation is found in the actions of everyday life; what helps bring healing and acceptance to Lewis is his ability to continue living his life. Lewis also shows his readers a faith that enables us to live with an acceptance of suffering. In Lewis's later writings, we have a greater sense of his belief in the intimate, abiding presence of God, his faith in the incarnation (knowing Christ suffered as he does), and a development of his understanding of providence that affirms his belief that there is a greater purpose and meaning for his life and all of humanity, even at a time when life seemed devoid of meaning. All of these beliefs help Lewis find light in the midst of his darkness. Throughout his writings, Lewis is also greatly consoled by his belief in the afterlife. He knows Joy lives on. He feels her presence, and he takes great comfort in knowing someday they will be together again. He also finds comfort in the midst of daily life. Even his ability to appreciate a sunny day and a good night's sleep offer him comfort and hope. They, too, are signs of life in the midst of death.

Lewis's gift to his readers is that he models the transformative nature of grief for a Christian. Like Taylor, he shows his readers how to *live* with grief. He models a process that leads to acceptance, but begins in anger and fear. The depths or heights of Lewis's anger are notable. As Beversluis writes, "Seldom has such a Christian writer assumed such freedom in refusing to pull his punches."[79] Banks identifies three important elements of Lewis's model: thinking through feelings, addressing unresolved experiences of grief (being aware of the cumulative effects of loss), and allowing aspects of our faith to be challenged and even shattered, so that they might grow stronger.[80] In a world where

79. Beversluis, *C. S. Lewis and the Search for Rational Religion*, 276.
80. Banks, 155–56.

technological advances lead to expectations of less suffering, the quick acceptance of Gregory, Julian, and Taylor may seem a relic and difficult to comprehend. Lewis offers a different approach. He offers an acceptance born out of a process that develops a richer theology. It is not that the fundamentals of Lewis's beliefs are changed; he does not stop believing in God or stop being a Christian. It is, as noted above, that his focus shifts—his relationship with God changes. God is no longer seen as a distant sovereign figure (as in *The Problem of Pain*) or a Cosmic Sadist (as in the early pages of *A Grief Observed*). God, particularly as manifest in Christ, is a gentle companion and guide. We can find acceptance because, while suffering is a given reality in a world where sin and evil are real, we are not alone. We can trust God's goodness triumphs, ultimately, over any evil in the world or any suffering we must undergo. Even Lewis's understanding of salvation and the afterlife take on more intimate qualities in his later writings. Salvation is found, in part, in the acts of daily living, and the afterlife is something to which Lewis feels a connection, a reality in which he believes, for he knows in his heart and in his soul that Joy lives on: he feels her presence. Lewis's theology—his understanding of God and his relationship to God—is transformed by the experience of grief. It is given new depth and definition, and through it all he comes to better understand his beliefs on a personal level.

CRITIQUE

There are those who do not believe Lewis is a strong model for Christians. Beversluis is one who is critical of Lewis. He does not believe Lewis lost his faith after Joy died, although he shares a belief that Lewis's faith was transformed by his grief.[81] What Beversluis finds is that Lewis's rediscovered faith lacks conviction. Beversluis argues that Lewis ends up failing to have "empirically meaningful assertions, the ordinary meaning of terms, and a God who is good 'in our sense.'" For Beversluis, Lewis is still an example of faith, but he has lost his status as an apologist or a man of logic. Lewis cannot let go of the Cosmic Sadist without

---

81. Beverslius, *C. S. Lewis*, 303. The claim Lewis lost his faith as a result of Joy's death was also perpetuated by the play and film *Shadowlands*. See Wayne Martindale, "Shadowlands."

ignoring or completely redefining a whole host of religious terms.[82] Beversluis may have a point. Language is necessary to talk about faith, and in order for there to be communication the meanings of words must be clear. Yet it does not seem fair to argue that Lewis is no longer a "man of logic." On the surface, *The Problem of Pain* may seem a work of logic, and *A Grief Observed* not, because one is scholarly and the other merely reflective. Yet to do so is to say experience did not inform Lewis's earlier writing and the theology that develops out of *A Grief Observed* is not logical. Neither of those statements are true. While it may be most evident in *A Grief Observed,* experience informs all of Lewis's works, and the theology of *A Grief Observed* is different than that of *The Problem of Pain*, but not less logical. Ann Loades, in fact, commends Lewis for the theology that develops from *A Grief Observed.* She writes that he "shows us someone who has the courage to let his passion and honesty pervade his theology. His theology arises from his engagement with himself and his loving, theology probed for its resources, tested for its adequacy, developed in some directions, made flexible and promising in unsuspected ways, still kindly in its astringency."[83] Loades argues that Lewis's theology is as sound and tested as any other. With Loades's argument in mind, the questions of Lewis in *A Grief Observed* are not only the questions of one who grieves, they are the questions of a theologian struggling to adjust his framework when new information has provided a challenge to it. *A Grief Observed* is not merely the musings of a man who has lost his wife, it chronicles the struggles of a theologian endeavoring to redefine his understanding of God and himself in relation to God in the midst of his grief.

CONCLUSION

Lewis shows Christians it is acceptable to be fearful and angry, to question God and to question our faith. He might say that those emotions should be felt, but we should not dwell on them, because the future is not there. Lewis shows the future lies in learning to live by faith and placing our focus on God, for in so doing our anger can be transformed into acceptance. Living by faith is Lewis's obligation to himself and to

82. Beversluis, 295 and 316–17.
83. Loades. "C. S. Lewis," 120.

Joy, but first and foremost to God. It is the path he chose when he became a Christian. As Banks notes, "Now, just as while Joy was alive his task had been to put God first, so he must do in her absence."[84] Lewis himself writes that, "there's no practical problem before me at all. I know the two great commandments, and I'd better get on with them."[85] Lewis "gets on," not only because it is his duty, but because he comes to understand that when he puts God first, everything else seems to fall into place. In the emphasis on maintaining our focus on God and the assurance of God's intimate, abiding presence in the midst of suffering, Lewis's theology echoes Julian's. As noted above, he has much in common with his predecessors in this book, but his theology is perhaps closest to that of Julian. What makes Lewis distinctive, however, is that he opens the door to the possibility of an acceptance that holds a trust in God's providence and a hope for the future while also leaving room for the intensity of our own grief. The question that remains is whether or not it is possible to construct a theology of suffering that holds onto the heights of Julian's optimism while also allowing for the depths of Lewis's grief. A theologian who shares Lewis's emphasis on embracing our own personal grief and in building our theology out of experience, is Ivone Gebara, and it is to her perspective we now turn.

---

84. Banks, "C. S. Lewis on Pain," 152.

85. Lewis, *AGO*, 81.

5

Transforming and Reframing Tradition

A Theology of Suffering and Loss in the Work of Ivone Gebara

UNTIL NOW, WE HAVE focused on voices that are established within and uphold the doctrines and beliefs of mainstream Western Christianity. In this chapter we shift to bring in a voice still within the tradition, but which is also sharply critical of it, particularly regarding the acceptance of suffering. The voice is that of Brazilian feminist theologian, Ivone Gebara. Gebara deals with the questions of why humanity suffers and how people should respond in the face of suffering. Ivone Gebara is a theologian who speaks from within the Roman Catholic tradition and who also critically engages with tradition. Focusing especially on the ways patriarchy and hierarchy have contributed to women's suffering, Gebara brings a strong voice of critical reflection to the conversation. Her focus on a particular population also helps highlight and clarify the important issue of unjust suffering—the times when acceptance is wrong and leads to complicity in causing suffering. Gebara's work, *Out of the Depths,* offers a way to understand when suffering is unjust, and, therefore, when it should be combated. Gebara also speaks from the perspective of a liberation theologian. She does not advocate jettisoning the tradition, but rather reframing it in ways that lead to flourishing rather than suffering.

Like the others in this conversation, Gebara writes out of the experience of particular suffering. Gebara writes as one who has experienced suffering herself and as one who has witnessed a great deal of suffering in the course of her daily life. Gebara acknowledges that she is by no means immune from the reality of evil in her own life. In fact, it is her own experience of evil that helps her recognize the depth of the problem. She writes that it is:

> when I surprise myself by being afraid of children, of their violence; when I see a neighbor set fire to another neighbor's stall out of jealousy and competition over trade; when I see my neighbor, who beats his wife and abuses her in public; when I see the carelessness of my neighbors, ignoring the common good, throwing garbage in the street; when I see dirty water coming out of our faucets; when I feel powerless and ignorant as to how to use my own abilities in my neighborhood, suffering becomes my daily bread, and I feel in my own skin the transcendence and immanence of evil.[1]

Gebara has also suffered greatly in her personal life. Early in her career, during the time of the dictatorship in Brazil, she was teaching philosophy, and rode home with a friend after a school meeting to find police at the friend's house. Her friend was involved in the resistance and suspected of being a dissident. The police came inside and searched through her friend's possessions for anything that might implicate her as an enemy of the state. One of the officers found a crucifix, and, upon finding it, remarked, "What I do, I do for him." This officer would later be responsible for the torture and death of this woman, Gebara's friend.[2] Gebara's desire to push back on the traditional theology of the church and to seek a new way forward is not merely an academic exercise. It is a calling deeply grounded in her own personal experience of suffering and loss.

Gebara is a Sister of Notre Dame (her order was founded in Lorraine, France, in the sixteenth century to educate poor girls).[3] She chose to spend her life living among the poor in Recife, Brazil, so she could be a voice for transformation in that community.[4] She is a voice that questions tradition and speaks of religion and theology as a force for change. The aim of this chapter is to engage with Gebara's perspective

1. Gebara, *Out of the Depths*, 57.
2. Ibid., "Changing Our Perceptions of God."
3. Gebara to Molly James, email. 2 February 2009.
4. Puleo, *The Struggle is One*, 205.

to understand how it might enrich a contemporary theological understanding of suffering and grief. Gebara provides an important reminder of the role of the church to be a voice for those on the margins and to seek to bring God's message of hope and liberation to the places where it is most needed.

LATIN AMERICAN FEMINIST CONTEXT

Gebara's perspective is that of a feminist in Latin America. She is not a lone voice; there are many others who stand with her. A useful window into understanding their perspective is "The Final Statement" from the Latin American Conference in 1985, a conference sponsored by the Ecumenical Association of Third World Theologians (EATWOT). "The Final Statement" is printed as the last chapter of *Through Her Eyes,* and its statements of commonality note how "women's theological activity strives to be." According to the statement, the work is "[m]arked by a sense of humor, joy, and celebration, virtues that safeguard the certainty of faith in the God who is with us," and this underscores the hopeful tone of the document. It looks toward the future with great optimism, because it is accompanied by a commitment to make the world different. The theology of the women there is also "[m]ilitant, in the sense of taking part in the totality of our people's struggles for liberation at local and global levels." It is significant to note this commitment to engagement and change. The women theologians in Latin America choose to ground their theology in experience and to work together in the hopes of making concrete differences in the lives of others. As with other feminists, experience is a fundamental part of their theological work. One of the tasks set forth by the conference is "To pay attention to the theological experience and reflection that is taking place in base-level groups, especially by women, to take on this experience and to allow ourselves to be challenged by it in the process of a mutual enrichment. . . ."[5] Of course, using experience to inform theology is not a new idea. Paul's letters in the New Testament and Augustine's *Confessions* are a testament to the long history of relying on experience to inform theology. What is significant for these women, and for theology as a whole, is that their work is about ensuring the inclusion of the experience of those who are on the margins, those whose voices

5. Tamez, *Through Her Eyes,* 150–53.

have often been absent in the preceding centuries. For Gebara, the experience of women points not only to the ways in which the Christian tradition has gone wrong, betraying the heart of the gospel and harming those on the margins, but also to how it might repair the damage done and do better going forward.

In *Out of the Depths,* Gebara explains her philosophy regarding the value of experience in doing theology:

> Starting with one's own story, one comes to see a broader picture, placing oneself in a particular time and culture. This is not a matter of absolutizing individual experience but of showing how each person exists in relation with others, with the larger world, with the earth, and with the whole ecosystem. . . . This kind of reflection is not an abstract act: it takes one's own experience as matter for thought, as a book to be studied, as a school in which one can develop personhood by using certain tools. This method receives little appreciation from those who advocate the scientific method in which the subject must be set apart and emotion plays no part in what is called objective knowledge. But for some feminist groups subjectivity, emotion, sensitivity, and interconnection among different levels of existence are fundamental to knowledge. I share this perspective.[6]

Gebara is critical of those theologians in the West, where science and reason are still highly prized, who seem to forget there are a variety of ways of knowing. Gebara is not implying that emotion or experience should replace reason as the primary mode of knowledge for theologians. Rather she is advocating an approach that puts experience as the starting point from which we reason our theology. Her understanding of the gospel comes through the lived experience of Christians (particularly women), and not just through intellectual engagement with the text. Gebara also values a plurality of voices—not only those who are in positions of power or have been accepted by the tradition, but also those voices from the margins who may bring a different perspective. Gebara believes that no longer should theology be limited to those in positions of power and influence in academia or the church. It is also limiting to assume theology is only done by men or it only happens in the academy or in the church. In discussing her life in her poor neighborhood in Recife, Gebara says, "Truly, I've learned more

6. Gebara. *Out of the Depths,* 45–46.

theology living in poor neighborhoods than in classrooms."[7] Gebara desires a world where gender and socio-economic status are not barriers to doing theology, to participating in the wider theological conversations of the church.[8] As a way of counteracting a long history of male interpretation of women's experience of suffering, she offers a feminist interpretation that often lets women speak for themselves. Sadly, the suppression of women's stories about their own experience of suffering is not only missing in the church; it is also missing throughout much of the history of the West. Gebara notes that "[f]requently, what men perceive is woman herself as evil: their view demonizes woman. We need only to consult the mass of works in the Western tradition that speak of women as witches or purveyors of wickedness. . . . Women's words are nowhere to be found: women are silent victims even when they succeed in gaining a mention in official history. Moving from silence to public speech is the purpose of this study [*Out of the Depths*]."[9]

In terms of the importance of men and women doing theology, Gebara believes women have a unique gift and voice to contribute to the theological discourse. "Above and beyond the academic theological formation" she writes, "there is something special in the way that women do theology." She goes on to say women's theology can give permission for people to express their own experiences with God in a way "that does not demand that reason alone be regarded as the single and universal mediation of theological discourse."[10] This is one of the important contributions of feminists like Gebara—a reminder of the diversity of sources for talking about God. Theological discourse is not only a cerebral exercise, it is also an emotive and spiritual one that involves our whole being and experience, not merely the use of our mental faculties. For Gebara, an approach to theology that is not strongly grounded in the experience of individuals is insufficient. Of course, feminist theology is not the only discipline that has endeavored to reshape the theological tradition; throughout history voices have been raised, endeavoring to direct the course of the tradition. Gebara's perspective is significant because of her work particularly on the issue of suffering through the lens of feminist and liberation theologies.

7. Puleo, *The Struggle is One*, 208.
8. Gebara. "Women Doing Theology in Latin America," 37.
9. Gebara, *Out of the Depths*, 7.
10. Ibid., "Women Doing Theology," 41.

Feminist theology focuses on what is vital, in the sense of what arises from, and is relevant to, the lived experience of women in daily life, and it does not remain at the level of the abstract or objective. Like many before her, Gebara argues for a reconnection to poetry and poetic language because of its use of symbols and the fact that it better acknowledges the element of mystery that is ever-present in theology. Gebara desires theology to also be expressive of the breadth and depth of human experience. Gebara objects to "purely rational concepts" that are not interpreted through our current existence and experiences, because those concepts in and of themselves seem to "not take into account the meaning, desire, flavor, pleasure, pain and mystery of existence." What Gebara seems to object to is the importation of a theological term or rational concept from the past into the present without getting "to know them and discover their meaning for today."[11] She can be seen as connected to the mystical tradition, whose writers freely expressed the emotions of their own spiritual journeys. Gebara desires an approach to theology that is communal, allowing the input of a multiplicity of voices and experiences and not limited to the perspective of one powerful individual. It is about accessing the deep issues of human experience —including suffering and grief—through the experience of many, rather than assuming the experiences of the few are universal. For Gebara, experience also informs how we understand tradition. She sees tradition as a process formed through experience and always grounded in and informed by the message of love and justice preached by Jesus. Tradition, therefore, is not a fixed or monolithic entity for her as it is for some. Gebara values tradition, but as long as the community is "faithful to the Spirit of God manifest in history and demanding absolute respect for life," elements of tradition can be "re-created" if they do not resonate with the community's current experience.[12]

In addition to the value of experience in theological discourse, a feminine way of doing theology also offers an open directness about the ways experience informs our theology. Gebara models this in her own work. She begins her essay in Tamez's collection by explaining her starting point: "To speak or write from northeast Brazil is to situate myself in a region where misery and exploitation take on extremely dehumanizing forms and where most people, especially women, are its victims. .

11. Ibid., 45.
12. Ibid., 46.

. . It is out of this situation, which sustains my being and my reflection, that I can speak of women's theology."[13] In much of her writing, Gebara speaks freely about her own context and the suffering she experiences and witnesses. The following is the beginning of Puleo's interview with Gebara, included in *The Struggle is One:* "I live with a small community in a poor neighborhood in order to feel more directly the pains of the impoverished. This allows me to do theology another way—trying to feel the meaning of being exploited in all ways."[14] As with so many others in the Christian tradition, Gebara realizes powerful theology and possibilities for transformation can come out of experiences of what is vital in the human condition. To be in the midst of suffering is also to enrich our theological discourse, since suffering and redemption are central elements of the Christian faith.

It is important to note Gebara's feminist convictions do not mean she sees the feminine as superior to the masculine. She does not seek to replace the old tradition with a new one that focuses solely on women. She seeks the liberation of all people. Her hope is for "a new synthesis in which the dialectic present in human existence can take place, without destroying any of its vital elements."[15] This sentiment is also expressed in *Out of the Depths*, where Gebara writes, "I have often heard it said that women are only one subject among others in theology, and that today it is a fashionable subject. Often too I have heard that the theological claims of women have no basis in tradition. But what tradition is that? Must we, while keeping intact the good things of our patriarchal tradition, cling to its harmful aspects and forget the primacy of justice and love?"[16] Gebara should not be seen as one who desires the overthrow of tradition, but rather, like her fellow liberation theologians, she seeks a reframing of tradition that is more inclusive and liberating. Gebara is not suggesting changing the tradition to fit some external standard; rather, she is calling for a returning of the tradition to its roots: to the message of justice and love preached by Jesus Christ.

13. Ibid., 38.
14. Puleo, *The Struggle is One*, 206.
15. Gebara, "Women Doing Theology in Latin America," 48.
16. Gebara, *Out of the Depths*, 53.

THEOLOGY OF SUFFERING IN THE WRITINGS
OF IVONE GEBARA

Humanity, Sin, and Evil

Gebara's book *Out of the Depths* is devoted to a discussion of women's suffering and the conviction that patriarchy (especially within the church) has increased that suffering. Gebara does not hesitate to name and confront evil and the suffering it causes. She delves right in on the opening pages: "The evil I want to talk about is not the evil we do personally, but the evil we undergo, that we suffer or endure, something not chosen, the kind of evil present in institutions and social structures that accommodate it, even facilitate it. . ." Gebara's focus is on giving voice to the experience of those who suffer and on questioning what has led to this unjust suffering. Gebara is also unafraid to acknowledge the pervasiveness of evil results in people, especially women, experiencing suffering and grief. She writes: "Moreover it often happens that this kind of evil is accepted as fate, as God's design or as punishment for hidden sins. Evil is so mixed with our existence that we can live in it without even taking account of it as evil."[17] While it is not difficult to acknowledge the immensity of suffering in the world, Gebara notes that there can be a hesitation to name as evil the source of some of that suffering, perhaps because an action began with good intentions or because it brought about a good result. While we might want to objectively define evil as that which is counter to God and God's will, Gebara argues that a discussion of evil is not that simple. Her work points to the fact that it is often challenging to discern evil on a personal level, particularly when evil has come to be embedded within social structures, such as the church. For Gebara, there are two kinds of moral evil. One is the evil that can be unintentional—bad consequences of good actions. The other is more pervasive and more problematic. It is the evil so embedded within institutions (like the church) that it is no longer recognized as evil.[18]

Gebara goes on to note how complicit the church has been in causing or worsening the unjust suffering women experience. "The church,

17. Gebara, *Out of the Depths*, 1.
18. Ibid., 1–2.

an institution created and dominated by men, has interpreted women's experience of evil, whether undergone or committed by women, in a way that bears little or no resemblance to what women feel or ask for, whether in theology or within the structures of the church."[19] The church's interpretation of women's experience of evil is part of the impetus behind Gebara's book. She hopes her book will be the beginning of a conversation about the ways the church's actions and interpretations have resulted in women experiencing injustice.[20]

What Gebara desires is the transformation of human society, and in order for that to begin, people must delve into the issue of suffering and identify its cause and root. Gebara believes "[e]nduring suffering imposed by the cross has been developed by religious traditions and social-religious systems as a veil to cover up different kinds of misery or unjust crosses. This veil does not allow us to distinguish between suffering caused by the wrongdoing of others and that existential anguish present in every human life."[21] There is an important acknowledgment in Gebara's statement, an acknowledgment that even if people succeed in combating human evils and transforming society, doing so will not mean an end to suffering. Like so many who have gone before her, she acknowledges that some suffering is endemic to the human experience. This ineradicable pain should not, however, stop people from fighting against human-caused or unjust suffering or engender discouragement. The nature of human experience is that people suffer. The continual and profound question of how to live with that reality is evident in Christian theologies of suffering and grief throughout the centuries.

Gebara offers the reminder that there is another question to ask: how and when can suffering be prevented? Gebara underscores the distinction between the existential anguish of being human and the unjust suffering that is a result of the abuse of power or acts of injustice and cruelty, or perhaps, even worse, acts of negligence and neglect. The model of Christ's ministry and the central tenets of the Christian faith call Christians to respond faithfully in the midst of pain, but also calls them to fight against what results in the unnecessary suffering of fellow humans. Sadly, this is a reality Gebara herself has witnessed: "I once conducted a workshop attended by some thirty or so women from poor

19. Ibid., 3.
20. Ibid., 177.
21. Ibid., 90.

neighborhoods in Recife and João Pessoa . . . For them, the cross was not just the suffering of their daily lives in poverty but also their condition as women. Christianity taught them to bear and even welcome their cross rather than to look for ways to be rid of it."[22] Unlike Gregory, Julian, and Taylor, Gebara does not see suffering as something to be welcomed for its cleansing or redemptive qualities. For Gebara, a blanket acceptance of suffering distorts the hopeful message of Christianity.

Human Experience of Grief: The Personal Story of Isabel Allende

On a number of occasions in *Out of the Depths,* Gebara draws on the writings of Isabelle Allende's memoir, *Paula.* The book was written over the course of a year as Allende's daughter Paula, suffering from a rare illness, lay in a coma and subsequently died. The book tells the story of that year and it is in many ways a reflection on suffering, grief, and loss—not only the suffering of Allende in losing her daughter, but the suffering she and her family had gone through living under and escaping from a dictatorship in Chile. As Gebara notes:

> She ties the events of her story to a broader background: family, nation, loves, and memories are all intermingled in the present sorrow. Grief evokes them and makes them live again in memory. Just to write about them seems to be a 'plank' of salvation. Her way of telling about herself reveals how significantly her experience of evil is mixed in with the rest of her life, and, even though her experience is similar to that of some men, it is marked by the absolutely determinative factor of being female. This factor reveals the originality of her life and her reactions as she faces her life story. What a struggle to find herself in a society in which men always have the last word! What a struggle to bring about good in a society ruled by a bloody dictatorship that upholds the well-being of a tiny privileged minority! The evil here is not something metaphysical or abstract, but a specific evil endured—no food, no freedom of expression, no equal access, no democracy. Here is a country and a continent inhabited by evil. And this lived evil, narrated later, is combined with the evil of dying, the serene tragic waning of her daughter's life.[23]

22. Ibid., 113.
23. Ibid., 24.

Gebara shows that Allende's description is not only important for its specificity, for the intimate portrait it paints of a mother's grief, but also for its insight into broader and more systemic evil. Gebara's interpretation of Allende's experience helps in further understanding when suffering is unjust. Suffering perpetrated by specific individuals in power or by a system of government created to privilege the few and torment the masses—this suffering, she says, is unjust. When there is "no food, no freedom of expression, no equal access, no democracy," when these are the daily realities of the people, their suffering is unjust. For Gebara, knowing when suffering is unjust is essential, because then we know what Christians are called to fight against.

Within this portrait of national and even continental suffering, there is also the specific suffering of Allende and her daughter. Allende's openness and vulnerability in her writing provide a window into a specific experience of suffering, which provides a place of engagement for Gebara on the themes of meaning, death, and salvation. This engagement, in turn, provides a greater understanding of Gebara's perspective on suffering and grief. Allende is not afraid to open up her heart and tell her daughter, and her reader, the pain she feels. She writes: "Since you fell ill I have had no strength for anything but you, Paula. You have been sleeping for a month now. I don't know how to reach you; I call and call but your name is lost in the nooks and crannies of this hospital. My soul is choking in sand. Sadness is a sterile desert. I don't know how to pray. I cannot string together two thoughts, much less immerse myself in creating a new book. I plunge into these pages in an irrational attempt to overcome my terror."[24] While Allende was raised Roman Catholic, she is not a particularly religious person or active member of the church. Even so, Allende is still a faithful person. She talks of God and Scripture. She wishes to pray, but the rituals of the tradition seem empty in the midst of her pain. Although Allende is neither an academic nor a self-declared believer, her memoir is still full of theology.

As Gebara has articulated in her writing, there is a sense in which humanity must come to grips with the reality of human suffering, at least with some forms of it. The suffering of Allende and her daughter is not that of the poor or oppressed. It may be horrible and seem completely unfair, but it is not the result of power imbalance or one person's unjust treatment of another. Gebara acknowledges the existence of physical

24. Allende, *Paula*, 9.

evil in the world. She writes that "[f]or Allende the evil of powerlessness is evident in the insurmountable limits of existence. And the evil that is present is not moral, an ethical failure, but embodied in the finitude of human existence, the evil everyone experiences at the loss of a loved one. Ultimately we are all caught in this kind of grief . . ."[25] Allende's experience is a universal one, a fact of human existence. Allende can be considered an example of how to face the reality of loss and grief that results from physical evil. As Gebara writes, Allende eventually reaches "a certain acquiescence to the inexorable that forms part of the mystery of human existence. . . . We give in to what is relative and provisional, to the unforeseeable, or even to what is foreseeable in the evil we have had to accept." Gebara does not believe accepting the mystery, accepting the unexplainable evil in human life, is a sign of weakness or of giving up; rather she sees it as an adjustment of our worldview. Acceptance speaks of a willingness to be open and flexible. Gebara sees in Allende's writing the willingness to acknowledge that life is "both miracle and enigma. There are only temporary and incomplete answers."[26] What is required for Allende, and for all, in the midst of the experience of grief and loss that is a result of physical evil, and which seems to shatter our way of understanding the world and making meaning, is a willingness to change and to accept. Changing our viewpoint is about coming to accept that the meaning of a given situation and the meaning of life and death cannot be defined the way they previously were.

Evil and suffering in the world have a concrete reality for Gebara. She focuses on her experience of the evil perpetrated by human institutions, particularly the church and totalitarian regimes in Latin America. She sees those institutions as having played a significant role in causing and perpetuating much suffering in the lives of women and those on the margins. For Gebara, a large part of the motivation of her own work and writing as a theologian is to raise this issue. She wishes to identify and name this evil in an effort to bring about transformation of society. She envisions a new world where the suffering endemic to human experience is not added to the sinful actions of human institutions. She grounds her work in the Christian faith and wishes to call the church back to the message of God's love and mercy that she believes is at the heart of the gospel. Through the story of Isabel Allende, Gebara also engages with the reality

25. Gebara, *Out of the Depths*, 43.
26. Ibid., 25–27.

of physical evil, of suffering endemic to the human experience, and how, in contrast to the moral evil perpetrated by institutions, we must find a way to accept that evil. Gebara advocates that acceptance comes through openness and a willingness to change our worldview.

Providence

There is less emphasis on the power and sovereignty of God in Gebara's writings than in the other participants in this conversation. This is largely due to her emphasis on the human experience, particularly on women's experience. She is less concerned with theological doctrine and more concerned with the ways in which that doctrine has been understood in and impacted on women's lives. This does not mean, however, that her work is devoid of any discussion of God's power and sovereignty. It is notable that, as in her discussion of Christ and the cross, Gebara advocates re-envisioning and reframing traditional understandings of providence. Gebara is interested in putting forth an understanding of God that is not limited by the restrictive terms the patriarchal tradition of the church has put forth over the centuries. The God she envisions is one who is critical of "those images frozen in a patriarchal world" where God is "likened to an army, to emperors and kings, to philosophical systems and theological treatises." Rather Gebara urges understanding God as one "who cries within us to be free from our prisons, who cries to be allowed to be simply God, the One who *is*." Gebara cautions her readers to remember that our understanding of and relationship to God are "tied to our life experience."[27] How we understand God cannot, in other words, be separated from our own experience. Gebara encourages an awareness of this connection between experience and understanding, but does not mean God is, thereby, limited to the understanding that develops out of experience. Gebara believes "the indisputable love of God, his trinitarian character, the communion of the divine persons, the basic goodness of the biblical God" are all elements of "an a priori view of God that must always be asserted." We can (and should) make strong claims about the nature of God and the goodness of God. Then we can cite our own experience "to confirm what is from all eternity or a priori."[28]

27. Ibid., 180 and 158.
28. Ibid., 160.

Gebara holds these truths about the nature of God and also affirms God's intimate involvement in human affairs. Gebara sees God as "mingled with the daily routine of poor women who cry to him/her in the midst of their struggle simply to survive."[29] Gebara does not focus on God as the source of suffering. As it is for C. S. Lewis, much of the suffering in the world is, for Gebara, of human origin. There is, of course, other suffering that is just a part of life, but Gebara does not talk of that suffering as being sent by God as the others do. For Gebara, like Julian, what matters more is the goodness of God and the affirmation of God's presence in the midst of suffering, and for Gebara what matters particularly is God's presence with those on the margins. She asserts that God is present with those who struggle, and it is through that presence, through that mystery of goodness that salvation can be found in the midst of struggle.

As is true of much of Gebara's theology, her emphasis is more on concrete reality than on the theoretical. She wishes to place more emphasis on the reality of God in people's experience than on the idea of God. What is important about Gebara's understanding of God is her emphasis, shared by the others, on the goodness and love of God. All five thinkers would agree that God's actions are motivated by love for humanity. Where Gebara differs is that she believes the tradition must put more emphasis on that love. She does not believe in talking of suffering as something sent by God for spiritual improvement. Doing so only reinforces the patriarchal tradition that has caused so much suffering among women and those on the margins. She wants the Christian tradition to focus on the way God's love can be manifest in the midst of suffering because it is through that love that individual salvation, as well as the institutional transformation she advocates, can happen.

Salvation

Death is not foreign to the experiences of Gebara, Allende, or the other Latin American women about whom she writes. We could argue there is perhaps a uniqueness to experiencing the death of a child because the parental instinct of protection is so strong. Allende points out, however, that it is a new phenomenon for parents to expect to outlive their

29. Ibid., 180.

children. "Only a group of privileged women—in very recent times and in advanced countries where health care is available to all who can afford it—can hope that all their children will live to be adults."[30] Acknowledging this fact, however, does not, of course, diminish her strong desire to keep her daughter alive, and her desire is palpable in her writing. In fact, as Gebara notes, Allende's writing, "becomes a means of salvation: writing to allay fear, to make sense of what is irrational. Writing to continue to struggle for her daughter's life and for her own life is a kind of salvation mixed with anguish, suffering, and the fear of death, a salvation of daily life's tedium in the midst of its sorrows and pleasures." This emphasis on salvation as a seemingly mundane and daily activity goes to the heart of Gebara's understanding of salvation. For Gebara, "Salvation is not outside but mixed in with suffering; it is where one would not think to find it. . . . Salvation is not a 'once and for all' solution but a solution for one time, then another time, and then a thousand times. Salvation is like the breath of the Spirit—it blows where it will and as it can." For Gebara, specifically, salvation is a recurring reality and not something that happened in the past. Gebara's work reminds contemporary Christians that there is a battle against evil in the here and now. Gebara also defines salvation as being about the here and now. For her, salvation is: "everything that nourishes love, our body, our life. It is more than happiness in the hereafter."[31] Discussion of evil and salvation cannot be, for her, only about a past event or only on a cosmic or theoretical level; discussion must be grounded in the present. This is because Gebara believes talking about the battle as if it is over and done with will not help those who suffer today.

Salvation through Acceptance

Gebara's discussion of Allende's writings offers a window into a concrete, lived experience of salvation. Although, as with Lewis, there is initially a struggle, and a desire to keep her daughter alive which is evident in Allende's writing and Gebara's interpretation of her, there also comes a peaceful acceptance of the reality of death. As Gebara writes, "At the end of an event or a life (and there may be several interpretations of this

---

30. Allende, 292.

31. Gebara, *Out of the Depths*, 26 and 124–27.

end), we have to give in to what happened, to this lack of outcome, or rather, to an outcome rather than the one for which we had hoped. We give in to what is relative and provisional, to the unforeseeable, or even to what is foreseeable in the evil we have had to accept."[32] Gebara sees this acceptance in Allende. She sees it is a resignation to the reality of physical evil and an acceptance that her previous understanding of life and death must be changed. As noted above, Allende must make new meanings for herself out of the reality she faces.

Like C. S. Lewis, Gebara has an understanding of salvation that is grounded in the concrete, everyday realities of life. She does not deny God's role in salvation nor the reality of an eschatological salvation, but she wishes to focus on the ways in which salvation is possible in the here and now. Gebara wishes to highlight the ways in which transformation, the ways an in-breaking of God's love, can happen in the present suffering and is not limited to the hereafter. For Gebara, what are most important are the ways salvation is manifest in the daily lives of women. Salvation is found for anyone when "the breath of the Spirit" blows into our lives, particularly in the midst of suffering. Salvation comes when hope is present and transformation happens, and for Gebara this must happen both on an individual and institutional level. Gebara's understanding of salvation is grounded in the lives of women, and it is not limited to the sacrifice of Christ on the cross.

Christ: Sacrifice and the Cross

One of the values long upheld in Western tradition is sacrifice. A willingness to die for our faith and our country has long been upheld by societies as a mark of courage and bravery, a noble act. The practice of sacrifice and a belief in its benefits can be found in many different cultures at many different times. What Gebara is most interested in engaging, though, is the Western ideology and theology, specifically in the Roman Catholic tradition, surrounding sacrifice. Gebara wants to show the ways in which that theology has been problematic for all people and for women in particular. The paramount symbol of sacrifice in the Christian tradition is the crucifix: the image of a bleeding, suffering Christ nailed to a cross. This image has served to reinforce the belief that Christianity shares with the Western tradition in the nobility of

32. Ibid., 25 and 27.

sacrifice. As Jesus says in John 15:13, "No one has greater love than this, to lay down one's life for one's friends," a statement which has been fully absorbed into Christian theology. Gebara does not necessarily want to deny any positive value of this belief but questions its negative effects.

One of Gebara's main concerns is that promoting sacrifice can end up harming the weak and reinforcing the privilege of the powerful. Her concern is for the weak, for those on the margins, who seem to be required by those in power to sacrifice, sometimes in an effort to get ahead, and often just to survive. She writes, "The need for sacrifice is always present, and this need is, for some people, a daily burden in keeping themselves alive. To live or just to survive becomes a sacrifice that is a terrible tragedy and injustice."[33] To constantly require sacrifice, particularly of those who are on the margins, is to misunderstand the redemptive act of Christ. Christian theology states that Christ's sacrifice was meant to be a once-and-for-all event. For the most part, Christian theology has held that Christ's sacrifice is the source of salvation for all and not an event to be repeated. As the Episcopal *Book of Common Prayer* articulates in Eucharistic Prayer A, "He stretched out his arms upon the cross, and offered himself in obedience to your will, a perfect sacrifice for the whole world."[34] Gebara is right to raise this issue and to question the practice of sacrifice. There is clearly something wrong with a theology that continually demands an imitation of Jesus's action on the cross, but leads only to suffering and not to redemption.

It is easy to want to join Gebara and cry a voice of protest against the belief that sacrifice should be advocated for its redemptive value. Unfortunately, the transformation of values and beliefs necessary to move away from an idealization of sacrifice has not yet been realized in the contemporary world. As Gebara notes, "[s]acrifice is the key to the happiness of living in accordance with the norms established by the new global culture." It might be tempting here to put the blame for this problem, for this reality, squarely on the shoulders of men and the wrongs of a patriarchal tradition. To do so, however, would entail the failure of self-reflection, and Gebara does not give in to this temptation. She is willing to acknowledge that all people, women included "can develop the same cruelty and jealousy that produce systemic violence in society."[35]

33. Gebara, *Out of the Depths*, 86.

34. *Book of Common Prayer*, 362.

35. Gebara, *Out of the Depths*, 89 and 98.

She believes Christ's sacrifice makes sense within the context of his own life and ministry, but being a follower of Christ need not be about repeating his sacrifice. For Gebara, being a disciple of Christ is about sharing his passion for justice, his love for all, his desire to reach out to those on the margins. It is also about calling authority to account for the ways in which the burden of suffering has been placed on the backs of the poor and the weak. It is certainly not about glorifying sacrifice, so destructive practices that harm those on the margins can continue. Therefore, Gebara advocates a different way, a different model, to understand Jesus' life "that does not stress suffering as redemptive or as the path to salvation. . . . [because] I believe some models of God and christological models hinder the self-determination of persons, especially of women." Following in the tradition of Gustavo Gutierez and others in the traditions of liberation and feminist theology, Gebara wishes to change the focus in the Christian tradition from one that emphasizes the sacrificial death of Jesus to one that emphasizes his life and teachings. The wish for a change of focus does not mean she ignores or devalues Christ's death, but his death must always be seen in the context of how he lived his life. She writes, "In this understanding we emphasize that the center of the life of Jesus was not sacrifice or suffering but works of justice, the arrival of relationships of mercy and solidarity. The core of Jesus' life was the battle against evil in all its manifestations."[36] For Gebara, the hope of Christianity lies not in focusing on images of bloody sacrifice, but in knowing God condemns the evils of human experience. The example for humanity to follow is Christ's mercy and his work to combat evil. These are to be guideposts for Christians who are to engage in acts of mercy and to join the fight against the evils of the world that result in such great human suffering.

Although Gebara wishes to move the focus of Christian theology away from the cross, she does not discount the positive role it can play in women's lives. Many women feel they can identify with Christ on the cross. There is a validation of their own experience in the knowledge that Christ knows what it is to suffer great pain. The redemptive nature of Christ's suffering can also help women find a sense of meaning in their suffering. Yet Gebara cautions against returning to the viewpoint that for the Christian tradition sacrifice is only a good. It is important to remember that for many Christians throughout history, and especially

---

36. Ibid., 87 and 107.

for women, seeing sacrifice as a good has resulted in the seeking of sacrifice or the confusion of sacrifice and pleasure. Another dark side to the belief in the positive, redemptive nature of sacrifice is coming to believe that all suffering is redemptive. Gebara cautions against emphasizing the belief that suffering leads to victory: "For women, the path to take us there is to contemplate the sufferings of this man on the cross and to accept our own crosses. The promises of the resurrection call us to bear our own sorrows and humiliations and even to renounce our basic human rights." Such a theology leads to the promotion of victimization and martyrdom among women, which runs counter to many central Christian beliefs. The conviction that suffering should be sought out would seem to fly in the face of Christian beliefs in a loving God, in the goodness of creation, and in the salvation of the world through God's love as expressed by the sending of Christ (John 3:16). As Gebara says, "I am persuaded that this unjust situation demands not only economic, social, and cultural reform but also a theological revision radically transforming the image of God as one who demands suffering as the price of happiness and exacts self-denial, with no attention to life's sources of pleasure."[37]

The image of Christ on the cross is central in Christian tradition, but for Gebara it is problematic. Gebara highlights the ways in which the cross and the ideal of sacrifice have prompted unjust and unnecessary suffering. Gebara wishes to change the focus of tradition from an act of sacrifice to the acts of love, mercy, and promotion of justice that she finds at the heart of Jesus' life and ministry. She acknowledges, as the others have, that the cross can be a point of connection with God. It can be a source of comfort in the midst of suffering to know God in Christ fully understands the reality of human suffering. Yet Gebara does not want a positive view of the Cross or sacrifice to be at the center of the Christian tradition because its centrality has only led to further suffering. She sees Christ's act of love and mercy and his calls for justice as worthy of imitation, not his sacrifice. It is through that kind of imitation the transformation she desires can begin.

37. Ibid., 88, 90, and 107.

Eternal Life

It is certainly fair to argue that there is far more emphasis on the here and now than any hereafter or other world in Gebara's writing. With her focus on the daily aspect of salvation, she seems to disregard the other side of the Christian tradition. Yet Gebara does not reject the reality of eschatological salvation, upholding that aspect of the Christian tradition, albeit with her own more ground-oriented vision of what it might look like. She pushes back on the "beyond" element of the Christian tradition in so far as it is a doctrine that has been used to promote or cause unnecessary or unjust suffering, not wanting to promote a reliance merely on the afterlife as a source of comfort in the midst of suffering. Whereas Gregory, Julian, and Taylor focus on the reward, on the joys of heaven that await the faithful, Gebara does not want a belief in the afterlife to distract us from the ways in which we can actively participate in the present. For Gebara, the kingdom of God is not merely a distant entity realized only in the end times; there is an in-breaking of the kingdom here and now, in which humanity can and should participate by imitating the acts of love and mercy that are central to Jesus' teachings.[38]

For Allende, the drive to save her daughter is eventually transformed into acceptance of her death. One of the ways this happens is through Allende's development of a theology of immortality. As Gebara notes, "*Paula* ends with a kind of theology of immortality in the form of a vision or mystical revelation."[39] Gebara then cites the following passage from Allende:

> I felt myself sinking into that cool water, and knew that the voyage through pain was ending in an absolute void. As I dissolved, I had the revelation that the void was filled with everything the universe holds. Nothing and everything, at once. Sacramental light and unfathomable darkness. I am the void, I am everything that exists, I am in every leaf of the forest, in every drop of dew, in every particle of ash that is carried by the stream, I am Paula, and I am also Isabel, I am nothing and all other things in this life and other lives, immortal. Godspeed Paula, woman. Welcome, Paula, spirit.[40]

38. Ibid., 130–31. Regarding the afterlife, Gebara writes, "I prefer, for my last sigh and my last repose, the arms of the earth—which according to the book of Genesis, is the place where God walks." (131).

39. Ibid., 156.

40. Allende, 330.

This theology of immortality Allende develops provides her a way of coping and understanding death that emphasizes how death is not the end. Allende's theology also articulates the reality and importance of the connectedness of all of creation in the past and future. The emphasis on connectedness highlights a belief in eternity, and it is an emphasis that Gebara believes Allende shares with mystic and theologian Hewig of Antwerp.[41] While Gebara argues for the value of insights and understanding gained from specific stories, such as Allende's, she also shares a belief in the connectedness of humanity, particularly among women. As she observes that there are "similarities among quite different experiences" and that "[t]he universal experience of distress and grief leads us to take note of a certain 'geography of evil,' which characterizes the life of women, especially poor women, everywhere. Moreover, an appeal to God or to a transcendent mystery occurs everywhere in these accounts of daily afflictions."[42] The value of Allende's story is not only in its specificity, which offers a concrete expression of themes in Gebara's book, but also in the ways—like other stories including Gebara's own—it points to themes and realities not unique to her experience but echoed in the experiences of other women, and even echoed in other elements of the Christian tradition.

Given the concrete nature of so much of Gebara's theology and her focus on the experience of the individual in the midst of daily life, she seems to be in stark contrast to the others. She does not share in the focus (particularly present in Gregory, Julian, and Taylor) on the joys and delights of eternal life with God. While that hope sustains those writers (and presumably many of their readers) in the midst of suffering, it is not strongly evident in Gebara's writing. A vision of the afterlife is certainly not entirely absent from Gebara's writing. She engages with Allende on the theme of immortality, and presents her own vision of life after death, wishing to rest "in the arms of the earth" because Genesis says that "is the place where God walks." Perhaps because her theology as a whole, like her vision of the afterlife, is more grounded and earthly focused, there is a notable absence of hell in her writing. Her emphasis on God's love and mercy, her acknowledgment that there is much beyond human knowing, and her intimate knowledge of suffering in the here and now, may lead her not to presume or even to

41. Gebara, *Out of the Depths,* 156–57.
42. Ibid., 12.

imagine horrible punishment and suffering beyond this life. Given her emphasis on human agency, she would likely share the belief of the others that we have the option to turn away from God, particularly given that she has witnessed so many choose evil over love and mercy in the here and now. Yet Gebara also shares with her companions in this conversation, a hopeful attitude that looks for an afterlife that is one of rest, free from the terrible realities experienced in this life.[43]

SUMMARY ANALYSIS

Gebara brings an important, critical lens to Christian theology and the Christian tradition. She provides a reminder not to let the human desire for power interfere with the foundations of the faith tradition. She laments and questions those structures and long-held beliefs that only serve a privileged few. She is a liberation theologian and a feminist who reminds the church that Christ preached liberation and sought to include those on the margins. She seeks to bring out into the light "a form of evil [that] has appeared not yet sufficiently recognized by Christian theology. It is the evil undergone and experienced especially by women at home and within social structures, like the church, which were originally founded to love and help people find dignity."[44]

It is her critical lens that makes Gebara stand in contrast to the four other thinkers, yet there is also room for acceptance within her theology of suffering. For Gebara, like Lewis, acceptance is arrived at after a journey. For Lewis, that journey is about feeling the depths of our grief, and for Gebara that journey is about examining the origins of the suffering we experience or witness. Once we have determined that the suffering in question is not the result of personal or institutional acts of injustice, that the suffering is, in fact, of the sort endemic to the human experience (a result of physical evil), then and only then can we arrive at a place of acceptance. Gebara does not discount nor deny the importance of acceptance, but for her it is not where the priority lies. Gebara's priorities lie in uncovering, exposing, and stopping acts of injustice that result in the suffering of those on the margins.

43. Ibid., 131 and 180.
44. Ibid., 176–77.

Given that her priority is not acceptance, her discussion of it is not as rich or nuanced as it is in Gregory, Julian, and Taylor. The main feature of Gebara's theology is a change in perspective and understanding in the face of suffering that must be accepted. As noted above, when the outcome of a situation is one of loss (e.g., the death of a loved one), then we must, like Allende, find new ways of making meaning. It may be our definitions of life and death have to change. For Gebara, coming to a place of acceptance also means an acknowledgment of mystery, of the fact that even a willingness to change our views does not necessarily mean we will have full understanding of the reality of suffering we experience. This acknowledgment of mystery is a facet her theology shares with the other thinkers. It is a humble acknowledgment of God's providence and the fact that there is much beyond human knowing. While we may be able to change our viewpoint or our definitions, and thereby enable us to live more easily with suffering, part of our acceptance will also need to be an acceptance of the limits of our own understanding.

CRITIQUE

The challenge of Gebara's discussion is the question of the centrality of the cross and sacrifice in the Christian tradition. As noted, Gebara wishes to emphasize the life and teachings of Jesus over his sacrifice. In her understanding, justice and mercy are at the heart of the Christian faith. She believes putting an act of male sacrifice at the center of the Christian faith has done damage because it has caused women to conflate pleasure and sacrifice rather than fight against oppression.[45] Her conviction, however, opens the question of whether it is possible to construct an understanding of the cross that acknowledges the centrality of its place in the Christian tradition and also appreciates the complex and ironic ways it has impacted piety and self-understanding of women over the centuries. Before that can be done, it is worth reviewing the place of the cross in the Christian tradition.

45. Ibid., 88.

Place of the Cross in Christian Tradition

The cross is a symbol shared across all the various branches of Christianity. It is, perhaps, one of the only symbols that has been central to the worship and self-identity of Christians since the early church. There is evidence of veneration of the cross on Good Friday dating from the fourth century.[46] From the early Middle Ages, the footprint of a church has often been made in the form of the cross.[47] In a newly constructed glass and steel mega-church, a sparse New England meetinghouse, or an ornate European cathedral, the cross will be there—on the walls, in the form of the building and/or worn by many worshiping there. Not only is the cross central to the visual, material life of Christian worship, it is also a central symbol of Christian piety that has been embodied by millions of Christians over the centuries. Many Christians cross themselves when entering a church, at significant moments in the liturgy, and frequently when receiving the Eucharist. The cross continues to be an integral part of modern worship. In Episcopal liturgies, for instance, when a minister gives a blessing, individual or collective, it is frequently accompanied by a sign of the cross, and many people cross themselves when receiving the blessing. On Ash Wednesday, marking the beginning of Lent, ashes are imposed in the form of a cross on our foreheads. Additionally, since the Middle Ages, a person was anointed with in the sign of the cross at death, a practice that is still done for those who are ill.[48] Its use and influence have even at times extended into agriculture. In the sixteenth century in North Wales, problems with cattle were seen as a result of forgetting to make the sign of the cross.[49]

The cross is also an important part of the liturgy of baptism, of initiation into the Christian faith. In a practice that has roots dating back to the third century, according to *The Apostolic Tradition* of Hippolytus, a person is usually anointed by the bishop or presiding minister at baptism in the form of a cross on the forehead (or in the past on the top of the head), symbolizing their new identity as a Christian.[50] This marking of the forehead was likely done by the earliest Christians as an out-

---

46. Hatchett, *Commentary on the American Prayer Book*, 232.

47. Risebero, *The Story of Western Architecture*, 48.

48. Hatchett, 464–65.

49. Thomas, *Religion and the Decline of Magic*, 31.

50. White, *Documents of Christian Worship*, 155.

growth of the Jewish practice of marking a newly baptized person with a "T" for the Hebrew letter Taw, which symbolized the name of God. In his commentary, Marion Hatchett notes that,"[t]he Taw was soon interpreted as the sign of the cross. In the early Church the devotional use of the sign of the cross was a reminder of one's baptism."[51]

The symbolism of the cross is not only externally important to the tradition and communities of worship, it is a symbol that has been embodied and internalized by individual Christians. It is foundational, Christianity's unifying and identifying symbol. Theologians do certainly differ on what the cross means or how it is to be understood by Christians, but given its centrality in the story and the practice of Christianity, the question in light of Gebara's criticism is how an understanding of the cross can be reformulated without losing its place at the heart of the Christian tradition.

Re-envisioning the Cross?

Gebara questions whether in this context the cross of Christ can still be the preeminent symbol of Christianity because it "ultimately affirms the path of suffering and male martyrdom as the only way to salvation and to highlight injustice toward women and humanity. All the suffering of women over centuries of history would be deemed useless by such a theology of history."[52] Although highlighting issues of injustice would always be valuable, at the heart of Gebara's statement is criticism of a masculine understanding of the cross. Additionally, we are left with the question of whether the cross only represents male sacrifice. Is male martyrdom indeed the only way? What about the idea, expressed in the gospel of John (notably John 3:16), in the letters of Paul, and in the writings of Julian, which affirms Christ's death on the cross was not for a select few, but for all of humanity? Julian affirms the crucifixion is an act of love. Is it not possible for the cross to be *both* a symbol of sacrifice and a symbol of redemption? Feminist critics, like Gebara, can provide a valuable call to Christians to return to their roots and to remember that which is central to their faith. The universal intention of Christ's sacrifice is eloquently expressed in the *Book of Common Prayer*: "Lord

51. Hatchett, 279–80.
52. Gebara, *Out of the Depths*, 118.

Jesus Christ, you stretched out your arms of love on the hard wood of the cross that everyone might come within the reach of your saving embrace . . ."[53] There is no doubt the universality of Christ's action has been ignored or forgotten at numerous points in Christian history; the history of violence among Christians and against others is a testament to that. The heart of the Christian message, however, has always been one of life and love. The Christian tradition and its symbolism need not be reinvented, only returned to its foundations.

Regarding the ways the cross has sanctified acts of sacrifice in the history of the church, Gebara does acknowledge the positive aspect of sacrificing oneself for another or for a good. She is only critical of the way this view of sacrifice has promoted undue or unnecessary sacrifice. Gebara acknowledges the traditional emphasis, as noted above, on Jesus's death as one of self-giving love, of laying his life down for his friends. She believes this interpretation can be true of intra-human relations, and she accepts it as a teaching of Christ and one that is significant for Christians. The understanding of the cross, therefore, need not to be completely redone. It seems possible (and valuable) to realign the cross, the most central symbol of Christian faith, with an interpretation that emphasizes love and self-giving, so as to balance and counter the ways in which it has been twisted and used in harmful ways.

It is important to point out, as Gebara does, that when the crucifixion is absolutized to such an extent that it eclipses the life and teachings of Christ, insights into the way of justice and mercy that can be learned from the gospels can be lost. Yet we cannot talk about Christ apart from the cross. We cannot omit the cross in consideration of Christ's acts of love or his desire for justice without editing out major sections of the gospel accounts, rejecting outright Paul's Christology and the kerygma of the early church, and dismissing centuries of reception of the story of Jesus Christ by Christians. Gebara states, "The core of Jesus' life was the battle against evil in all its manifestations."[54] For her, this statement is a call to action for Christians, a call to mimic his fight for social justice. Could the cross, with its self-giving act of love, be seen as the paramount example of Christ's battle against evil? For centuries in the Christian church, one way of understanding the cross was to describe it as the means of Christ's victory over the devil. It might be helpful

53. *Book of Common Prayer,* 101.
54. Ibid., 87.

though, to draw on the "Christ as Victor" model in the contemporary battle. To see Christ's suffering on the cross as a battle against evil is to understand that we do not fight alone. The battle against evil in the here and now is not a losing battle. Evil cannot triumph because Christ has already won. That reality may not yet be manifest in human time, but we can be confident our own efforts contribute to hasten that reality. As Jeremy Taylor writes in *Holy Living and Dying*, "But He who restored the law of nature, did also restore us to the condition of nature, which, being violated by the introduction of death, Christ then repaired when He suffered and overcame death for us; that is, he hath taken away the unhappiness of sickness, and the sting of death. . . . If therefore we can well manage our state of sickness, that we may not fall by pain, as we usually do by pleasure, we need not fear; for no evil shall happen to us."[55] This quote offers great hope in believing Christ has been victorious over evil. As is evident in the theology and experiences of the thinkers presented here, it is not an empty hope, but one that can have real impact in the midst of suffering.

An important theme in Gebara's writing is the belief that salvation is a ground-level, daily reality; salvation is not merely a transcendent idea, but a reality that must be lived out daily. Gebara states that salvation happens "through promoting relationships of justice, respect, and tenderness among human beings."[56] This is not a radical idea in the Christian tradition. It is an idea that has theological roots in Paul's letter to the Philippians, where he writes, "work out your own salvation with fear and trembling; for it is God who is at work in you, enabling you both to will and to work for his good pleasure."[57] There is no doubt these traits are important hallmarks of the Christian tradition; there is no doubt they are an important part of how salvation is lived out. Gebara focuses on the relational, human-to-human aspect of salvation because she wants to criticize the view that salvation is something that can be imposed from above by an imperial power. Yet to only focus on the relational is to miss an important theological aspect. As Paul notes, our salvation is worked out because God is at work in each person; salvation is not an entirely human endeavor. Gebara's criticism of imposed salvation is justified, but in pushing her reader to the relational end of the

55. Taylor, *Holy Living and Dying*, 352.
56. Gebara, *Out of the Depths*, 113.
57. Philippians 2:12b–13.

spectrum, the theological reality of salvation as a divine/human coop-erative endeavor should not be lost. For Gebara, the quest for salvation is not a single monolithic event, rather it is a daily activity: "In practice we must always begin again every day the search for salvation just as every day we have to begin again the actions of eating and drinking." Salvation, by this measure, is a gift from God, and it is a gift in which humans can participate. In addition to being aware of the ways we can be complicit in the suffering of others, Gebara exhorts Christians to be inspired and reassured that we can also be a part of the healing of others and the transformation of the world. Transformation can happen if we can also come to the realization "that salvation experienced by Jesus, as well as our own salvation, does not occur automatically through the cross imposed by an imperial power but through promoting relation-ships of justice, respect, and tenderness among human beings."[58] These are meant to be the hallmarks of Christians—justice, respect and ten-derness, and it is through actions that express these beliefs that people can be a force for good and help bring healing into the lives of others. This is a point at which Gebara could seem to be far removed from the thinking of theologians in the previous chapters.

For the mainstream of the Christian tradition, salvation is also inextricably linked to the death of Christ. This does not mean salvation is not also worked out and lived out in human relationships, nor does it disregard the value of the Incarnation or the life and ministry of Jesus, but it does mean a theological understanding of salvation, for main-stream Christianity, cannot leave out the cross and the self-sacrifice of Christ. It is a view articulated by Gregory the Great in his *Moralia*: "He offered a sacrifice in our behalf, He set forth His own Body in behalf of sinners, a victim void of sin, that both by human nature He might be ca-pable of dying, and by righteousness be capable of purifying."[59] This is a view also shared by Taylor and expressed in *The Worthy Communicant*. Taylor writes, "there is no other sacrifice but that of Himself offered upon the cross; it follows that Christ in heaven perpetually offers and represents that sacrifice to His heavenly Father, and in virtue of that obtains all good things for His Church."[60]

58. Gebara, *Out of the Depths*, 113 and 123.

59. Gregory, *The Books of the Morals, Vol II.iv.*

60. Taylor and Carroll, 209.

This emphasis on salvation through Christ's self-giving has its foundation in Scripture in the story of the Last Supper. Matthew 26:27–28 tells of Christ sharing the cup with the disciples: "'Drink from it, all of you; for this is my blood of the covenant, which is poured out for many for the forgiveness of sins.'" These words, which are found with some variation in all four gospels and in Paul's letters, and their focus on the blood of Christ, serve as a charter for how the church has received the meaning of the cross, and for the Eucharistic rite, which has been observed by all branches of the church over the centuries with only rare exceptions. The blood imagery threads its way through Scripture and is central to the rite, which in turn is central to Christian worship. These facts serve to reinforce the central place of the cross for Christian identity across history.

The emphasis on blood, particularly Christ's blood, has led, in Gebara's thinking, to the belief that "[m]ale sacrifice is the only kind that redeems and restores life; male blood is the only blood of any value." If for all Christians it is Christ's blood that is the source of redemption, if that blood has a place of reverence and is a source of life and salvation, then, Gebara argues, male blood is seen as worthwhile by tradition, whereas, "[w]omen's bleeding is filthy, impure, dangerous." [61] This highlights another difficulty with the image of Christ on the cross for Gebara. While, as noted earlier, many women identify with Christ's act of sacrifice (because there experiences have been filled with a need to sacrifice for the sake of others), because women's blood is not seen as redemptive by the tradition, it may be difficult for them to understand the Cross as a symbol of redemption and salvation, and not just one of sacrifice.

Gebara's call for justice and mercy, her call to Christians to follow Christ's teaching rather than mimic his sacrifice, is a noble and valuable call. Her emphasis on love and mercy is a fair criticism of the Christian tradition, as there is no doubt over the centuries a predominately male leadership that often used the cross as a symbol of their power and authority has also perpetuated the subjugation of women and those on the margins. Yet it is not possible to talk about Jesus' life and teachings apart from his death, apart from the cross. The gospel writers find in his own preaching frequent references to his death and expressions of his willingness to sacrifice himself for others. A belief in Christ's willingness to give himself over to death on a cross for the salvation of all

61. Gebara, *Out of the Depths*, 7.

points to the reality that God's will for humanity is for life and salvation, not for further sacrifice. This is evident in many aspects of the Christian tradition, including the Eucharistic prayer cited above, and Gebara's own writing. She writes that she envisions a future where "all people, lifting their eyes, will see the earth shining with brotherhood and sisterhood, mutual appreciation, true complimentarity . . ."[62] A belief that God wishes human flourishing for all people is a belief Gebara certainly upholds, and one that can be supported by an understanding of the cross as a symbol of love and salvation. Therefore, it would seem Gebara could use Christ's death on the cross as further support of her argument.

While Gebara rightfully points out what and who is missing in some of the traditional doctrines of the crucifixion, it is also possible to see the cross as an act of love. The cross is evidence of God's desire for human flourishing and a symbol of hope to those who are suffering. The cross is not meant to encourage sacrifice, but to show that God's will is for health and life. The image of a crucified Christ can be a source of comfort in the midst of grief, for it is a reminder that God knows the pain of human suffering. The cross represents Good Friday, the depths of anguish and despair, and it also represents Easter morning. It represents the possibility that new life and hope can be born from suffering. One might counter, of course, that it is still a *male* body that is resurrected on Easter morning, which is an important criticism.[63] It is Christ's body, however, the body of God's Son, that is resurrected, and just as Christ died for all humanity, his resurrection is for all: male and female. It is important that theologies of the cross emphasize redemption and salvation are real and for *all* people. For these and many other reasons, we cannot separate the cross from the Christian tradition, and particularly not from a theological discussion of grief and suffering. In fact, as Christians, we cannot think about suffering apart from the cross—not only because the cross *is* suffering, but also because the cross offers the reminder that suffering can be transformed. The cross is central to making sense of suffering and grief in the Christian tradition because it is a point of empathetic connection and ultimately a source of hope. It offers Christians an assurance that the love of God will have the last word. It is possible to view the cross not as an act of pain and

---

62. Gebara, "Women Doing Theology in Latin America," 48.
63. Gebara to Molly James, email. 2 February, 2009.

sacrifice that should be imitated, but as the ultimate act of love—it is the love and not the suffering that is to be imitated.

Gebara is not a lone voice. There are like-minded voices crying out from the depths of the Christian tradition that embolden her argument that the cross is not to be a symbol of power or pain. As seen in the chapter on Julian, her conclusion at the end of her writings is that the ultimate meaning of her visions and all she has learned in her contemplations is: love. Love is and was and will be Christ's meaning. Not sacrifice, not suffering, not pain. As evidenced in her vision of Christ on the cross in which she sees joy on his face, Julian believes that as Christ's suffering was transformed into joy, so too will the present suffering of humanity be transformed into joy. For Julian, suffering is redemptive, and it is a truth Julian asserts from her own experience: "And for this little pain which we suffer here we shall have an exalted and eternal knowledge in God which we could never have without it."[64] This statement of Julian's is thought provoking; but it could be seen to be advocating suffering as good, because it leads to a greater knowledge of God. In fact, Julian is saying that suffering is redemptive, but she is not promoting suffering. Suffering is a fact of life for Julian, a daily reality for those in the fourteenth century as it is for people in the twenty-first. Julian's goal of finding ways to cope with the reality of suffering, ways to understand it that lead to joy and redemption rather than more pain, is a goal Gebara shares. Gebara writes, "While we must treat suffering seriously, we should also try to redeem it, to transform it into a sign of salvation." Gebara acknowledges that the cross can also be seen as a "call to redemption and salvation," and need not always be a symbol of sacrifice.[65] Given this acknowledgment of how the cross can be a positive symbol, we wonder why she does not seek to put greater emphasis there instead of on criticisms of the ways the cross has traditionally been viewed and portrayed. Without a doubt, the cross is a positive symbol for Julian, a symbol of love, new life, and transformation. While Julian and Gebara certainly have their differences, there is also solidarity across time among these two women who both seek to correct the tradition that says the cross is meant to promote sacrifice or suffering. On this score, they provide a powerful voice to assert, "love was his meaning."

64. Julian of Norwich, *Showings*, 215.
65. Gebara, *Out of the Depths*, 107 and 112.

CONCLUSION

There are many valuable themes that arise from the work of Ivone Gebara that can be important elements in a Christian theology of grief. Gebara's feminist and liberation perspectives bring critical questions to the conversation, offering the reminder to critically assess traditional beliefs, practices, and power structures. Those that are detrimental to the poor, the oppressed and those on the margins, and those that result in unjust suffering, should be revised. According to Gebara, special attention should be paid to the ways traditional Christologies that upheld the value of sacrifice and maleness have been detrimental to women. Gebara also underscores the value of story and experience because she believes they are valuable tools in doing theology, and she offers a reminder to be aware of how personal experience impacts our theology.

Gebara's writings additionally offer the important reminder to critically engage with tradition in order to ensure that theologies seek to uplift and strengthen believers rather than divide or harm them. She reminds Christians they are called to fight with and for those on the margins, and called to stand in opposition to unjust suffering. She also encourages acceptance of suffering that is not the result of injustice. With the contributions of voices such as Gebara's, Christians may work to regain the emphasis of love and mercy at the heart of their tradition as they seek to deal with the reality of grief and loss in the human experience.

While Gebara's contribution, particularly her critical voice, is a valuable and important part of the conversation on the reality of suffering within the Christian tradition, we wonder how her voice can meld with the other participants in this conversation. Can we, in fact, begin with a framework such as Gebara's, one that highlights questions of injustice and the experiences of those on the margins, while building a nuanced understanding of acceptance regarding the reality of endemic suffering? Is it possible, for instance, to be critical of the way human sin results in suffering while also believing suffering has a purgative and cleansing quality, as Gregory does? Can we focus both on suffering as the path to union with God in heaven, as Julian does, while simultaneously being committed to fighting injustice in the here and now? Can we practice Taylor's patient endurance and be committed to action as well? And is there room in Gebara's framework for the depth of grieving Lewis advocates? There are many questions and tensions raised by

Gebara's critical perspective. The task of the concluding chapter is to develop a theology of suffering that draws on all these thinkers and seeks to find a path in the midst of the tensions raised. It is to that task we now turn.

Conclusion

A Contemporary Theology of Suffering

HAVING HAD OUR "CONVERSATION" with the five theologians, it is time to develop a contemporary theology of suffering that draws on their work. Each thinker offers a different type of acceptance. For Gregory, acceptance of suffering is shown through an ascetic discipline that promotes spiritual cleansing and growth. For Julian, suffering is accepted with joy because it is through suffering we attain union with God. For Taylor, acceptance is manifest through the practice of patient forbearance in the face of suffering. For Lewis, acceptance is understood as a place of rest after the challenging work of grief. For Gebara, acceptance is only promoted as a response to suffering that is endemic to the human experience, because in the face of unjust suffering we are called to engage in the opposite of acceptance: we are called to fight. The typology offered through the works of these five thinkers provides a framework with which to develop a contemporary theology of suffering, a "type" of acceptance for those who currently struggle with the reality of suffering.

The contemporary theology is developed out of and for the cultural context of twenty-first century America, and it is a theology that seeks to nuance the belief that all suffering is good in order to state that suffering and sacrifice *can be* good. It is true that acts of sacrifice and the experience of suffering can do much to deepen our faith and bring us closer to Christ, yet the possibility of gaining virtue does not mean we should blindly accept the reality of suffering. We need to engage in discernment with a critical lens, as Gebara does, and ask whether the suffering we experience is endemic or whether it is the result of sin and injustice. If it is the latter, the pain of suffering should be seen not as something to be borne with patience, but as a call to a different kind of virtuous action—that of following Christ's teachings of justice, love and mercy; combating unjust suffering is equally, if not more, noble as patiently enduring it. This is, of course, not the only message regarding suffering that can be valuable to contemporary Christians. Even as much of Western Christianity still promotes a strong message of acceptance of suffering—as it has for centuries—there is a growing and paradoxical cultural message in America that any suffering is wrong. The belief that suffering is an aberration is one that can certainly be theologically backed up by an argument in the goodness of creation and God's desire for human flourishing. It is a small step from seeing suffering as an aberration to a belief that life is supposed to go along swimmingly; we are not supposed to get ill or die, we are not supposed to experience tragedy or loss, and we are not supposed to commit violent acts or to ignore the needs of our neighbors. Particularly as medical technology has advanced, an expectation has grown in America that any life can be saved and that much suffering can be prevented. Like the belief that all suffering is good, this expectation, too, needs to be nuanced through the critical voices of the thinkers in this conversation as I construct a contemporary theology of suffering. This expectation can be nuanced by reminding contemporary American Christians of the value in seeing endemic suffering as a given reality, as a possibility for spiritual growth, and as the way to a great reward. It can also be nuanced by the reminder that suffering is of value to patient endurance; though, it may also need to be reiterated that to come to a place of patience and acceptance does not mean ignoring the gravity of experience or the depth of our pain. As Lewis suggests, sometimes the best way to acceptance begins with anger.

A contemporary theology of suffering, then, is one that finds a way to hold onto and live with the tensions of suffering. On the one hand, it must heed Gebara's call to remember the distinction between the types of suffering and to take action in the face of unjust suffering. It must heed the call of the liberation theologians not to allow Jesus's teachings of justice, love, and mercy to be disregarded or pushed to the sidelines. On the other hand, it must not fall into the trap of believing life can (or should be) free from suffering; suffering is a reality of the human experience, and it can be a good. Endemic suffering can be borne in such a way as to bring great spiritual riches to our lives.

A contemporary theology of suffering is one that takes seriously the acceptance of suffering so strongly advocated by Gregory, Julian, and Taylor. It takes seriously the gifts and virtues they argue can be gained, while also acknowledging, with Gebara, an appreciation of those gifts does not have to mean a blind acceptance of all suffering. Nor is the road to acceptance necessarily a simple or easy one. As Lewis shows, we may only come to a place of acceptance after a struggle in one's relationship with and understanding of God. In the end, we may arrive at a theology that, at its heart, is about acceptance, but acknowledges that in order to best face current challenges, acceptance must be nuanced by a discerning mind and a tolerance for the depth of emotion that can come with the reality of suffering. The practical models and approaches offered by all five theologians are important and will now be considered in the development of a theological framework for contemporary Christians to think about and live with the realities suffering and grief.

SUMMARY OF TYPOLOGIES

Gregory the Great

For Gregory, suffering is to be accepted because it is an ascetic discipline through which we can grow in virtue. Gregory places a strong emphasis on the reality of human sinfulness, and for him an important aspect of seeing suffering as an ascetic discipline is his view of it as an opportunity to engage in repentance. Suffering is scourge that can cleanse humanity of its sins, if we take the opportunity to repent and to amend our lives. According to Gregory, we must not disregard the gift of God's discipline by adding to our sins by grieving. God is, for Gregory, the great disciplinarian who seeks to school humanity, so people may be more Christ-like in their stature. We can take comfort in the knowledge that no matter how harsh God's discipline may seem, humanity's sufferings always pale when in comparison with Christ's. God seeks to reward those who submit to the scourge of discipline (suffering) with eternal life in heaven, but salvation is not guaranteed. For Gregory, the possibility of eternal damnation is real, and it must be held up as a deterrent to sinful behavior. We can take comfort in the hope of an eternal reward, but we must never become complacent. Suffering, for Gregory, is to be seen as a gift from God, and perhaps even as an experience to be sought, for it is through suffering we are cleansed from sin and brought closer to Christ.

Julian of Norwich

For Julian, suffering is to be accepted because it is the path to a blissful union with God in Christ. Julian's theology is notable for its optimism, but that does not mean she discounts the reality of human sinfulness. Julian has an awareness of her own sinful tendencies and that of her fellow Christians, but for her we cannot view human sinfulness apart from the mercy of God. God is always present with humanity and seeking to bring humanity to that blissful union. The fall, therefore, is seen as a happy event because it results in humanity's salvation by Christ, in humanity's being brought to bliss through unity with God in Christ. It is in Christ's fall (in becoming human) humanity is raised up, and the sinfulness of Adam is transformed into the blamelessness of Christ. Julian sees God as a mother who allows her children to fall so they may be brought to a reward greater than if they had not fallen. While that reward is fully realized in heaven through the joy of eternal union with God, we can find glimpses of joy when God's love is manifest in the here and now. Julian does acknowledge the possibility of damnation, but her overwhelming emphasis is on her belief that God desires to bring all of humanity to that place of blissful union. In Julian's view, there is hope in the midst of suffering, because God, like a loving mother, is always present and is ultimately leading us to bliss.

Jeremy Taylor

For Taylor, suffering is to be accepted because it grants us the opportunity to live a more holy life through the practice of patient forbearance. Taylor's view of the world is somewhat pessimistic, as he encourages his readers to meditate on the miseries of the world and to be grateful that human lives are short. Yet Taylor is also hopeful. His hope is grounded in a belief in the importance of a lifelong cultivation of virtue. Taylor does not believe in deathbed repentance because he believes we must spend our whole lives seeking to cultivate virtue, particularly the virtue of patient forbearance in the midst of suffering. Cultivating patient forbearance is an opportunity to imitate Christ and to participate with God in our salvation. Taylor has great confidence in God's providence, believing all that happens is good in God's eyes, no matter how it may seem from humanity's perspective. Much of Taylor's hope lies in his confidence that all is good and all we love is eternal; therefore, we need not despair in the midst of suffering. We need only practice patient forbearance, for suffering does not last, and if we have lived a holy life then we will be granted the reward of eternal life with God and those we love.

C. S. Lewis

For Lewis, acceptance of suffering comes as a matter of respite after the struggle of grief. Lewis's writing, particularly in *The Screwtape Letters*, attests to the fact he believes in the reality of evil and humanity's tendency toward sin, yet this does not mean he has an ultimately dark view of God or humanity. In the midst of his grief, Lewis wonders if God is a Cosmic Sadist, but ultimately he comes to a positive view of God. In his acceptance of suffering, Lewis comes to realize that while there is much he does not understand, he can have faith that God desires good for humanity and seeks to bring all to a great reward. Lewis's belief in God's loving care and willingness to sacrifice for the salvation of humanity is most evident in the character of Aslan (the Christ figure) in *The Chronicles of Narnia*. The unsurpassed beauty of the reward awaiting the faithful is portrayed in the closing pages of the *Chronicles*, but Lewis does not believe it is the fate of all. While he believes God offers the reward to all, he also has a strong view of human freedom and believes we can refuse God's offer and choose eternal separation from God (hell). Lewis also believes the nature of human sinfulness does not merit an easy reward, and believes human sinfulness requires a belief in purgatory, a cleansing of the soul at the end of our lives. While the reality of sin remains in Lewis's worldview, and he fully acknowledges the pain and suffering of grief, he ultimately comes to a place of peace and trust: in the end good can triumph.

Ivone Gebara

Gebara's theology has room for an acceptance of suffering only after it has been firmly established that a particular instance of suffering is endemic to the human experience and not the result of injustice. Gebara's main concern is to address the reality of human and institutional sin and the ways in those realities have caused or contributed to the suffering of those on the margins, particularly women and the poor in Latin America. She believes the Christian understanding of the cross and Jesus's ministry needs to be re-envisioned in order to place less emphasis on the value of sacrifice and more emphasis on the love and mercy of God that are, for her, at the heart of Jesus's ministry and message. Gebara also does not want salvation to be understood only as a single or simply eschatalogical reality. For salvation to have meaning to those who suffer in the here and now, it must be able to be realized in the midst of suffering and in the midst of daily life. Gebara places much less emphasis on the afterlife than the others, although she does see it as a time of eternal rest after the struggles of this life. Gebara's main concern is to call Christians to fight against the unjust suffering present in the here and now.

THEOLOGICAL TOUCHSTONES OF A CONTEMPORARY THEOLOGY

As is evidenced in the preceding discussion, the writings of these five theologians provide insight into five significant theological themes or touchstones: humanity, sin and evil, God's providence, salvation, Christ, and eternal life. Each thinker emphasizes the themes differently, and in many cases they have widely divergent views on those themes as they relate to the issues of suffering and grief, yet there are also many points on which common ground can be found. Gregory, Julian, and Taylor all strongly advocate acceptance of suffering, albeit in different ways and for varied reasons. For Gregory, suffering is a matter of ascetic discipline. For Julian, suffering is the path to blissful union with God. For Taylor, suffering is an opportunity to live a holy life through the practice of patient forbearance. While their approaches differ somewhat, in examining each of their theologies we are left with the same two challenges. First, is it possible to hold a strong view of acceptance (as they do) while also leaving room for the anguish felt in the midst of grief? Second, is it possible to hold a strong view of acceptance while also engaging in the fight to alleviate unjust suffering in the world? Lewis offers a way to engage fully with the emotions of grief while still finding a way to ultimately accept the reality of suffering. Gebara's critical approach advocates fighting against unjust suffering and coming to acceptance only once it has been discerned the suffering is endemic to the human experience. The challenge that remains then, is to develop a contemporary theology of suffering that endeavors to build a synthesis drawing on the rich views of acceptance found in Gregory, Julian, and Taylor, but also seeks to leave room for the anguish of grief, as Lewis does, and heeds the call to fight against unjust suffering, as Gebara does.

Humanity, Sin, and Evil

The story of the fall and its consequences mean Christians must grapple with the reality of sin in the world. Living in a fallen world means living with the reality of evil, and it means there are diseases and natural disasters; people die—sometimes after long and full lives, sometimes after very short ones. These realities illustrate the suffering endemic to the human experience. Living in a fallen world also means humanity is prone to sin, on an individual and an institutional level. As Lewis and Gebara particularly remind their readers, sin is the cause of much suffering in the world, and suffering as a result of human sin must be brought out into the light; it must be faced and fought against. While this distinction between endemic and unjust suffering may seem to be only a modern one, the approaches of Gregory and Taylor do have some bearing. Gregory and Taylor have strong views on the depths of human sinfulness. They both note how when humanity puts its own selfish desires first and falls away from a focus on God, it is possible to contribute to or even cause suffering. They both advocate using suffering to change our ways and move toward living a holy and devout life. It would seem, therefore, we could raise a call to fight unjust suffering that not only draws on Gebara's distinction, but also advocates the rigorous approaches of Gregory and Taylor as a way to cleanse and heal from sin, whether it be from sin on an individual or an institutional level.

Even if we have found a way to address the reality of unjust suffering in the world, we must still face the reality of the suffering endemic to the human experience. Julian understands suffering as a fall that obscures humanity's vision and prevents people from seeing their true status as beloved children of God. Julian particularly affirms how God not only desires goodness for humanity, but also desires to bring humanity to a bliss partially realized on earth and fully realized in heaven. If we are to follow Julian and to focus on the hope of bliss, then we must also follow her in seeing the fall as a happy event. It may take a leap of faith to follow Julian, but doing so is also an affirmation of God's goodness and of Christian hope. To say the fall was a happy event is to first acknowledge the depth of suffering it has led to and then to affirm the hope of a reward, which is greater for having gone through suffering. We can also affirm the good in suffering, that the good can be realized in the midst of humanity's fallen state, when we join Gregory and Taylor in affirming its cleansing and educative value. Emphasizing the good that can come of it can help us accept the reality of endemic suffering as a part of the human experience in which we must live.

This contemporary theology of suffering offers a vision of the human condition that acknowledges its fallen state and the suffering that ensues—both as a result of living in a fallen world and as a result of sin. Following Gregory, Julian, and Taylor, we can advocate a belief that life should be ordered around our desire for God and to follow God's will, but with Gebara's perspective we can also push this vision to say our lives should also be ordered by God's desire for human flourishing. While we can affirm God is at work in the world, caring for creation and bringing salvation, we must also affirm Christians have a duty to order their own lives in such a way as to seek to participate in God's work and to promote the flourishing of all. Because of the goodness of God and God's providence, Christians can have great hope even in the midst of the reality of endemic suffering.

God's Providence

This contemporary Christian understanding of suffering affirms, as Scripture does again and again, God's intimate involvement in human affairs. Additionally, of course, at the heart of the Christian faith is the Easter story—the story of God transforming suffering and death into new life. These five thinkers affirm God's connection with humanity. For Gregory, the emphasis is on God as schoolmaster teaching his pupils a new way of living. Julian sees God as the loving lord who seeks to reward his servant after the fall. Taylor's God is the one who has humanity's best interests at heart even when it might not seem that way from the human perspective. For Lewis, God is initially a more distant figure and one who is the subject of Lewis's questions and anger, and while he toys with calling God a Cosmic Sadist, he ultimately comes to see God as a loving and wise parent who is caring for his children. Gebara also affirms God's goodness and finds goodness is particularly in evidence when love and mercy are present in the midst of suffering.

We may want to push back on Gregory in particular for his emphasis on suffering as divine punishment or discipline, in part because the image of God as a harsh taskmaster does not fit with the loving, compassionate image of God prevalent in the other thinkers, and in part because advances in knowledge and modern science can help people understand diseases and natural disasters are not acts of divine punishment or retribution. Modern science, however, does not weaken Gregory's argument of suffering as a learning experience that holds great potential for spiritual growth. Coupling this potential with the image of God as a loving and wise parent, an image particularly evident in Julian and Lewis, we can affirm a belief in God's providence in the midst of suffering. God allows suffering, as a loving parent does, because God can see the good and the growth that will come of it. Humanity is to trust, as Taylor and Lewis do, that even in the midst of pain and loss, there is more to the situation than can be comprehended. Without God's vision, suffering may not make sense in the here and now, but we can have faith the ultimate end toward which we (and all of creation) are heading is good. Where Lewis and Taylor disagree, however, is to what extent our faith in God's providence should govern our response to suffering. While Taylor's trust in God means we should be almost happy in the face of loss, Lewis comes to affirm God's providence more fully after having struggled with the anguish of grief. If one is to leave room for the grieving process, then, we must be willing to moderate Taylor's prescription for a perpetual practice of patient forbearance. In constructing a contemporary theology, we need not let go of a belief in God's providence, for even Lewis comes to a place of being able to affirm it, but we do need to allow the space (missing in Taylor) for the questions and emotions that can come with grief.

Melding and modifying the approaches of the five theologians, we can build a contemporary belief in God's providence that envisions God as a teacher and loving parent who allows us to suffer so we will learn and grow. A contemporary theology can affirm there is cause for great hope in the midst of suffering. No one is left alone because, like the lord in Julian's parable, God is ever present, ever compassionate and merciful. Given God's compassionate presence with humanity, we can affirm God will also be patient as we struggle with the anguish we feel in the midst of suffering and loss. If we are able to express our emotions, and we are able to grow spiritually as a result of suffering, then we can move toward a joyful union with God.

Salvation

The knowledge of God's participation in human life is inextricably linked with the hope of salvation. Gregory and Julian particularly emphasize salvation as a predominately divine activity and one only realized in the hereafter; for them, salvation is a gift from God awaiting the faithful at the end of their earthly lives, and any present joy is merely a glimpse, a foretaste, of that gift. Beginning in Taylor there is a shift in emphasis to the way humanity participates in salvation and the ways salvation can be manifest in the here and now. Although Taylor does have some Pelagian tendencies, none of the thinkers say we can accomplish our own salvation. Even Gebara, who places the greatest emphasis on the ways salvation is manifest in daily life, agrees salvation is accomplished by God; humanity is not capable of saving itself. What humanity can do, however, is participate in the reality of salvation. For Taylor, this participation, this striving after a holy life, is not accomplished by a single act of repentance, but by a lifetime of practice—practicing an awareness of death, a purity of intention, and an attitude of contentment. We are to live our whole lives with repentant and humble hearts. In Lewis, we begin to see the ways salvation can manifest in the midst of daily life; for example, he realizes the value of a sunny day or a good night's sleep in bringing him out of his grief. For Gebara, the focus on daily life goes even further. She notes how writing is a form of salvation for Isabel Allende and focuses on the importance of hope and new life being realized in the midst of women's daily sacrifice and suffering. Hope can also be realized through the work of combating unjust suffering. Gebara is, in fact, critical of a theology that speaks only of salvation as something realized in the hereafter; the depth of suffering she has witnessed has shown her such an approach is insufficient. Instead, for Gebara, the hope and healing possible because of a simple daily activity such as Allende's writing show how salvation is not limited to the hereafter.

While Gebara, like Taylor and Lewis, particularly believes salvation can be realized (at least in part) in the here and now, a contemporary understanding of salvation need not choose between an old and new way of looking at salvation. Gregory and Gebara's views are not inherently incompatible, and we can, in fact, hold the essentials of both perspectives to be true. Mainstream Christianity affirms salvation as accomplished once and for all by Christ's salvific act on the cross. It is possible, therefore, to affirm a belief in salvation as fundamentally God's action, as Gregory and Julian do, while also holding, as Lewis and Gebara do, to the conviction it is possible for salvation to be *manifest* in the midst of daily life. We need not share in Taylor's Pelagian tendencies, nor assert we can actually have a role in accomplishing our own salvation. We can affirm, however, the reality of God's work of salvation, while only realized fully in the hereafter, is evident and can be experienced in the midst of daily living. Through daily gifts and blessings one begins to see the depth of God's generous love for humanity, a love most profoundly evident in Christ himself.

Christ

The story of Christ's suffering on the cross has long been a point of identification and comfort for Christians in the midst of suffering. Gregory focuses on the magnitude of Christ's suffering and the fact that our own suffering can only pale in comparison. Julian focuses more on how Christ suffered joyfully and willingly out of love for humanity. There is also in Julian an emphasis on Christ's suffering as the source of salvation because it is through his actions humanity is brought from its fallen state to bliss. Julian sees Christ's suffering as a positive event, not only because it offers comfort in the midst of suffering, but also because it is the source of humanity's salvation. In Taylor, the emphasis is on how Christ's own endurance offers a model for humanity; remembering the sufferings of Christ is meant to inspire patient endurance. We are to respond to suffering as Christ did, because to do so, in Taylor's mind, is to exhibit Christian virtue in the midst of suffering. While Lewis does certainly focus on Christ's suffering (in Aslan's act of vicarious suffering, particularly), Lewis's emphasis is on Christ's relationship with humanity. Through the character of Aslan, we come to see Christ's role as companion and guide as Aslan leads the children throughout their adventures and ultimately to heaven. As in Julian, there is emphasis on the way Christ is present with humanity throughout the experience of suffering and brings humanity to its great reward in heaven. Gebara does not discount the value of Christ's suffering on the cross as a point of connection and inspiration for Christians; however, in her discussion of the cross, she does remind us how we cannot look at the cross without the context of Christ's whole life and ministry. Gebara is particularly critical of the way the maleness of Christ and the redemptive nature of his sacrifice have been emphasized by the Christian tradition because she sees this as having contributed to the marginalization and unjust suffering of many, and women in particular. Gebara wishes to emphasize how anyone's suffering (regardless of gender) can be valuable and redemptive. She also wishes to discount the ideal of sacrifice, at least in the sense that sacrifice is the act of Christ we should imitate. For Gebara, it is the acts of love and mercy evident throughout Jesus's ministry we should imitate. Doing so offers the possibility of actually alleviating suffering, rather than just accepting it blindly.

In developing an understanding of Christ and suffering for contemporary Christians, we must explore a reconciliation between the ideals put forth by the first four thinkers and the criticisms of Gebara. It is essential to maintain a view of Christ's suffering as a point of connection for humanity, as all these thinkers would agree doing so can provide hope in the midst of suffering. To know Christ suffered means God knows the fullness of human pain. If we add to this the images of Christ as lord and as Aslan, in Julian and Lewis respectively, we may also find comfort in seeing Christ as companion and savior in the midst of our suffering. Although Gregory likely meant it as a chastisement to keep us from grieving or expressing self-pity in the midst of suffering, the knowledge our suffering pales in comparison with Christ's could also be a source of comfort, as it helps one keep one's pain in perspective. The emphasis, found particularly in Julian and Lewis, on the willingness of Christ to suffer (doing so even joyfully) is also important. It is perhaps in this willingness, in this emphasis on Christ's selfless act of love, we can find a way of reconciling Taylor and Gebara. Taylor advocates imitation of Christ as a response to suffering, particularly imitation of Christ's patient endurance, but, as Gebara points out, this response can perpetuate or even cause greater suffering. What if we followed Taylor's advice to imitate Christ, but rather than focusing on his patient endurance, we focused on his self-giving love? Certainly Christ is a model for Christians in the midst of suffering, but it does not mean we should accept all suffering willingly. Rather, we can focus on Christ's actions of justice, love, and mercy and imitate those in the midst of our own or another's suffering. We should not throw out Taylor's model of patient endurance entirely, of course, for there are times when there is nothing to be done and the suffering must be endured. Patient endurance, therefore, can be coupled with the additional attributes of love and mercy, and doing so will multiply the virtues exhibited in the face of suffering. In this coupling we can reconcile the criticisms of Gebara with the views of the other thinkers. A focus on the suffering of Christ is held as essential to a Christian theology of suffering because it provides a point of connection with God, hope in the midst of suffering, and an opportunity to model Christ-like virtues of patient endurance, justice, love, and mercy.

Eternal Life

Gregory, Julian, and Taylor emphasize heaven as the reward to the faithful for having lived virtuous lives. The hope of eternal life in heaven is meant to provide great comfort in the midst of suffering. As Gregory writes, "For unless it was his plan to give them an inheritance after correction, he would not concern himself to educate them through affliction."[1] We can have hope in the midst of suffering because the suffering we undergo can be seen as a sign of the divine inheritance that awaits. There is also hope, as Taylor particularly emphasizes, in keeping our perspective. We are to hold on to the reality of death and the hope of eternal life because they show how suffering does not last and there is more to our existence than the here and now. These thinkers' descriptions of heaven—Julian's evocation of a state of eternal bliss with God, Taylor and Lewis's shared conviction that those we love and

---

1. Gregory the Great, *Pastoral Rule*, 115.

all that is truly precious in this life will be met again, Lewis's vision of the unsurpassed beauty and perfection at the close of *The Chronicles of Narnia*, and Gebara's vision of eternal rest in the place where God dwells—certainly also provide great hope. How could we not be hopeful if those visions describe the future awaiting us?

If this was all there was to it, if we could say with confidence that those beautiful visions of heaven come close to describing the fate that awaits, then we would indeed have great confidence and hope in the midst of suffering. We cannot, however, discount the reality of hell, because the possibility of spending eternity suffering—or at the very least separated from God—has a strong presence in the Christian tradition. For Gregory and Taylor, the possibility of punishment beyond the grave is very real. This reality was meant to serve as a deterrent to sin and as inspiration to live faithfully. For Julian and Lewis, the focus is not on the possibility of punishment, but rather on the possibility of eternal separation from God. There is a strong emphasis in both Julian and Lewis on the reality of human freedom and the ability of humanity to turn away from God, and so, for them, the option of rejecting God's continual offers of love and mercy is an eternal option. Saying no to God, with its resultant separation, is clearly not a choice any of the theologians would advocate, but if we are to accept the reality of human freedom, we must also accept the possibility we can choose to reject God.

Many contemporary Christians would agree with Gregory and Taylor and would hold to a belief in eternal damnation as a deterrent from sinful behavior. Others would prefer to share Julian and Lewis's emphasis on the possibility of eternal separation from God as a result of our own choice to reject God. There would seem to be a tension here between damnation and separation. If we only speak of separation, as Julian and Lewis do, then is there a lack of accountability for sin? One way to balance this tension is to believe in purgatory, as Lewis does. While he holds to a belief in hell as eternal separation from God, purgatory provides a state in which one can be cleansed of sin, and, like his portrayal of Eustace and the dragon skin in the *Chronicles*, there is reason to believe this cleansing will be quite painful.

This contemporary theology has already emphasized the mercy and compassion of God, and it continues to do so by rejecting the emphasis on damnation found in Gregory and Taylor, in favor of the emphasis on separation found in Julian and Lewis. A belief in the possibility of eternal separation from God because it is an inherently negative experience, can still serve as a deterrent to sin and an inspiration to live a godly life, as a belief in damnation does for Gregory and Taylor. Siding with separation does not have to mean a belief in purgatory, however; for as noted in the chapter on Lewis, we can view death as cleansing without actually holding to the traditional doctrine of purgatory, which was rejected by Anglicans and other Protestants during the Reformation. To believe in the possibility of eternal separation, rather than damnation, is to remain in continuity with the beliefs expressed earlier in a God who is always reaching out in love, desiring to offer the reward of heaven to all, and who also values human freedom to the extent we are allowed to refuse the invitation.

Gebara does not devote much of her book to a discussion of eternal life, and a discussion of hell is notably absent, so this is one area where she offers little criticism or push back. Given her focus on here and now, particularly on the way salvation can be manifest in the midst of daily life, we can see she does offer a caution when formulating our belief in eternal life. If we are in the midst of suffering, we can find great comfort, as Julian did, in the possibility of a reward in heaven. While a focus on eternal life can certainly be a source of hope and of great value in broadening our perspective in the midst of suffering, we should not keep one's focus entirely there, as it may prevent us from acting with love and mercy in the here and now. We should reach out and do what we can to combat unjust suffering so a foretaste of the heavenly reward can be realized and does not remain a distant hope for those who have been the victims of injustice. There is an important balance to be struck in holding a belief in eternal life, and this balance is found in Taylor who advocates living with an awareness of the afterlife while also being present in the here and now. Life in the here and now must also involve imitating God's love and mercy as Gebara advocates. A contemporary theology regarding eternal life can be a source of comfort and hope for the future, while also affecting how we choose to live in the present.

CONCLUSION

What we have, in the end, is a theology of suffering retaining many of the foundational elements established in Gregory, Julian, Taylor, and the tradition of mainstream Christianity, while also being nuanced and adjusted to enable us to address the concerns and criticisms raised by Lewis and Gebara. The reality of sin and evil in the world can be upheld while also acknowledging the importance of distinguishing between suffering as the result of human sin and suffering endemic to the human experience. Heeding the call of Gebara and what she identifies as the central message of the Christian tradition, Christians should highlight this distinction, so they are reminded of their obligation to work vigorously through actions which imitate Christ's self-giving love and passion for mercy and justice to combat the sinfulness resulting in unjust suffering. Not all suffering is to be accepted, but even if we work against suffering, there will still be suffering with which we must live. The nuanced acceptance, therefore, at the heart of this contemporary theology of suffering is an acknowledgment of the reality that in this fallen world, we will experience suffering, without diminution of the desire to work for transformation in the world to bring an end to unjust suffering caused by human sinfulness.

This nuanced acceptance also contains humility about humanity's tendency toward sinfulness balanced by a belief in God's providence, a deep and abiding trust that our own fate and the world's is ultimately under God's control and God brings all things to a positive end. In this understanding, God is the benevolent parent and teacher who allows his children to suffer because he can see the redemptive value of suffering and can also see the glorious bliss awaiting the faithful. Those who are reflective in the midst of suffering will find an opportunity to grow in faith, and in their knowledge of and relationship with God. Salvation has been accomplished by Christ's sacrifice on the cross, and God continually reaches out (as the lord does in Julian's parable) with love and mercy toward humanity. In this theology of suffering, God seeks to bring all people to fulfillment, to eternal life in heaven. Yet the existence of free will means people suffer the consequences of their actions and have the eternal option to reject God's gestures of love, mercy, and the offer of eternal life in heaven.

This contemporary theology affirms how in the midst of all suffering we can have hope. In the midst of the suffering that results from human sinfulness, we can find hope in the fact that Christians can and should do something to bring suffering to an end. In the midst of any suffering we can find comfort in the ways our suffering is Christ-like and in the reward awaiting the faithful. For centuries the church has emphasized hope was to be found in the Christ-like nature of our suffering. While this belief may have led, at times, to a justification of unjust suffering, at its heart is a message still of value to contemporary Christians: the sufferings of Christ show how God fully understands the reality and pain of human suffering. An additional source of hope has been the church's long-held affirmation that in the afterlife there would be no suffering. The challenge such an affirmation poses for contemporary theology is it can lead to devaluing earthly life. Contemporary theology can still hold to the belief that in heaven there awaits a bliss surpassing our earthly experiences, if it also emphasizes how the joys and comforts found in the here and now offer a foretaste of this bliss. As the thinkers attest, there are in fact many blessings to be had, even in the midst of suffering. This contemporary theology, therefore, urges Christians to remember blessings can be found: in the cleansing power of suffering (as Gregory did), in recovery from an illness (as Julian did), in the gift of children (as Taylor did), in the simple joy of a good night's sleep or a beautiful day (as Lewis did), and in working to alleviate suffering (as Gebara did). These blessings and others we may find show how, even in the midst of suffering, there is joy in life, and we can relish those blessings in their own right because they point to the future reality of a blissful union with God in heaven.

The theology of suffering developed through engagement with the five thinkers, Gregory the Great, Julian of Norwich, Jeremy Taylor, C. S. Lewis and Ivone Gebara, regarding the theological touchstones provides, for contemporary American Christians, a framework for thinking about and living with suffering. It is theology possessing an awareness of human sinfulness, asking Christians to live in such a way as to combat the suffering resulting from it. This means heeding the call to action at the heart of the gospel, a call to reach out in love and mercy and to act for justice in the face of unjust suffering. As the breadth of the Christian tradition explored in this book attests, even if we seek to combat the reality of suffering resulting from human sinfulness, life does not become free from suffering, no matter how or when we live. Despite the cultural messages of contemporary American life, it is not possible to have a life free from suffering. As has been discussed, suffering and grief are not limited to the experience of death, disease, or tragedy; they come in the face of any experience of loss. Christians are, therefore, called to live with the reality of endemic suffering and to seek comfort in the knowledge that while the experience of suffering can be challenging and painful, it can also be spiritually fruitful. Suffering can be redemptive because it can prompt reflection and amendment of life. Having an awareness of our own frailty and mortality can also help us have a wider perspective that can lead to a greater appreciation of the blessings in the here and now, as well as joyful expectation of the blessings beyond the grave. Suffering can also prompt a sense of compassion for others, which can provide a connection with them and with God through reaching out to those in need. This contemporary theology affirms that the Christian story has at its heart a message that suffering can lead to new life and new possibilities. In the midst of experiences of grief and suffering, Christians can affirm the promise of new life found in the Easter story is not limited to that single event, but rather the promise points God's continual work in the world, seeking to offer new life to all. The theology formulated in this book understands God as having issued an invitation to humanity. It is an invitation to participate with God in the work of combating unjust suffering, while also learning to trust, in the midst of suffering endemic to the human experience, that God, like the lord in Julian's parable, is ever present, leading humanity toward the reality of endless bliss in the divine presence.

Bibliography

Achtemeier, Paul J., editor. *Harper Collins Bible Dictionary.* New York: Harper, 1996.

Aers, David. *Salvation and Sin: Augustine, Langland, and Fourteenth-Century Theology.* Notre Dame: University of Notre Dame Press, 2009.

Aers, David, and Lynn Staley. *The Powers of the Holy.* University Park, PA: Pennsylvania State University Press, 1996.

Ahlgren, Gillian T. W. "Julian of Norwich's Theology of Eros." *Spiritus: A Journal of Christian Spirituality* 5:1 (2005) 37–53.

Allchin, A. M., editor. *Four Studies to Commemorate the Sixth Centenary of the Revelations of Divine Love.* Oxford: SLG, 1973.

Allende, Isabel. *Paula.* New York: Perennial, 1996.

Augustine. *City of God.* Translated by Henry Bettenson. London: Penguin, 2003.

———. *Confessions.* Edited by Henry Chadwick. Oxford: Oxford University Press, 1998.

Baker, Denise Nowakowski. *Julian of Norwich's Showings: From Vision to Book.* Princeton: Princeton University Press, 1994.

Banks, Robert. "C. S. Lewis on Pain." In *The Consolation of Theology*, edited by Brian S. Rosner, 131–58. Grand Rapids: Eerdmans, 2008.

Batiffol, Pierre. *Saint Gregory the Great.* Translated by John L. Stoddard. London: Burns, Oates & Washbourne, 1929.

Bauerschmidt, Frederick Christian. *Julian of Norwich and the Mystical Body Politic of Christ.* Notre Dame: University of Notre Dame Press, 1999.

———. "Julian of Norwich—Incorporated." *Modern Theology* 13 (1997) 75–100.

Beaty, Nancy Lee. *Craft of Dying: A Study in the Literary Tradition of the Ars Moriendi in England.* New Haven: Yale University Press, 1970.

Beer, Frances. *Women and Mystical Experience in the Middle Ages.* Woodbridge, UK: Boydell, 1992.

Beversluis, John. *C. S. Lewis and the Search for Rational Religion.* Grand Rapids: Eerdmans, 1985.

Book of Common Prayer. Edited by the Episcopal Church. New York: Church Publishing, 1979.

Bradley, Ritamary. *Julian's Way: A Practical Commentary on Julian of Norwich.* London: Harper, 1992.

———. *Not for the Wise: The Prayer Texts of Julian of Norwich.* London: Longman, 1994.

Brinkley, Roberta Florence, editor. *Coleridge on the Seventeenth Century.* New York: Greenwood, 1968.

Brown, Peter. *The Rise of Western Christendom.* Malden, MA: Blackwell, 2003.

Bibliography

Browning, W. R. F., editor. *A Dictionary of the Bible*. Oxford University Press, 1997. http://www.oxfordreference.com/views/ENTRY.htmlsubview=Main&entry=t94. e1407.

Bush, Michael, editor. *This Incomplete One: Words Occasioned by the Death of a Young Person*. Grand Rapids: Eerdmans, 2006.

Bynum, Caroline Walker. *Jesus as Mother*. Berkeley: University of California Press, 1982.

Carpenter, James C. "Accepting Death: A Critique of Kubler-Ross." *The Hastings Center Report* 9:5 (1979) 42–43.

Catto, Jeremy. "Currents of Religious Thought and Expression." In *The New Cambridge Medieval History, vol. VI*. Cambridge, UK: Cambridge University Press, 2000.

Cavadini, John C., editor. *Gregory the Great: A Symposium*. Notre Dame: University of Notre Dame Press, 1995.

Childress, James F., and John Macquarrie, editors. *The Westminster Dictionary of Christian Ethics*. Philadelphia: Westminster, 1986.

Christopher, Joe, and Joan Ostling. *C. S. Lewis: An Annotated Checklist of Writings about Him and His Works*. Kent: Kent State University Press, 1973.

Clark, David G. *C. S. Lewis: A Guide to His Theology*. Malden, MA: Blackwell, 2007.

Cohn, Samuel K. *The Black Death Transformed: Disease and Culture in Early Renaissance Europe*. London: Arnold, 2003.

Conn, Marie A. *C. S. Lewis and Human Suffering: Light Among the Shadows*. Mahwah, NJ: Paulist, 2008.

Cross, F. L., and E. A. Livingstone, editors. *The Oxford Dictionary of the Christian Church*. Oxford: Oxford University Press, 1997.

Davies, Oliver. "Late Medieval Mystics." In *The Medieval Theologians: An Introduction to Theology in the Medieval Period*. Oxford, UK: Blackwell, 2001.

Demacopoulos, George E. *Five Models of Spiritual Direction in the Early Church*. Notre Dame: University of Notre Dame Press, 2007.

Dickinson, J. C. *An Ecclesiastical History of England: The Later Middle Ages: From the Norman Conquest to the Eve of the Reformation*. London: Black, 1979.

Dudden, F. Holmes. *Gregory the Great: His Place in History and Thought*. New York: Russell & Russell, 1967.

Duffy, Eamon. *The Stripping of the Altars*. New Haven: Yale University Press, 1992.

Duriez, Colin. *The C. S. Lewis Encyclopedia*. Santa Monica: Azure, 2002.

———. *C. S. Lewis Handbook*. Sussex: Monarch, 1990.

Edwards, Bruce. *The Taste of the Pineapple*. Bowling Green: Bowling Green State University Popular Press, 1988.

Elwes, Teresa. *Women's Voices*. London: Marshall Pickering, 1992.

Evans, Gillian Rosemary. *The Thought of Gregory the Great*. Cambridge: Cambridge University Press, 1986.

Faria, Miguel. "Medical History—Plagues and Epidemics." *Medical Sentinel* 7:4 (2002) 119–21. Online: http://www.haciendapub.com/faria4.html.

Fellowes, Robert. *Manual of Piety*. London: Poultry, 1807.

Gatta, Julia. *Three Spiritual Directors for Our Time*. Cambridge, MA: Cowley, 1986.

Gebara, Ivone, and Maria Bingemer. *Mary, Mother of God, Mother of the Poor*. Maryknoll: Orbis, 1989.

———. "Changing Our Perceptions of God." Hartford Seminary, Hartford, CT, June 4, 2007.

———. *Out of the Depths*. Minneapolis: Fortress, 2002.

Gibbs, Jocelyn, editor. *Light on C. S. Lewis*. New York: HBR, 1965.

Gilchrist, K. J. *A Morning After War: C. S. Lewis and WWI*. New York: Lang, 2005.

Gittings, Clare. "Sacred and Secular: 1558–1660." In *Death in England: An Illustrated History*, edited by Peter C. Jupp and Clare Gittings, 147–73. New Brunswick, NJ: Rutgers University Press, 2000.

Green, Roger Lancelyn, and Walter Hooper. *C. S. Lewis: A Biography*. New York: HBJ, 1974.

Greer, Rowan A. *Christian Hope and Christian Life: Raids on the Inarticulate*. New York: Crossroad, 2001.

Gregory the Great. *The Books of the Morals of St. Gregory the Pope Or An Exposition on the Book of Blessed Job*. Translated by John Henry Parker. London: Oxford, 1844. http://www.lectionarycentral.com/GregoryMoraliaIndex.html.

———. *The Book of Pastoral Rule*. Translated by George E. Demacopoulos. Crestwood, NY: St. Vladimir's Seminary Press, 2007.

———. *Forty Gospel Homilies*. Translated by Dom David Hurst. Kalamazoo, MI: Cistercian Publications, 1990.

———. *Pastoral Care (Regula Pastoralis)*. Vol. 11 of *Ancient Christian Writers*. Translated by Henry Davis. New York: Newman Press, 1978.

Gresham, Douglas H. *Jack's Life: The Life Story of C. S. Lewis*. Nashville: Broadman & Holman, 2005.

Harvey, Van A. *A Handbook of Theological Terms*. New York: Simon & Schuster, 1992.

Heber, Reginal. *The Whole Works of The Right Rev. Jeremy Taylor, D.D.* London: Darton, Longman and Todd, 1854.

Hatchett, Marion J. *Commentary on the American Prayer Book*. San Francisco: HarperSanFrancisco, 1995.

Hauerwas, Stanley. *God, Medicine, and Suffering*. Grand Rapids: Eerdmans, 2000.

Heimmel, Jennifer P. *God is Our Mother: Julian of Norwich and the Medieval Image of Christian Feminine Divinity*. Salzburg, Austria: Institut für Anglistik und Amerikanistik Universität Salzburg, 1982.

Herbert McAvoy, Liz. *Authority and the Female Body in the Writings of Julian of Norwich and Margery Kempe*. Cambridge: Brewer, 2004.

Hide, Kerrie. *Gifted Origins to Graced Fulfillment: The Soteriology of Julian of Norwich*. Collegeville, MN: Liturgical, 2001.

Hildesley, C. Hugh. *Journeying with Julian*. Harrisburg, PA: Morehouse, 1993.

Holloway, Julia Bolton. *Julian of Norwich: Showing of Love*. Collegeville, MN: Liturgical, 2003.

Holmer, Paul L. *C. S. Lewis: The Shape of His Faith and Thought*. New York: Harper & Row, 1976.

Hooper, Walter, editor. *C. S. Lewis Collected Letters*. New York: HarperCollins, 2006.

———. *C. S. Lewis: A Companion and Guide*. London: HarperCollins, 1996.

Houlbrooke, Ralph. "The Age of Decency: 1660–1760." In *Death in England: An Illustrated History*, edited by Peter C. Jupp and Clare Gittings, 174–75. New Brunswick, NJ: Rutgers University Press, 2000.

Howorth, Henry H. *Saint Gregory the Great*. London: Murray, 1912.

Hughes, H. Trevor. *The Piety of Jeremy Taylor*. London: Macmillian, 1960.

Huntley, Frank Livingstone. *Jeremy Taylor and the Great Rebellion: A Study of His Mind and Temper in Controversy*. Ann Arbor, MI: University of Michigan Press, 1970.

Bibliography

Jacobs, Alan. *The Narnian: The Life and Imagination of C. S. Lewis.* New York: HarperCollins, 2006.

Jantzen, Grace. *Julian of Norwich: Mystic and Theologian.* New York: Paulist, 2000.

———. *Power, Gender, and Christian Mysticism.* Cambridge Studies in Ideology and Religion. Cambridge: Cambridge University Press, 1995.

Julian of Norwich. *The Showings.* Edited by Georgia Ronan Crampton. TEAMS: Middle English Texts Series. Kalamazoo, MI: Western Michigan University, 1994.

———. *Showings.* Translated by Edmund Colledge and James Walsh. Classics of Western Spirituality Series. New York: Paulist, 1978.

Kaufman, Sharon R. *And a Time to Die: How American Hospitals Shape the End of Life.* New York: Scribner, 2005.

Kerby-Fulton, Kathryn. *Books Under Suspicion.* Notre Dame: University Notre Dame Press, 2006.

Kierkegaard, Søren. *Christian Discourses.* Translated by Walter Lowrie. New York: Oxford University Press, 1961.

———. *Works of Love.* Translated by Howard Hong and Edna Hong. New York: Harper & Row, 1962.

Klapisch-Zuber, Christiane. "Plague and Family Life." In *The New Cambridge Medieval History, vol. VI.* Cambridge, UK: Cambridge University Press, 2000.

Kreeft, Peter. *C. S. Lewis: A Critical Essay.* Grand Rapids: Eerdmans, 1969.

Kübler-Ross, Elisabeth. *On Death and Dying.* New York: Scribner, 1997.

Kushner, Harold. *When Bad Things Happen to Good People.* New York: Avon, 1983.

Kuykendall, George. "Care for the Dying: A Kübler-Ross Critique." *Theology Today* 38:1 (1981) 37–48.

Leibniz, Gottfried Wilhelm. *Theodicy.* Lexington: Bibliobazaar, 2007.

Lesser Feasts and Fasts. Edited by Church Publishing. New York: Church Publishing, 2003.

Lewis, Charlton T., and Charles Short. *A Latin Dictionary.* Oxford: Clarendon, 1958.

Lewis, C. S. *C. S. Lewis's Letters in Latin.* Translated by Martin Moynihan. London: Collins & Sons, 1988.

———. *The Chronicles of Narnia.* New York: HarperCollins, 2001.

———. *The Great Divorce.* San Francisco: HarperSanFrancisco, 2001.

———. *A Grief Observed.* London: Bantam, 1983.

———. *Letters to Malcolm: Chiefly on Prayer.* San Francisco: Harcourt, 1964.

———. *The Problem of Pain.* San Francisco: HarperSanFrancisco, 2001.

———. *The Screwtape Lettters.* New York: Macmillian, 1961.

———. *Surprised by Joy.* New York: Harcourt, 1955.

Lindskoog, Kathryn. *C. S. Lewis.* Chicago: Cornerstone Press Chicago, 2007.

———. *Sleuthing C. S. Lewis: More Light in the Shadowlands.* Macon, GA: Mercer University Press, 2001.

Lindsley, Arthur. *C. S. Lewis's Case for Christ: Insights from Reason, Imagination, and Faith.* Downers Grove, IL: InterVarsity, 2005.

Livingstone, E. A., editor. *The Oxford Dictionary of the Christian Church.* Oxford: Oxford University Press, 1997.

Llewlyn, Robert, editor. *Julian, Woman of Our Day.* London: Darton, Longman and Todd, 1985.

Loades, Ann. "C. S. Lewis: Grief Observed, Rationality Abandoned, Faith Regained." *Journal of Literature and Theology* 3:l (1989) 107–21.

Macdonald, Michael et.al. *The Riddle of Joy.* Grand Rapids: Eerdmans, 1989.

Macquarrie, John. *Principles of Christian Theology.* New York: Scribner, 1977.

Magill, Kevin J. *Julian of Norwich: Mystic or Visionary?* London: Routledge, 2006.

Markus, Robert Austin. *Signs and Meanings: World and Text in Ancient Christianity.* Liverpool: Liverpool University Press, 1996.

———. *Gregory the Great and His World.* Cambridge: Cambridge University Press, 1997.

Martindale, Wayne. "Shadowlands." In *C. S. Lewis: Lightbearer in the Shadowlands,* edited by Angus Menuge, 33–53. Wheaton: Crossway, 1997.

Matthews, Melvin. "Two Women Facing Death, Julian of Norwich and Etty Hillesum." The Julian Lecture, the Julian Centre, Norwich, UK, May 10, 2008.

Maynard, Jane. *Transfiguring Loss.* Cleveland: Pilgrim, 2006.

McAdoo, H. R. *The Structure of Caroline Moral Theology.* London: Darton, Longman and Todd, 1949.

McSheffrey, Shannon. *Gender and Heresy: Women and Men in Lollard Communities, 1420–1530.* Philadelphia: University of Pennsylvania Press, 1995.

Menzies, Lucy. *Mirrors of the Holy: Ten Studies in Sanctity.* Milwaukee: Morehouse, 1928.

Mitchell, Kenneth R., and Herbert Anderson. *All Our Losses, All Our Griefs: Resources for Pastoral Care.* Louisville: Westminster John Knox, 1983.

Moorhead, John. *Gregory the Great.* London: Routledge, 2005.

Morgan, Philip. "Of Worms and War: 1380–1558." In *Death in England: An Illustrated History,* edited by Clare Gittings and Peter Jupp. 119–46. New Brunswick, NJ: Rutgers University Press, 2000.

Moorman, J. R. H. *A History of the Church in England.* London: Black, 1967.

Mountney, John Michael. *Sin Shall Be a Glory: As Revealed by Julian of Norwich.* London: Darton, Longman and Todd, 1992.

Muller, Richard A. *Dictionary of Latin and Greek Theological Terms.* Grand Rapids: Baker, 1985.

Murrin, Michael. "The Dialectic of Multiple Worlds: An Analysis of C.S. Lewis's Narnia Stories." *Seven* 3 (1982) 93–112.

Nicholi, Armand, Jr. *The Question of God.* New York: Free, 2002.

Niebuhr, H. Richard. *Christ and Culture.* San Francisco: HarperSanFrancisco, 2001.

Nuth, Joan M. *Wisdom's Daughter: The Theology of Julian of Norwich.* New York: Crossroad, 1991.

———. *God's Lovers in an Age of Anxiety.* Edited by Philip Sheldrake. Traditions of Christian Spirituality Series. Maryknoll, NY: Orbis, 2001.

Oden, Thomas C. *Care of Souls in the Classic Tradition.* Philadelphia: Fortress, 1984.

Ortega, Ofelia. *Women's Visions.* Geneva: World Council of Churches, 1994.

Oxford English Dictionary Online. 2nd ed. Oxford: Oxford University Press, 1989. http://dictionary.oed.com/entrance.dtl

Palliser, Margaret Ann. *Christ, Our Mother of Mercy: Divine Mercy and Compassion in the Theology of the Shewings of Julian of Norwich.* Berlin: de Gruyter, 1992.

Pelphrey, Brant. *Christ Our Mother: Julian of Norwich.* Wilmington, DE: Glazier, 1989.

Phipps, William. *Death: Confronting the Reality.* Atlanta: John Knox, 1987.

Pui-Lan, Kwok, and Elisabeth Schüssler Fiorenza, editors. *Women's Sacred Scriptures.* London: SCM Press, 1998.

Puleo, Mev. *The Struggle is One: Voices and Visions of Liberation.* Albany: SUNY Press, 1994.

Purtill, Richard. *C. S. Lewis's Case for the Christian Faith*. San Francisco: Harper & Row, 1985.

Radford Ruether, Rosemary. *Visionary Women: Three Medieval Mystics*. Minneapolis: Fortress, 2002.

Richards, Jeffrey. *Consul of God: The Life and Times of Gregory the Great*. London: Routledge, 1980.

Risebero, Bill. *The Story of Western Architecture*. Cambridge, MA: MIT Press, 2002.

Rogers, Rolf E. *Max Weber's Ideal Type Theory*. New York: Philosophical Library, 1969.

Ross, Ellen M. *The Grief of God: Images of the Suffering Jesus in Late Medieval England*. New York: Oxford University Press, 1997.

Sayer, George. *Jack: C. S. Lewis and His Times*. San Francisco: Harper & Row, 1988.

Schultz, Jeffrey, and John West. *The C. S. Lewis Readers' Encyclopedia*. Grand Rapids: Zondervan, 1998.

Sibley, Brian. *Shadowlands*. London: Hodder & Stoughton, 1990.

———. *Through the Shadowlands: The Love Story of C. S. Lewis and Joy Davidman*. Grand Rapids: Revell, 1994.

Sister Mary Paul. *All Shall Be Well: Julian of Norwich and the Compassion of God*. Oxford: SLG, 1976.

Skinner, John. "The Lord and His Servant." The Julian Lecture, the Julian Centre, Norwich, UK, May 8, 1999.

Smith, Julia. *Europe after Rome: A New Cultural History 500–1000*. Oxford: Oxford University Press, 2005.

Smith, Robert Houston. *Patches of Godlight: The Pattern of Thought of C. S. Lewis*. Athens, GA: University of Georgia Press, 1981.

Soelle, Dorothee. *Suffering*. Minneapolis: Fortress, 1984.

Spearing, Elizabeth. *Medieval Writings on Female Spirituality*. New York: Penguin, 2002.

Spurr, John. "Taylor, Jeremy." *Oxford Dictionary of National Biography*. Oxford University Press, 2004. Online: http://www.oxforddnb.com/view/article/27041.

Stranks, C. J. *The Life and Writings of Jeremy Taylor*. London: SPCK, 1952

Stranks, C. J., and Thomas Carroll. *Selected Works*. New York: Paulist, 1990.

Straw, Carole Ellen, and Roger Collins. *Gregory the Great*. Vol. 9, no.12 of *Authors of the Middle Ages*. Aldershot, UK: Variorum, 1996.

———. *Gregory the Great: Perfection in Imperfection*. Berkeley: University of California Press, 1988.

Tamez, Elsa, editor. *Through Her Eyes: Women's Theology from Latin America*. Maryknoll: Orbis, 1989.

Taylor, Jeremy. *Holy Living and Dying: With Prayers Containing the Whole Duty of a Christian*. New York: Cosimo Classics, 2007.

———. Jeremy Taylor. 29 August 1657. British Library. RP 2595.

———. Jeremy Taylor to Lady Annabella Howe. 29 August 1657. British Library RP 2785.

Thomas, Keith. *Religion and the Decline of Magic*. New York: Scribner, 1971.

Thouless, Robert H. *The Lady Julian: A Psychological Study*. New York, Macmillan, 1924.

Tuchman, Barbara. *A Distant Mirror: The Calamitous Fourteenth Century*. New York: Ballantine, 1987.

Turner, Denys. "'Sin is Behovely' in Julian of Norwich's *Revelations of Divine Love*." *Modern Theology* 20:3 (2004) 407–22.

Upjohn, Sheila. *In Search of Julian of Norwich*. New York: Morehouse, 2007.

———. *Why Julian Now? A Voyage of Discovery.* Grand Rapids: Eerdmans, 1997.

Vanauken, Sheldon. *Severe Mercy.* New York: Bantam, 1979.

VandenBos, Gary R. *APA Dictionary of Psychology.* Washington, DC: American Psychological Association, 2007.

Vaus, Will. *Mere Theology: A Guide to the Thought of C. S. Lewis.* Downers Grove, IL: InterVarsity, 2004.

Volz, Carl. *The Medieval Church: From the Dawn of the Middle Ages to the Eve of the Reformation.* Nashville: Abingdon, 1997.

Walsh, James. *The Revelations of Divine Love of Julian of Norwich.* New York: Harper Brothers, 1961.

Watkin, E. I. *On Julian of Norwich; and In Defence of Margery Kempe.* Exeter, UK: University of Devon, 1979.

White, Hugh. "Langland, Milton, and the Felix Culpa." *The Review of English Studies, New Series* 45:179 (1994) 336–56.

White, James F., editor. *Documents of Christian Worship: Descriptive and Interpretive Sources.* Louisville: Westminster John Knox, 1992.

Wilhelm Westhoff, Elbert, editor. *S. Gregorii Papae I. Cognomento Magni De Pastorali Cura Liber.* Monasterii Westphalorum, 1860.

Williams, Rowan. "Christianity and the Ideal of Detachment." Lingdale Papers 12, Frank Lake Memorial Lecture, Oxford, Clinical Theology Association, 1988.

———. *Tokens of Trust.* Louisville: Westminster John Knox, 2007.

Williamson, Hugh Ross. *Jeremy Taylor.* London: Dobson, 1952.

Willis, John Randolph. *Pleasures Forevermore: The Theology of C. S. Lewis.* Chicago: Loyola University Press, 1983.

Wilson, A. N. *C. S. Lewis.* New York: Norton, 1990.

Wolterstorff, Nicoholas. *Lament for a Son.* Grand Rapids: Eerdmans, 1987.

Subject/Name Index